TEILHARD DE CHARDIN'S THEOLOGY OF THE CHRISTIAN IN THE WORLD

TEILHARD DE CHARDIN'S THEOLOGY OF THE CHRISTIAN IN THE WORLD

by ROBERT L. FARICY, S.J.

SHEED AND WARD : NEW YORK

© *Robert L. Faricy, S.J., 1967*

Library of Congress Catalog Card Number 67-13767

Imprimi potest:
    Very Reverend Edward J. Sponga, S.J.
    Provincial, Province of Maryland

Nihil obstat:
    Reverend Ernest E. Larkin, O. Carm., S.T.D.
    Censor Deputatus

Imprimatur:
    ✠ *Patrick A. O'Boyle*
    Archbishop of Washington
    March 21, 1966

The nihil obstat and imprimatur are official declarations that a book or pamphlet is free of doctrinal or moral error. No implication is contained therein that those who have granted the nihil obstat and the imprimatur agree with the content, opinions, or statements expressed.

Manufactured in the United States of America

*To Mademoiselle Jeanne Mortier, who has
done so much for the Church in making
known the ideas of Father Teilhard de Chardin.*

PREFACE

THE PURPOSE of this study is to present an outline synthesis of a central theme in the writings of Pierre Teilhard de Chardin: the relation between human endeavor and Christian revelation. In diverse letters, essays, and books, Teilhard tries to unify in a way meaningful to contemporary man the idea of activity directed toward human progress and the idea of activity directed toward salvation. The result is a theological reflection on human endeavor, a Christian theology of human effort thought out in the modern perspectives of a world in evolution.

This theological reflection is fragmented in Teilhard's works. Perhaps the closest he ever came to a complete statement of his views on the religious value of human endeavor is *The Divine Milieu,* written in 1927. The book, however, is less a theological work than a spiritual essay; it presents a broad point of view but without extensive treatment of the theological underpinnings of that viewpoint or of the theological problems that it raises. What is more, Teilhard de Chardin's religious thought developed over the years. Toward the end of his life, a reading of what he had written years before in *The Divine Milieu* surprised him—all the essential characteristics of his Christo-cosmic vision were already in those days well in place. But he was just as surprised to discover to what point his view of the universe was vague and undetermined. At that early date, the main outlines of his ideas of evolution, of cosmic convergence, the law of complexity-consciousness, an Omega point, had not yet appeared to him distinctly.[1]

The present study is an attempt to integrate the somewhat scattered elements of Teilhard's complete vision of the place of man's endeavor in a universe that is centered on Christ. The purpose is neither to attack nor to defend Teilhard's general perspectives or any of his ideas, but simply to set forth a coherent summary of his views on a subject that he considered of the highest importance. Teilhard's views will not appeal to all Christians, but they are Christian views and they surely have their place within the many-mansioned edifice of Christian thought. There is, Hans Urs von Balthasar writes, not merely the one common Christian perspective but also particular insights into the nature of Christian life.

This way there can be a multiplicity of viewpoints in the Church, provided they are contained in the over-all unity. The harsh conflicts in Christian history, which arose because people could not see how different viewpoints could be reconciled, have their prototype in the warlike history of the apostles, whose conflicts can be traced to differing divine mandates. Origen said repeatedly that there must be many

[1] See "Le coeur de la matière," 1950, 26.

schools of thought and viewpoints in the Church so that the fulness of the one Word can blossom forth in it in human form. The fathers had a lively, often intransigent, awareness of the unity of the Church; yet they clearly defended the individuality of her great teachers.[2]

Teilhard de Chardin writes of his own particular understanding of the Christian life. It is a contemporary understanding, for Teilhard was a man very much of this century, and as such it appeals to many men today. Nevertheless, Teilhard would be the last to suggest that his is *the* Christian point of view, the only valid perspective for a twentieth-century Christian. It is only one Christian view of man and the world, but it is a view that is carefully thought out and that deserves to be taken seriously.

I would like to thank the Rev. Ernest E. Larkin, O. Carm., for his kind help and encouragement in writing this book. I am indebted also to the Paris Province of the Society of Jesus for making it possible for me to make use of the unpublished writings of Teilhard de Chardin. In studying Teilhard's unpublished works, I used copies of the documents in the collection of Father Christopher F. Mooney, S.J. Father Mooney also made his recent book, *Teilhard de Chardin and the Mystery of Christ* (Harper and Row, 1966), available to me in manuscript form before its publication. I would like to express gratitude to Father Mooney especially for his help in several conversations and for the helpfulness of his book. I would also like to thank Sister Emily Joseph, S.S.J., and Mrs. Marilyn Durrant for their help in preparing the manuscript, and Mr. Fred Wieck of Harper and Row, Publishers, for his aid

[2] H. Urs von Balthasar, "The One True Spirituality of the Church," *Theology Digest* 10 (1962) 191, translated and condensed from "Spiritualität," *Geist und Leben* 31 (1958) 340–52; a full translation of this article can be found in H. Urs von Balthasar, *Word and Redemption*, tr. A. Littledale (New York, Herder and Herder, 1965), 87–108.

in matters concerning quotations from Teilhard's writings. Finally, I would like to thank Mr. Harry K. Rosenfield for his special help in bringing this book to publication.

Acknowledgment and grateful appreciation are due to Harper & Row, publishers of the works of Pierre Teilhard de Chardin, for permission to quote copyrighted material from the following books by Teilhard de Chardin: *The Divine Milieu*, copyright © 1960 by Wm. Collins Sons & Co., London, and Harper & Row, Publishers, Incorporated, New York; *Letters from a Traveller*, copyright © 1962 by Wm. Collins Sons & Co., London, and Harper & Row, Publishers, Incorporated, New York; *The Future of Man*, copyright © 1964 by Wm. Collins Sons & Co., London, and Harper & Row, Publishers, Incorporated, New York; *Hymn of the Universe*, copyright © 1965 by Wm. Collins Sons & Co., London, and Harper & Row, Publishers, Incorporated, New York; *The Phenomenon of Man*, copyright © 1959 by Wm. Collins Sons & Co., London, and Harper & Row, Publishers, Incorporated, New York (revised English edition, 1965); *The Appearance of Man*, copyright © 1965 by Wm. Collins Sons & Co., London, and Harper & Row, Publishers, Incorporated, New York; *The Making of a Mind*, copyright © 1965 by Wm. Collins Sons & Co., London, and Harper & Row, Publishers, Incorporated, New York; *Man's Place in Nature*, copyright © 1966 by Wm. Collins Sons & Co., London, and Harper & Row, Publishers, Incorporated, New York; *The Vision of the Past*, copyright © 1967 by Wm. Collins Sons & Co., London, and Harper & Row, Publishers, Incorporated, New York; *Writings in Time of War*, copyright © 1968 by Wm. Collins Sons & Co., London, and Harper & Row, Publishers, Incorporated, New York.

Acknowledgment and grateful appreciation are also due to Editions du Seuil, Paris; Wm. Collins Sons & Co., London; Harper & Row, Publishers, Incorporated, New York, for permission to quote from the following works of Teilhard de Chardin: *L'énergie humaine, L'activation de L'énergie, Science et Christ, La parole attendue,* and *Le Christ Evoluteur.*

Excerpts from The Constitution on the Church in the Modern World are taken from *The Documents of Vatican II,* published by Guild Press, America Press, Association Press, and Herder and Herder, and copyrighted 1966 by The America Press. Used by permission.

For an overall view of writings by and about Teilhard de Chardin and for more complete information on material cited in shortened form in the footnotes to this study, consult the Bibliography at the end of this volume.

CONTENTS

xiii

ABBREVIATIONS

AM   P. Teilhard de Chardin, *The Appearance of Man*, tr. J. Cohen.

Archives H. de Lubac, S.J., "Maurice Blondel et le Père Teilhard de Chardin, mémoires échangés en décembre 1919, présentés par H. de Lubac," *Archives de philosophie* 24 (1961) 123–56.

Cuénot C. Cuénot, *Teilhard de Chardin*, tr. V. Colimore.

DM   P. Teilhard de Chardin, *The Divine Milieu*, tr. B. Wall, A. Dru, N. Lindsay, D. MacKinnon, *et al.*

Ecrits P. Teilhard de Chardin, *Ecrits du temps de la guerre (1916–1919)*.

FM   P. Teilhard de Chardin, *The Future of Man*, tr. N. Denny.

HU   P. Teilhard de Chardin, *Hymn of the Universe*, tr. S.
          Bartholomew.

LT   P. Teilhard de Chardin, *Letters from a Traveller*, tr. B.
          Wall, R. Hague, V. Hammersley, N. Lindsay, *et al.*

MM   P. Teilhard de Chardin, *The Making of a Mind*, tr. R.
          Hague.

MPN   P. Teilhard de Chardin, *Man's Place in Nature*, tr.
          R. Hague.

OE 6   P. Teilhard de Chardin, *L'énergie humaine*, vol. 6 of
          the "Oeuvres de Pierre Teilhard de Chardin."

OE 7   P. Teilhard de Chardin, *L'activation de l'énergie*, vol.
          7 of the "Oeuvres de Pierre Teilhard de Chardin."

OE 9   P. Teilhard de Chardin, *Science et Christ*, vol. 9 of the
          "Oeuvres de Pierre Teilhard de Chardin."

PM   P. Teilhard de Chardin, *The Phenomenon of Man*, tr.
          B. Wall.

VP   P. Teilhard de Chardin, *The Vision of the Past*, tr. J.
          Cohen.

TEILHARD DE CHARDIN'S THEOLOGY OF THE CHRISTIAN IN THE WORLD

I · THE PROBLEM OF THE TWO FAITHS

PIERRE TEILHARD DE CHARDIN was a priest and a scientist, a man of God and a man of his time. His life was directed toward forming a synthesis between Christianity and the spirit of our age, a synthesis that it was his life effort to live, to think out, and to put into words and pass on to others. His writings on the subject stretch from early in World War I, a few years after his ordination to the priesthood, when he was serving as an enlisted man in the French army, through his long and distinguished career in France, China, Africa, and the United States as a geologist and paleontologist, to his death in 1955.

In 1916 he writes to a friend that the reconciliation of Christianity and the contemporary spirit "has always been the problem of my interior life—a little like the question of Rome for Newman . . .

3

I mean the reconciliation of progress and detachment, of the passionate and legitimate love of this great earth and the single-minded pursuit of the kingdom of heaven."[1] And again: "I would like to be able to have a great love for Christ in the *very act* of loving the universe. Is that a dream, or a blasphemy? Besides union with God and union with the world, isn't there a union with God through the world?"[2] It was the coming together of these two currents, love of God and love of the world, that was responsible for the progress and also for the struggles of his interior life.[3] Precisely because he shared normally in the ideas and the interests

[1] Letter of March 15, 1916, quoted in H. de Lubac, S.J., *La pensée religieuse du Père Teilhard de Chardin,* 349. On Teilhard's interior life, see H. de Lubac, S.J., *Teilhard de Chardin, the Man and His Meaning,* tr. R. Hague, 3–130. By far the best biography of Teilhard is the long and heavily documented work by C. Cuénot, *Teilhard de Chardin,* tr. V. Colimore. There are several short accounts of Teilhard's life. See, for example, M. Murray, *The Thought of Teilhard de Chardin,* 1–8. The recent literature on the life and thought of Teilhard de Chardin is vast. A complete bibliography of all works in all languages published each year on Teilhard since 1956 appears annually in the July–December issue of *Archivum Historicum Societatis Iesu.*

[2] Letter of March 15, 1916, in H. de Lubac, S.J., *op. cit.,* 350. See letter of July 22, 1916, *ibid.,* 352–3: "More and more, it seems to me, there is a healthy reconciliation—and how profound a reconciliation—to be made between the adorers of Christ and those of the world." In another letter written on the same day Teilhard writes: "And once again, I was conscious within myself of the inspiration that calls me to the great work of reconciling the supreme and absolute love of God with the lower (but still legitimate and necessary) love of life embraced under its natural forms." (P. Teilhard de Chardin, *The Making of a Mind,* tr. R. Hague, 114, hereafter cited as *MM.*) In a letter of March 29, 1917, he writes: "For my part, I told you the frame of mind in which I was going back to the front: more sharply aware that for the rest of my life my task is to develop in myself, humbly, faithfully, doggedly,—and at the same time to impart it as much as possible to others—the sort of mysticism that makes one seek passionately for God in the heart of every substance and every action." (*MM,* 190.)

[3] "Le coeur de la matière," 1950, 24.

of his time, he was able to find a balanced interior life only in an organically unified conception of the world and of Christ, and in that conception he found "peace and limitless room to expand."[4] Teilhard felt that his own interior effort to unite in himself the elements of his double role in life was the experience on a personal and individual level of the contemporary struggle of mankind to unify its perspectives and its action.[5] He felt that his personal solution was a small-scale outline of the solution to the great spiritual problem confronting all mankind today.

The originality of his personal faith was that it had its roots in two sectors of life that are usually thought to be opposed. He stood at a privileged crossroads of the world where, in his double role as priest and scientist, he could let form in himself a lived synthesis between Christian faith and what is best in contemporary culture. Placed by life at the heart of two worlds whose thought patterns and feelings he knew intimately from experience, he placed no partition between them. The two forces that drew him reinforced one another so that he could say that he believed better than ever in God and more than ever in the world. He was conscious that his own life was, at a personal level, at least the sketch of the solution to "the great spiritual problem that, right now, is troubling the front ranks of mankind."[6]

[4] "Mon univers," 1924, P. Teilhard de Chardin, *Science et Christ*, vol. 9 of the "Oeuvres de Pierre Teilhard de Chardin," 65–6, hereafter cited as *OE* 9. See Teilhard's letter of January 21, 1936, P. Teilhard de Chardin, *Letters from a Traveller*, tr. B. Wall *et al.*, 218–9, hereafter cited as *LT*: "As a purpose in life, my science (to which I owe so much) seems to me to be less and less worthwhile. For a long time now, my chief interest in life has lain in some sort of effort towards a plainer disclosing of God in the world."

[5] "Le Christique," 1955, 1.

[6] "Comment je crois," 1934, 1. See "The Heart of the Problem," 1949, P. Teilhard de Chardin, *The Future of Man*, tr. N. Denny, 261, hereafter cited as *FM*.

Teilhard de Chardin's effort of synthesis has several overlapping aspects; it is an effort to make a synthesis of love of God and love of the world, of faith in Christ and faith in man, of religion and science, of Christian detachment and immersion in the world, of the kingdom of God and human achievement.

From the time of his earliest writings he points out the necessity of reconciliation between Christianity and the pursuit of progress in the world. A point of view must be found in which Christ and the universe are seen to stand so related that possession of one means possession of the other, that union with one means union with the other, that a person cannot be fully Christian without being profoundly human.[7] In an essay on "the Kingdom of God and the mastery of the world," religion and earthly progress are compared to the summit and the base of a pyramid. They should be "neither confused nor separated; they are destined to form a vital unity where their respective lives can be prolonged and subordinated, where they can be mutually complementary. Since it is in our age that the duality has become manifest, it is up to us to make the synthesis."[8] This same duality and the same need for synthesis are expressed in 1929 and after in terms of "the Christian point of view" and "the human point of view."[9]

---

[7] "La vie cosmique," 1916, P. Teilhard de Chardin, *Ecrits du temps de la guerre (1916–1919)*, 46, hereafter cited as *Ecrits*.

[8] "La maîtrise du monde et le règne de Dieu," 1916, *Ecrits*, 80. See "A Note on Progress," 1920, *FM*, 11–24, where Teilhard speaks out for a Christian faith in the movement of the world, in human progress.

[9] Intégration de l'homme dans l'univers," fourth lecture, 1930. In "Le coeur de la matière" (1950, 1) Teilhard groups several seemingly synonymous terms: "sens humain" (which I have translated as "human point of view"), "sens de la consistance," "sens cosmique," "sens de la terre," and "sens Christique." All of these appear to mean about the same thing in Teilhard's writings except for "sens Christique." Certainly in Teilhard's own outlook the "human point of view" and the "Christic point of view" were one. But they are conceptually different; the Christic point of view is the specifically Christian development of the human point of view.

It seems to me clear above all else, setting aside the countless minor divergences, and ignoring the dull, inert mass of those who believe in nothing at all, that the spiritual conflict afflicting Mankind today arises out of the division of minds and hearts into the two profoundly separated categories of:

(a) Those whose hopes are directed towards a spiritual state or an absolute finality situated beyond and outside this world;

(b) Those who hope for the perfection of the tangible Universe within itself.

The first of these groups, by far the older, is pre-eminently represented in these days by the Christians, protagonists of a transcendent and personal God.

The second group, comprising those who for a variety of reasons have dedicated their lives to the service of a Universe which they conceive as eventually culminating in some form of impersonal and immanent Reality, is of very recent origin. Throughout human history this conflict between the "servants of Heaven" and the "servants of earth" has gone on; but only since the birth of the idea of Evolution (in some sort divinising the Universe) have the devotees of earth bestirred themselves and made of their worship a true form of religion, charged with limitless hope, striving and renunciation.

Are we to disdain the world and put it behind us, or live in it in order to master and perfect it? Mankind is rent asunder at this moment by these two concepts or rival mysticisms; and in consequence its vital power of adoration is disastrously weakened.

Such in my view is the nature of the crisis, more profound than any economic, political or social struggle, through which we are passing.[10]

A short examination of each of these two rival mysticisms or understandings of reality, beginning with "the human point of view," will prepare us for a further study of the need for their synthesis.

[10] "Some Reflections on Progress," 1941, *FM*, 76–7.

The Human Point of View and Its Limitations

Teilhard uses the phrase "human point of view" to designate the total outlook of the contemporary man, who has, but in a contemporary and much more developed way, what Tertullian called "the naturally Christian soul." He describes the "human point of view" as "the consciousness of earthly thought that it forms an organized totality which is endowed with the power of growth and which is equal to and responsible for a future."[11] The development of this "human point of view" is comparatively recent, and its rise and growth have revolutionized thought patterns, particularly the thought patterns of western civilization.

There are three principal phases in the history of the "human point of view."[12]

Speaking generally, our modern way of looking at the universe has its roots in the Copernican revolution. By the simple admission that the earth revolves around the sun, the idea of a mechanical earth-centered universe was destroyed; "all the magic of the celestial spheres disappeared and man was left facing an amorphous mass to be totally rethought."[13]

In a second period, the eighteenth and nineteenth centuries, there were the beginnings of the study of genesis in several fields: the study of genetics in biology and zoology, the study of the genesis of human institutions and of ideas in history.

Finally, the modern idea of evolution was born, grew, spread. And with this, supported by the formation of the new sciences of modern physics and chemistry, the "human point of view" took

[11] "Le sens humain," 1929, 1.

[12] "Du cosmos à la cosmogénèse," 1951, P. Teilhard de Chardin, L'activation de l'énergie, vol. 7 of the "Oeuvres de Pierre Teilhard de Chardin," 261–5, hereafter cited as OE 7. See "La mystique de la science," 1939, P. Teilhard de Chardin, L'énergie humaine, vol. 6 of the "Oeuvres de Pierre Teilhard de Chardin," hereafter cited as OE 6.

[13] "Du cosmos à la cosmogénèse," 1951, OE 7, 262.

form. The form is that of a conception of a world in movement, in evolution, growing always more complex and more highly organized, moving as a totality in space-time toward some Future. The human point of view is, as a matter of fact, much more than a point of view. It is a belief in man and in the world and in progress, and it is a call to service and to self-sacrifice in helping to shape the future. It is really a new kind of religion. It is "the religious power of the Earth that is, at this very moment in us, undergoing the definitive crisis of its own discovery."[14] This new religion of the world may be confused in its dogmas, but it is perfectly clear in its moral orientations: the priority of the common good over individual interest, a vigorous faith in the value and the potential of human activity, a reverence for all forms of research.[15]

In the years 1929 through 1936, Teilhard was preoccupied with the religious importance of the modern "religion of earth." It is not surprising that an essay written in 1932 compares this western natural religion, the mystique of the West, with oriental mysticism.[16] Speaking very broadly, in the mysticism of the East the multiplicity of things and of desires is a bad dream from which we should awaken; we should suppress efforts to know and love and further develop our individuality, for these add to the strength of the bad dream. In the silence that follows the suppression of

[14] "Le sens humain," 1929, 7.
[15] "L'incroyance moderne," 1933, *OE* 9, 150-1. See "L'esprit de la terre," 1931, *OE* 6, 25-7, where Teilhard speaks of faith in the world as "le sens de la terre," the acute sense of common destiny that carries ever further the thinking portion of life.
[16] "La route de l'ouest," 1932. For a later and more developed treatment of the same theme, see "L'apport spirituel de l'extrême orient. Quelques réflexions personnelles," *Monumenta Nipponica* 12 (1956) 2-11. Note that the "route of the West" is, for Teilhard, Christian in its origins and in its term in spite of appearances. See also "Le Christianisme dans le monde," 1933, *OE* 9, 135-7.

multiplicity, we attain the one Substance. This kind of mysticism means the death of constructive activity and is the affirmation of the radical meaninglessness of the universe.

To this admittedly schematic description of oriental mysticism, Teilhard opposes the "route of the West." The search for unity is the central theme in the mystique of the modern world of the West, just as it has always been for the East. But the approach is much different. It is natural to the contemporary western person, living in a culture permeated with the ideas of scientific research and evolutionary time, to seek unity through the constructive effort of unifying the multiple; not a negation of multiplicity, then, but a building of unity out of the multiple. Only the idea of a growing and converging unity can be at the foundation of religion and morality in a world based on research and progress. Influenced by his own taste for action, contemporary man doesn't want any control of his activity other than that which directs his activity toward further building the world, that integrates him actively in the building up of the world. The "mystique of the West" is a mysticism of construction and conquest directed to some supreme unification of the universe.[17]

The human and cosmic point of view, man's sense of unity with mankind and with the whole universe in movement, is expressed in the modern "religion of earth."[18] The modern spirit sees two dimensions that are new; the modern spirit has a sense of the *universal* and a sense of the *future*. The discovery of the immensity and the unity of the universe has given modern man a sense of the

[17] "Le Christianisme dans le monde," 1933, *OE* 9, 135–7.
[18] "Esquisse d'un univers personnel," 1936, *OE* 6, 69–114. Teilhard here sets forth his views on the person and the person's relations to all around him. The "human point of view" and the "cosmic point of view" are considered as affective and unity-directed manifestations of human consciousness. See "Quelques réflexions sur la conversion du monde," 1936, *OE* 9, 157–66.

universal, and the discovery of the immensity and the noncyclic nature of time has given him a sense of unlimited possible progress, a sense of the future. A sense of the universal that is a total view of the universe, and a sense of the future that is a faith in the possibilities of progress: these two, a comprehensive view of reality and a faith, define for Teilhard the essential elements of a religion.

He sees, then, the modern spirit as a basically religious spirit, the spirit of a new "religion of earth." The problem is not, as some have thought, that the world is growing cold to religion. "In fact, the world has never been more religiously ardent. It is beginning to burn, however, with a new fire, a fire that is not yet clearly distinguished and identified, . . . a faith and a hope in some salvation that is tied to the evolutionary building up of the earth. No, the modern world is not irreligious; just the opposite."[19] For the first time in its history Christianity is confronted not with a heresy, nor with a schism, nor even with paganism. In the face of Christianity there is today a new and growing "religion of earth."[20] Teilhard sees this confrontation of two religions, the modern "religion of earth" and the Christian religion, as the contemporary religious problem.

At its most intense and most typical, the religion of earth is found in the blind faith in progress that goes with the scientific

[19] "Christianisme et évolution," 1945, 1–2. Long sections of this unpublished essay are quoted in C. Cuénot, *Teilhard de Chardin*, tr. V. Colimore, 139–44, hereafter cited as *Cuénot*. In a letter of December 10, 1952, Teilhard writes: "Whatever may be said, our century is religious—probably more than any other (how could it fail to be with such vast horizons opening before it and with such problems to be solved?). The only thing is that it has not yet the God it can adore." (Quoted in *Cuénot*, 368.)

[20] "Quelques réflexions sur la conversion du monde," 1936, *OE* 9, 157–9. This essay was written as a confidential report at the request of "some high officials" in Rome. See L. Swan, "Memories and Letters," *Teilhard de Chardin, Pilgrim of the Future*, ed. N. Braybrooke, 44.

mystique, the hope in a limitless future based on the explorations and conquests of science. Writing in 1939, Teilhard finds this religion of science to be at the root of many of the materialistic philosophies and of all the totalitarian social ideologies of the time, Marxism, Fascism, Nazism.[21] But even in 1939, when the practical effects of the religion of science are more manifest than ever, it is clear that blind faith in progress cannot stand by itself. There is an intellectual and moral crisis in the religion of science; among many, faith in progress is discredited. In fact, he states that "the religion of science is dead."[22] By 1939, then, the problem of the two faiths is complicated by the fact that the religion of earth is in a state of crisis, and blind faith in science is dead. The moral and intellectual crisis through which the religion of the world is passing manifests itself in anxiety. And parallel to his description of faith in the world is his analysis of contemporary anxiety.

In *The Phenomenon of Man* Teilhard admits that human anxiety is bound up with human consciousness and is as old as man himself. Nevertheless, contemporary anxiety is something more than this. It is bound up somehow with modern man's sudden confrontation with space-time and with his increasing socialization. "Conscious or not, suppressed anguish—a fundamental anguish of being—despite our smiles strikes the depths of all our hearts and is the undertone of all our conversations. This does not mean that its cause is clearly recognized—far from it. Something threatens us, something is more than ever lacking, but without our being able to say exactly what."[23]

[21] "La mystique de la science," 1939, *OE* 6, 203–23.
[22] *Ibid.*, 219.
[23] P. Teilhard de Chardin, *The Phenomenon of Man*, tr. B. Wall, 226, hereafter cited as *PM*. See P. Teilhard de Chardin, *Man's Place in Nature*, tr. R. Hague, 100–4, hereafter cited as *MPN*; in these pages Teilhard writes of "the essential fear of the reflective element when it faces an apparently blind whole, whose vast layers enfold it as though to re-absorb it while still in the fullness of life." (100.) Today, Teilhard goes on, this

In several essays, from 1949 to 1954, he analyzes modern anxiety. The human race, after millions of years of expansion over the face of the earth, has suddenly entered into the compressive phase of its existence. The results seem to be that the elites are giving way to the rise of the masses, that nature and solitude are disappearing amid the cities and factories, that business has replaced more human forms of exchange, that the person is more and more collectivized, mechanized, dehumanized.[24]

At a more profound level, modern man suffers from the general conditions of his existence. He is overwhelmed by immensity, by the infinitely small in the structure of matter, by the infinitely large in the structure of the universe, and by the seemingly infinite axis of time that stretches back millions of years and reaches forward indefinitely. Further, he is crushed by the airtightness of the world; vast as the universe is, we are imprisoned in its space-time. What is more, man senses his own fragility in the face of a hostile world that he knows determines his destiny, in spite of himself, in many ways—even reaching into his most interior self. He is intimidated, too, by the immensity of the human mass, by the difficulty in communicating with others, by the impersonal blind hostility of large human institutions. In the face of all this, contemporary man is afraid.[25]

---

essential fear is more acute than ever owing to the compressive forces of contemporary civilization. See also "Does Mankind Move Biologically upon Itself?" 1949, *FM*, 249: "Confronted by this technico-social embrace of the human mass, modern man, insofar as he has any clear idea of what is happening, tends to take fright as though at an impending disaster." Teilhard is speaking of a general existential anxiety; for a psychotherapist's view of the same phenomenon, see V. Frankl, *Man's Search for Meaning*, 151–214.

[24] "Réflexions sur la compression humaine," 1953, *OE* 7, 357–8. See "The Singularities of the Human Species," 1954, P. Teilhard de Chardin, *The Appearance of Man*, tr. J. Cohen, 208–9, hereafter cited as *AM*.

[25] "Un phénomène de contre-évolution en biologie humaine, ou la peur de l'existence," 1949, *OE* 7, 189–97.

What is the root of this fear; what is at the core of mankind's present unrest and anxiety? Ultimately, Teilhard points out in a section of *The Phenomenon of Man* that deals with modern disquiet, it is the fear of death, the fear of the death of mankind itself; not simply fear of the future, but—at bottom—the fear that there will finally be no future.

Tomorrow? But who can guarantee us a tomorrow anyway? And without the assurance that this tomorrow exists, can we really go on living, we to whom has been given—perhaps for the first time in the whole story of the universe—the terrible gift of foresight?

Sickness of the dead end—the anguish of feeling shut in.

This time we have at last put our finger on the tender spot.

What makes the world in which we live specifically modern is our discovery in it and around it of evolution. And I can now add that what disconcerts the modern world at its very roots is not being sure, and not seeing how it ever could be sure, that there is an outcome—*a suitable outcome*—to that evolution.[26]

Mankind is not sure of an outcome, of a way out of what appears to be a blind alley, a closed universe. Teilhard more than once uses the figure of a group of miners trapped underground. Before they can decide to climb back up the mine shaft, they have to presuppose two things: that there is an opening at the end of the

[26] *PM*, 228. See "The End of the Species," 1953, *FM*, 298–303, where Teilhard says that twentieth-century man is haunted by the possibility of the extinction of the human species. "Darwinism, as it was then called, however naive its beginnings, came at exactly the right moment to create the cosmological atmosphere of which the great technico-social advance of the last century stood in need if it was to believe passionately in what it was doing. Rudimentary though it was, Darwinism afforded a scientific justification of faith in progress. But today, by a development natural to itself, the movement has come to look like a receding tide. . . . Following that exalted vision of species in growth, (man) is now confronted by an accumulation of scientific evidence pointing to the reverse—the species doomed to extinction." (299.)

shaft, and that on the other side of that opening are light and fresh air. In the same way, the present generation is confronted with the reality of a long and painful effort to be made, the effort of human progress. The effort won't, can't be made if the world is thought to be hermetically sealed, if the end is thought to be total death, if there is no opening, no way out.[27] It is true that most men never ask themselves the question, "Is living worth the effort?" Life carries them along automatically. The problem, however, exists, and it will stand out more and more sharply as the burden of human progress becomes heavier and more important. Is man making something that will endure, or are his efforts ultimately worthless? If it could be proved to men that nothing will remain of their work because there will be, finally, not just the death of the individual and of the earth but the death of the universe, then the very source of human action would be killed. "Free will cannot be put in movement except by the attraction of a lasting result."[28]

Mankind is just beginning to formulate the question of whether or not it is worthwhile to go on. What has changed mankind in a few centuries, what has made men so different from their fore-bears, not only more in control of nature and more ambitious but also more anxious and worried, is this: men are more and more conscious of the movement that is carrying them along. They are therefore realizing more and more the importance of knowing whether or not that movement is going somewhere, of knowing whether or not there is "a way out." Man is coming of age and having doubts; he is becoming critically conscious of his situation; and he will not go on acting, serving the world, if he sees the universe as closed, if he cannot find a suitable outcome to his efforts of progress. If man were to foresee somewhere in the future

---

[27] "Le phénomène chrétien," 1950, 5. See "La biologie, pensée à fond, peut-elle nous conduire à émerger dans le transcendant?" 1951, *OE 9*, 279–80.

[28] "Mon univers," 1924, *OE 9*, 70.

a total death of all human consciousness, a blank wall, his activity would simply stop, its mainspring broken. "Man will never take a step in a direction he knows to be blocked. There is precisely the ill that causes our disquiet."[29]

This, then, is the root cause of contemporary anxiety: man's uncertainty in face of the future, his fear that the direction he takes might be blocked, his fear of the possibility of a future total death of all human consciousness, his fear of a blank wall. A few months before his death in 1955, Teilhard writes of what he labels "the death barrier"; as mankind grows more conscious of the barrier of death, the need grows for some kind of basic evidence that the death barrier can be broken through.[30]

Faith in the world, in progress, in man, taken by itself, is inadequate. The religion of earth is crippled if it stands alone, because it cannot guarantee permanence to man's efforts, because it cannot guarantee a suitable outcome, a way out, to the universe. The more man progresses, the more conscious he becomes of the question "Where will it all end, and is it worth it?"

Christianity and Modern Unbelief

Teilhard's analysis of the religion of earth and the limitations of that religion has its counterpart in his analysis of contemporary Christianity. Just as the religion of progress is basically limited by

[29] *PM*, 229. See "L'esprit de la terre," 1931, OE 6, 50, where Teilhard writes that a universe that would continue to act laboriously while waiting consciously for an absolute death would be a monstrous and stupid world. See also "From the Pre-human to the Ultra-human," 1950, *FM*, 296: "The grand enigma presented by the phenomenon of man is not the question of knowing how life was kindled on earth, but of understanding how it might be extinguished on earth without being continued elsewhere. Having once become reflective, it cannot acquiesce in its total disappearance without biologically contradicting itself."

[30] "Barrière de la mort et co-réflexion," 1955, *OE* 7, 419–29.

its built-in ambiguity, by its incapacity to guarantee a successful outcome for human effort, so does Christianity as it is presented in the twentieth century have serious defects. The defects, however, are not in Christianity but in the way in which it is presented and understood.

In his essays written during the first World War he asks why the world seems to be becoming less Christian.[31] The traditional explanation for the rejection of Christianity by people is that they reject Christ because they do not love the truth enough, because they lack generosity, because they do not love enough or because they love badly. This has been the usual Christian explanation of heresy, agnosticism, modern paganism: there is something lacking not in the presented Christian message but in those who reject it.

But in this century there seem to be more and more people who reject Christianity *because* they are generous and Christianity does not ask enough of them, because they want to love more and better and Christianity does not appear to offer them a greater and better love. More and more sincere and truly religious men reject organized Christianity not because they are too small, but because Christianity seems too small for them; Christianity is not big enough for their generous desires. The natural charity of these people is not dead, nor even cold; it is being turned toward ideals that seem higher, purer, more human than the Christian ideal. Christianity is seen by many as something extrinsic to real life, something that can be added on for those who want to add it on, but not a belief concerned with real issues. It seems something for those who want that sort of thing; it answers needs that are particular, not universal. "Let us not fool ourselves. The Christian ideal (as it is usually presented) is no longer the common ideal of

[31] See "La vie cosmique," 1916, *Ecrits*, 42–6; "La maîtrise du monde et le règne de Dieu," 1916, *Ecrits*, 73–6; "L'âme du monde," 1918, *Ecrits*, 221–2; "Forma Christi," 1918, *Ecrits*, 335; "Note pour servir à l'évangélisation des temps nouveaux," 1919, *Ecrits*, 369–71.

Mankind. . . . To more and more men, Christianity appears invincibly inhuman and inferior."[32]

More and more men see the Christian message as promoting egotistic individualism and interest in one's own private salvation, as leading to lack of interest in the common effort of the world. In this century, people are more interested in social justice than in charity, in work and progress rather than in detachment, in full development of human powers rather than in mortification. The notions of "human" and "Christian" no longer coincide, and they seem to be diverging.

Men are more and more indifferent to the Christian message, not because Christianity is too difficult or too elevated but because it just does not seem important. In other times Christianity was a force and was presented as a force; today it is simply avoided, like a burden or a chain. Why is it that Christianity in its modern presentation seems so narrow, small, stifling? Because, says Teilhard, "the human point of view" believes in a magnificent future for this world and the Gospel appears to disdain this world. By temperament and formation contemporary man believes in the world; to all appearances, the Church does not.[33]

Unbelievers, searching for a name to give to the God that they feel, turn to the Church. And then they turn away from a Church that does not answer their questions nor their hopes, that does not seem relevant to the world they live in. The Church is meeting resistance and rejection not because her teaching is too elevated and her morality too difficult, but because men, not recognizing in the Church what they are seeking, drift further away and wait for something better.[34]

[32] "Note pour servir a l'évangélisation des temps nouveaux," 1919, *Ecrits*, 370.
[33] "Le sens humain," 1929, 8–12, 15–6. Also, "Comment je crois," 1934, 22.
[34] "L'incroyance moderne," 1933, *OE* 9, 151–2. From now on in this study, when two or more phrases or sentences are quoted from the same

What is more, Christianity seems less and less important not only to non-Christians but also to believers. Even the faithful do not find in their religion the total meaning of their lives; many remain Christian only because there is nothing better. More and more Christians are interiorly divided between their religion and their faith in the world. Teilhard is severe in his criticism of the Church's official reaction to the crisis in which she finds herself. Ecclesiastical authority has never really been interested in science, or in tangible human progress, or even in world unity. Faith in progress, in human effort, in research, has continually been mocked or condemned by the clergy. He suggests that the Church's motto is: "There is nothing more to look for; everything has been discovered."[35] "Most of the clergy are now in favor of giving human activities a larger place in Christian life. But for them this 'larger part' is never more than an addition, a 'plus,' an overflow of this supernatural life into the natural." The Church has lost contact with reality. "The ecclesiastical directives and the preoccupations of the faithful are slowly sealing the Church in a closed artificial world of rituals, of routines, of pious practices, a world completely separated from the mainstream of life."[36] This

---

passage and placed in close succession in the text, the reference will be indicated by only one footnote number in the text, placed immediately after the last phrase or sentence quoted.

[35] "Le sens humain," 1929, 10. See Teilhard's letter of February 4, 1934, to Father A. Sertillange: "I am convinced that if Christianity often has so much difficulty in keeping its true place in the consciousness of the faithful and also in converting the 'Gentiles,' it is chiefly because it often gives the *impression* of despising or of fearing the grandeur and the unity of the universe." [Quoted by P. Chauchard in "Teilhard de Chardin et Saint Thomas d'Aquin," *Revue Teilhard de Chardin* 1, no. 1–2 (1960) 12.] Ignace Lepp writes that "for a noteworthy number of educated men of today, it is the Church that represents the greatest obstacle to faith. . . . (because the Church) often gives the impression of refusing to understand the essence of the modern world and its spiritual needs." (*Teilhard et la foi des hommes*, 248–9.)

[36] "Le sens humain," 1929, 15.

may seem exaggerated or too harsh to us, but it was probably not too harsh for 1929 and still has a certain validity.[37]

Briefly, the present age believes in human effort and the building of the world; the current presentation of the Christian message tends in just the opposite direction: to discourage human effort and to devalue the building of the world. The Christian faith, at odds with the contemporary religion of earth, seems unappealing, small; it is losing ground. Teilhard's criticism of the way in which the Church today speaks about human effort and progress stresses the inadequacies in the manner in which the ideal of Christian holiness is understood and presented, especially the tendency to undervalue the material world and the weaknesses in the current Christian understanding of renunciation and detachment. The Christian ideal of detachment is often presented as a sort of derivative of the mysticism of the East, emphasizing flight from the world, withdrawal from material things, evasion of the natural and escape into the supernatural.[38]

In its classic and ancient form, the theory of Christian holiness rests on the idea that nature (in contrast to supernature) is complete—*fulfilled*. Numerically, of course, spirit still grows on earth (multiplication of souls). But qualitatively (in its natural powers), it spreads out and goes nowhere; it maintains itself; it simply endures. Under these conditions, holiness for men cannot consist in anything other than taking flight alone into the supernatural. Anything else is of no interest to the kingdom of God, except insofar as it is needed, for an arbitrary period of time, to assure that life goes on through the

[37] The contrast between the official Church attitude that Teilhard criticizes and the official Church attitude expressed in the documents of the Second Vatican Council is indeed great. See especially the *Pastoral Constitution on the Church in the Modern World*.

[38] In a letter of January 10, 1953, Teilhard writes: "Why is it that nine times out of ten a believing Christian is, as regards man, a 'sceptic'? That is the great stumbling-block for the Gentiles." (Quoted in *Cuénot*, 363.)

ages. And even for this, the children of the world are enough. Essentially, the Christian is more purely a Christian the sooner he detaches himself from the world, the less he uses creatures, the more he approaches spirit.[39]

Furthermore, the insistence on the absolute gratuity of creation and the utter contingency of creatures tends to discourage any interest in the world. How can man act if he is convinced of the uselessness of what he does? If man's efforts toward earthly progress are meaningless, why should he make those efforts?[40] If the ideal of holiness is presented as peace and silence and subjugation of matter through mortification rather than the perfection of human effort cooperating with God, then human effort and progress will be, as they often are, made little of and thus discouraged.[41]

Christianity is plagued by a spiritual dualism, by a conflict between the Church's teaching on the Christian duty to work and the notion that the world is vanity. It is one thing to point out that there is a divine precept to labor and to develop the earth. But if it is immediately added that the results of that labor are perishable and useless, that the world is given to man as a wheel is put in a squirrel's cage, chiefly to help him to exercise and to go through the motions of living, how can man have any enthusiasm for his work or for life itself? For man to give himself wholeheartedly to

[39] "Note sur la notion de perfection chrétienne," 1942, 1. This attitude is an inheritance from the Middle Ages and the earlier times that helped to form the medieval outlook. See A. Auer, "The Christian Understanding of the World," tr. C. Gusmer, *The Christian and the World*, 6–9. Auer writes that "the basic attitude of the Middle Ages was one-sidedly that of flight from the world. . . . Medieval Christianity was predominantly shaped by monks. Its ideal of life had a fascinating effect also upon laymen; one thought he could serve God best and most uncompromisingly when he bade farewell to the world." (6.)

[40] "Contingence de l'univers et goût humain de survivre," 1953, 3.

[41] "Introduction à la vie chrétienne," 1944, 11–2.

the work of the universe, he has to be convinced not only of the merit of what he does, but of its value. He has to believe in what he is doing.[42] Christianity seems to discourage that belief rather than support it. These ideas are from an essay written in 1916, when Teilhard was serving at the front as an enlisted man and becoming increasingly conscious of the changes needed if the gospel is to reach contemporary man. In a letter written soon after, he restates the problem:

How can one be fully a Christian and at the same time be fully a man? It is all very well to study the sciences, philosophy, sociology, in order to please God and to fulfill the assigned task. But it is not enough. Unless I recognize in my studies or my job the possibility of loving my work, unless I see the necessity of giving myself to it completely, unless I see that I consolidate my progress toward an Absolute by reason of my conquests themselves (and not just by the moral value of my efforts), unless the world means more to me than just an occasion for gaining merit . . . then I will be lukewarm among men, and they will regard me because of my religion as a deserter and only half a man. Who can say that they will be completely wrong?[43]

Two years later, in a short paper explaining his particular point of view to his friends and guides, he underlines his own need to

[42] "La vie cosmique," 1916, *Ecrits*, 45–6. Interestingly enough, the great Jewish mystic, Simone Weil, who was so close to Christianity, uses the same squirrel and wheel metaphor when writing of the mysticism of work. She uses it to illustrate a point of view that is the precise opposite of that of Teilhard de Chardin: "A squirrel turning in its cage and the rotation of the celestial sphere. Extreme misery and extreme grandeur. It is when a man sees himself as a squirrel turning round and round in a circular cage that, if he does not lie to himself, he is close to salvation." (*Gravity and Grace*, tr. A. Wills, 234.)

[43] Letter of March 15, 1916, quoted in H. de Lubac, S.J., *La pensée religieuse du Père Teilhard de Chardin*, 349.

unify his interior vision, and he feels that need so strongly that he is sure that there must be many others like himself.[44] The difficulty is a real and practical one. The supernaturalization of the world brings more than abstract problems for the theologians; it introduces an appearance of duality at the very heart of everyday Christian life. In the first place, a Christian who wants to truly live his religion is blocked by a dualism in his effort. How can he reconcile the detachment from the world that is so necessary to life in Christ with the taste for the things of earth that is indispensable to human effort? Further, there is an even more serious dualism of religious tendency; the Christian feels himself caught between two absolutes: the Universe of his experience and the transcendent God of revelation.

Teilhard's most complete description of the modern Christian spiritual conflict is found in the first part of *The Divine Milieu*.[45] On the one hand, the Christian is told that all his actions can and should be sanctified. This applies not just to strictly religious actions but to even the most mundane. We are obliged to perform the duties of our state in life and to perform them as well as we can, and the teaching of the Church has always been that these duties are sanctified when performed in union with Christ. "It is the whole of human life, down to its most natural zones, which, the Church teaches, can be sanctified. . . . The general influence and practice of the Church has always been to dignify, ennoble and transfigure in God the duties inherent in one's station in life, the search for natural truth, and the development of human action."[46]

On the other hand, the Christian knows that this present life is nothing compared to the life to come; what is really important is not this world but the next. This would perhaps be enough to take

[44] "Mon univers," 1918, *Ecrits*, 278.

[45] P. Teilhard de Chardin, *The Divine Milieu*, tr. B. Wall, A. Dru, N. Lindsay, D. MacKinnon, *et al.*, 50–6, hereafter cited as *DM*.

[46] *Ibid.*, 50–1.

away our interest in and our taste for this world, but to this is added the knowledge that this world is fallen and spoiled. " 'Perfection consists in detachment; the world around us is vanity and ashes.' The believer is constantly reading or hearing these austere words."[47]

So there is a conflict set up in the hearts of many Christians; they are drawn by their taste for life and by their love of whatever exists to learn and to create; but they want to love God above all things, and they are afraid of dividing their allegiance. They are torn between God and the world. Some choose God, and some choose the world. But the great majority of Christians give up trying to achieve interior unity. They never resolve their spiritual conflict. They go through life divided, victims of a spiritual dualism, never belonging wholly to God, never belonging wholly to the world.[48]

[47] *Ibid.*, 51.

[48] It is interesting to compare Teilhard's lifelong stress on the need for a synthesis of the two faiths with the writings of Thomas Merton, who vigorously opposes the idea of any such synthesis. Merton writes, for example: "The tendency of our modern society and of all its thought and culture is to deny and to deride this simple, natural awareness (of the reality of God), and to make man from the very beginning both afraid of faith and ashamed of it. The first step to living faith is then, as it has always been one way or another, a denial and a rejection of the standards of thought complacently accepted by rationalistic doubt. And in actual practice what this usually amounts to is not the rejection of 'reason' and the acceptance of 'faith' but rather a choice between two faiths. One, a human, limited, external faith in human society with all its inert patrimony of assumptions and prejudices, a faith based on fear of solitude and on the need to 'belong' to the group and to accept its standards with passive acquiescence. Or, in the second place, a faith in what we do not 'see,' a faith in the transcendent and invisible God, . . ." (*Life and Holiness* [New York, Herder and Herder, 1963], 96–7.) See also L. Bouyer, *Introduction to Christian Spirituality*, tr. Mary Perkins Ryan, 143: "The highest goods that it (creation) contains, instead of leading us beyond them to the Creator, screen Him off from us." For an expansion of this general point of view see, among the many works of Father Bouyer, especially his *The Meaning of the Monastic Life*, tr. K. Pond.

The Problem of the Two Faiths

Having briefly examined what Teilhard calls the religion of
earth and the fact that by itself it is intrinsically crippled by the
growing anxiety of the dead end, and having reviewed his criticism
of the contemporary presentation of the Christian message and of
the present-day Christian spiritual conflict, we can return to his
insistence on the need for the synthesis of the "two religions."
There are three phases in his thought on the problem. A first
period, which includes the essays written in the army during World
War I, from 1916 to 1928, stresses the urgency of the problem;
but the vocabulary is often inadequate and somewhat variable and
vague, and the thought is sometimes in poetic form.[49] In a second
period, especially from 1929 to 1936, he analyzes the religion of
earth, the "human point of view," and compares it with "the Christian point of view" as it exists today, with its weaknesses. It is the
third phase of his study of the problem, when his religious thought
has reached maturity and his vocabulary is clear and consistent,
that we are interested in now. From 1945 to 1955, from the end of
World War II until his death, the effort to better formulate the
problem of the "two religions" and to outline their synthesis becomes increasingly important in his writings.[50]

In a paper on "Christianity and Evolution" written in 1945,
Teilhard for the first time considers the problem in terms of "faith
in God" and "faith in the world."[51] Two years later he writes
again of "the two kinds of faith in the transcendent action of a

[49] See, for example, "La vie cosmique," 1916, *Ecrits*, 1–61; "L'éternel
féminin," 1918, *Ecrits*, 249–62.

[50] Teilhard writes in a letter of March 2, 1952: "Interiorly, the interest
of my life is concentrated more and more on the effort to find and if
possible to give voice to the final formulation (the last testimony) in
which I wish to express the 'soul' of my two-fold vision of the 'Upward'
and the 'Forward.'" (*LT*, 323–4.)

[51] "Christianisme et évolution," 1945.

personal God and the innate perfectibility of a world in progress."[52] The same year, in a talk given to fellow Jesuit priests, he
speaks of "the problem of the two faiths."[53] A faith in some evolutionary future of the world seems to be interfering with the traditional faith of Christianity. A humanist mysticism of "the Forward"
is in apparent conflict with the Christian mysticism of "the Upward." In this opposition between faith in a transcendent God and
faith in an immanent universe is to be found the root source of
the contemporary religious crisis. "The problem of the two faiths.
How can we approach it?"[54] To begin with, he continues, we can
establish that the two faiths under consideration are not really
in opposition; on the contrary, they are the two essential components of a complete human and Christian mysticism. From
this time on, Teilhard identifies faith in the world as the religion
of "the Forward" and Christianity as the religion of "the Upward."
The need for a synthesis of the two faiths becomes a need for the
synthesis of "the Upward" and "the Forward," between a Christian
upward movement toward God and a natural human movement
forward toward the future, between a vertically moving faith in
God and a horizontally moving faith in the world.[55]

In a series of essays written between 1948 and 1950, Teilhard
states the question clearly.[56] The most complete statement of the
need for a synthesis of the two faiths is "The Heart of the Prob-

[52] "Turmoil or Genesis?" 1947, *FM*, 224. See "Faith in Man," 1947,
FM, 191–2.

[53] "Sur la valeur religieuse de la recherche," 1947, *OE* 9, 260.

[54] *Ibid.*, 261

[55] "The Forward" and "the Upward" are in French "l'en haut" and
"l'en avant."

[56] "Trois choses que je vois," 1948, 4–7; "Comment je vois," 1948,
21–4; "The Heart of the Problem," 1949, *FM*, 260–9; "Le coeur de la
matière," 1950, 3. Also, "Le néo-humanisme moderne et ses réactions sur
le Christianisme," notes taken at a talk given by Teilhard de Chardin in
1948, 1–6; "Le phénomène chrétien," 1950, 4–6; "Pour y voir clair. Réflexions sur deux formes inverses de l'esprit," 1950, *OE* 7, 229–36.

lem," a confidential report sent to his superiors; it sets forth Teilhard's views on the source of religious unrest in the modern world.[57] "Among the most disquieting aspects of the modern world is its general and growing state of dissatisfaction in religious matters. . . . For some obscure reason something has gone wrong between Man and God *as in these days He is represented to Man.*"[58] One has the impression of a growing dechristianization of the world. At the source of the contemporary religious crisis, writes Teilhard, is a conflict of faith, a conflict between "the Forward" and "the Upward." This conflict is present more or less consciously in the heart of everyone as a result of the tension between the modern forward impulse toward progress and the traditional impulse of religious worship. But faith in the world can neither justify itself nor even sustain its momentum; for it offers no way out ahead, no escape from total death. It cannot guarantee that the world has a purpose. "Worldly faith, in short, is not enough in itself to move the earth forward; but can we be sure that the Christian faith in its ancient interpretation is still sufficient of itself to carry the world upward?"[59]

The Church has as its function to Christianize all that is human. But what is more human than the growing faith in the world? Nevertheless, ecclesiastical authority continues to ignore and even to condemn this faith; and so the Church, not embracing everything that is human, is for the time incompletely human and becomes less capable of fully satisfying believers and of converting unbelievers. Why is it that there is so much unease among mem-

---

[57] In a short paper entitled "Ce que le monde attend en ce moment de l'Eglise de Dieu," Teilhard writes in 1952 that four years earlier he had sent "The Heart of the Problem" to his superiors in Rome in order to advise them of what he considered to be the true source of religious unrest in the world. He adds that the report was rejected as being not in accord with current ideas in Rome.

[58] "The Heart of the Problem," 1949, *FM*, 260.

[59] *Ibid.*, 265.

bers of religious orders and among priests and seminarians; why does the Church in many countries fail almost wholly in attracting the working classes; why are there so few conversions when there are so many missionaries? Because Christian charity lacks a quality it needs to be effective: *"Human* faith and hope, without which, in reason and in fact, no religion can henceforth appear to Man as other than colourless, cold and inassimilable."[60]

Neither faith in the world nor Christianity can achieve its full development without the other; yet they appear to be irreconcilable and even mutually exclusive. But, asks Teilhard, is this intense opposition real or only apparent? On the one hand, even the Communists who represent an extreme case, a caricature of faith in the world, reject a God who is extrinsic, a *deus ex machina* whose existence could only detract from the dignity of the world and weaken the motive power of human effort; but Christians, too, reject the existence of such a God. On the other hand, Christianity is based on Christ, it is rooted in the Incarnation; and for this reason it has traditionally asserted the values of matter, explicitly condemning opinions to the contrary. Just as the source of the contemporary religious crisis is the conflict of the two faiths, the solution to the crisis lies in their coming together to form one faith.

Outline of Teilhard's Thought

Teilhard de Chardin's lifetime effort to work out this synthesis intellectually falls into three steps or phases, developed simultaneously and together forming a unified Christian vision.[61] The first

---

[60] *Ibid.*, 266.

[61] In "Quelques réflexions sur la conversion du monde," 1936, *OE* 9, 161–2, Teilhard lists what he considers the three steps necessary to reach and to guide at its most profound level the modern religious current: the development of a generalized physics of evolution, of a Christology that

phase or level of his thought is a sort of scientific phenomenology, a generalized physics of evolution. This part of his thought does not depend on revelation but is an attempt to formulate a general theory of evolution, an attempt based on scientific data. He finds that evolution has a direction: toward higher degrees of material complexity, of organization, and toward correspondingly higher degrees of consciousness. Further, he finds that evolution is converging toward some already existing center that is somehow personal. The universe, then, has a structure and a direction; it is evolving according to a law of "complexity-consciousness" in the direction of greater spiritualization toward a point, a center, that is somehow already in being and that is somehow personal.

On this generalized physics of evolution as on a base Teilhard, in a second phase of his thought, uses the data of revelation to construct a Christian apologetic that is at the same time a Christology. The personal center toward which evolution is converging he identifies with Christ. The personal center of convergent evolution, the new "God of the Forward," is, then, the same as Christ, the incarnate traditional "God of the Upward."[62] The entire uni-

---

would take this hyperphysics into account, and of a morality and a mysticism of conquest based on the Christology. In "La pensée du Père Teilhard de Chardin," 1948, *Les études philosophiques* 10 (1955) 580–1, a short article written by Teilhard himself, he explains his own thought as consisting of three phases: a phenomenology of evolution, a Christian apologetic that identifies the focal point of convergent evolution as Christ, and a mystique of communion with God through the evolving universe. For a brief discussion of the *temporal* phases in the development of Teilhard's thought, see G. Crespy, *La pensée théologique de Teilhard de Chardin*, 50–2.

[62] Besides the two articles noted in reference 61 *supra*, see "Un sommaire de ma perspective phénoménologique du monde," *Les études philosophiques* 10 (1955) 569–71. It is possible to compare Teilhard's synthesis of "the Forward" and "the Upward," of evolutionary perspectives and Christianity, with the synthesis of St. Thomas Aquinas. St. Thomas's synthesis, of course, is a total theological system, whereas Teilhard considered only a few selected questions for theological development. Still, there is a parallel

verse is evolving toward Christ. Teilhard considers his theology of Christ, of a Christ who has attributes that are cosmic and universal as well as human and divine, to be not only proportioned to the modern conception of the universe but to be in striking harmony with the most fundamental texts of St. Paul and St. John and with the theology of the Greek Fathers of the Church.

At a third level, Teilhard outlines a positive morality, a Christian mystique of human conquest. He bases this mystique of human conquest directly on his Christology; the one follows from the other. Christ is the summit of the evolution of the universe, the point of convergence of that evolution; from that fact, the supernatural value of human effort carried out in Christ is clear. The most direct route to heaven is not, then, a route that would by-pass earth. It is through the building up of the world, a world larger and more unfinished than we realized, that heaven is to be attained. Because this is true, the most fundamental Christian attitudes, without deviating from tradition, are enriched and made much more dynamic.

The Cross is no longer only the symbol of expiation, but also the sign of the growth that is accomplished in pain.

Detachment no longer means exactly to despise and to reject, but to work through and to sublimate.

---

between an effort that aims at combining evolution and Christianity in one view and an effort that aims at integrating Aristotle and Christianity. See J. Pieper, *Guide to Thomas Aquinas*, tr. R. and C. Winston, 106–18. Pieper writes that "almost as soon as Thomas awoke to critical consciousness he recognized that it was his life's task to join these two extremes which seemed inevitably to be pulling away from one another. And I have labeled the extremes . . . 'Aristotle' on the one hand and the 'Bible' on the other. The name 'Aristotle' was meant to serve as a cryptic word for natural reality as a whole. . . . 'Bible' was meant to include the whole realm of the supernatural." (106.) It is interesting too that both Teilhard and Thomas base their efforts of synthesis ultimately on the fact of the Incarnation; see Pieper, 116.

Resignation is the final form of the fight against evil, the transformation in God of inevitable defeats.

Charity does not ask us to just bandage wounds; charity pushes us to build here below a better world and to be the first to throw ourselves into every attack carried out for the betterment of Mankind. . . .

And personal salvation is important not precisely because it will beatify us, but because it makes us save the world in saving ourselves.[63]

[63] "Quelques réflexions sur la conversion du monde," 1936, *OE* 9, 162.

2 · EVOLUTION AND ITS DIRECTION

THE CHRISTIAN mysticism found in the writings of Father Teilhard de Chardin is a mysticism of human endeavor; it combines faith in human effort and in human progress with faith in God. It is a spirituality that finds God in and through the world, or, more exactly, in and through the building up of the world. This spirituality has as its base a theology of Christ as the center of the universe. Teilhard's theology of Christ is in turn rooted in two sources: Christian revelation and a hyperphysics of evolution, a sort of scientific phenomenology or generalized physics of evolution. There are, then, three steps or levels of Teilhard's thought:

1. a scientific phenomenology of evolution,
2. a theology of Christ as center of the universe, and
3. a Christian mystique of human endeavor.

In this chapter we will briefly outline step one of Teilhard's thought; an examination of this first step, his phenomenology of evolution, will prepare the way for a study of the second, his theology of Christ, in the next chapter. It is these two parts of his thought that describe the structure of the universe as seen by Teilhard, and it is this structure that gives the unity and the consistency to his vision. Subsequent chapters will be devoted to the third step, his spirituality of human effort.

Christian dogma during the first fifteen centuries of the Church's existence was formulated according to the dimensions of the universe as it was understood in those times. This was the Greek cosmos, a contained universe limited in extension and in duration, made out of objects more or less arbitrarily placed in space and time. With the Copernican revolution in the sixteenth century, man's understanding of the universe began to change. Gradually space came to be understood as unlimited, time was conceived of as organic duration, and all the elements of the universe were seen more and more as interdependent and as understandable only in relation to the entire system of which they are parts. Today, in the general human vision of the world, a universe in evolution has taken the place of the static universe of the ancient and medieval worlds. In the words of the Second Vatican Council, "the human race has passed from a rather static concept of reality to a more dynamic, evolutionary one. In consequence, there has arisen a new series of problems, a series as important as can be, calling for new efforts of analysis and synthesis."[1] Many of these problems are theological, for—unfortunately—the universe of the theologians has tended to remain the old static universe.

Because Christian dogma was formulated within the structure of a static cosmos, many Christians have felt it necessary to approach evolution with great caution. Catholics have generally held that

[1] *Constitution on the Church in the Modern World,* "Introductory Statement," no. 5.

evolution is a plausible hypothesis but by no means proven, a fragile theory that does not necessarily have to be completely rejected. A large part of this hesitation is founded on the fear that Catholic dogma, framed within the confines of a static conception of the world, is threatened by evolution. Teilhard claims that this fear has no real basis; Christology, in particular, is much freer to develop in the context of a universe in evolution than in that of a fixed world. The great cosmic attributes of Christ as described by St. John and especially by St. Paul lose their grandeur within the framework of a merely juridical explanation of the relation of the universe to Christ. It is only when seen in the perspectives of a universe in evolution that Christ's cosmic attributes take on their full dimensions. Christianity and evolution are not two irreconcilable visions; they are "made to fit together and to mutually complement one another."[2]

Let us proceed to outline Teilhard's phenomenology of evolution, for it is this phenomenology that is the framework for his Christology.

The Nature and Method of Teilhard's Scientific Phenomenology of Evolution

Teilhard de Chardin distinguishes three degrees of meaning of the idea of evolution.[3] At a primary and general level, the idea of evolution simply implies the affirmation of the fact that every thing and action and event in the world is preceded by some antecedent that conditions its coming-to-be among other phenomena. Nothing comes to be in the universe except by way of birth. We perceive everything as necessarily having something else before it in time

[2] "Catholicisme et science," 1946, *OE* 9, 240.
[3] "Sur les degrés de certitude scientifique de l'idée d'évolution," 1946, *OE* 9, 245–9.

and something else beside it in space; in our understanding of the universe, the totality of things forms a sort of net from which our experience cannot escape and in which objects, like the knots in a net, cannot be arbitrarily transposed. At this primary level, evolution means simply that the universe is an organic totality both in space and in time. "The distribution, succession and solidarity of objects are born from their concrescence in a common genesis. Time and space are organically joined again so as to weave together the stuff of the universe. That is the point we have reached and how we perceive things today."[4] It is our modern age that has first seen this dimension of the universe; at this level, evolution is seen as an *evidence*. In this sense, evolution is not just a hypothesis or a theory.[5] "It is much more: it is a general condition to which all theories, all hypotheses, all systems must bow and which they must satisfy henceforward if they are to be thinkable and true. Evolution is a light illuminating all facts, a curve that all lines must follow."[6]   At a second level or degree of meaning, evolution is seen as a current according to which matter takes the form of

[4] *PM*, 218. See "Du cosmos à la cosmogénèse," 1951, *OE* 7, 264–5; also, the essay referred to in reference 6 *infra*.

[5] Teilhard takes this position consistently in his later writings. In 1917, however, he considers this primary meaning of evolution to be a postulate, although "no postulate seems to me to be established on such a broad base of experience and observation . . . as that of evolution." ("L'union créatrice," 1917, *Ecrits*, 176.)

[6] *PM*, 219. For a statement almost identical to this one, see "Sur les degrés de certitude scientifique de l'idée d'évolution," 1946, *OE* 9, 246. See also the letter to Father Dallaire of October 10, 1942, quoted by J. Dallaire, S.J., "Teilhard et l'évolution," *Revue Teilhard de Chardin* 5, no. 19 (1964) 29–31. This statement of the first degree of meaning of the idea of evolution, that it is simply a dimension of contemporary understanding of the universe, is sometimes misunderstood. A typical misunderstanding is that of R. Nogar, O.P., in *Evolutionism, Its Power and Limits*, 45–7, and of W. Wallace, O.P., in "The Cosmogony of Teilhard de Chardin," *The New Scholasticism* 36 (1962) 360, both of whom apparently think that Teilhard elevates his own scientific *hypothesis* of evolution to the level of a world view to which all other ideas must bow.

increasingly complex organisms where a certain psychic interiority appears and increases in function of the degree of organization. As to the importance of this second meaning of evolution, there is room for discussion. But, according to Teilhard, as to the existence of this evolutionary current there is no question.

It is at the third level of meaning of evolution that we find evolution as a scientific hypothesis. Teilhard's theory of evolution is at the level of this third meaning of the term. The question here is not whether there *is* evolution; the question is, "Where is evolution going?" Will the current of evolution continue to rise in the future; is evolution divergent or is it convergent; in other words, does evolution have a direction? It is basic to Teilhard's scientific hypothesis of evolution that it does have a direction. Mankind in its march "is marking time at this moment because men's minds are reluctant to recognize that evolution has a precise *orientation* and a privileged *axis*. Weakened by this fundamental doubt, the forces of research are scattered, and there is no determination to build the earth."[7] It is this hypothesis of evolution, Teilhard's hyperphysics or scientific phenomenology of evolution, that we want to examine in this chapter.

In the first place, Teilhard's scientific phenomenology is not a philosophy or a metaphysics. The object of his study is phenomena, and the method is a generalized scientific method. There is no recourse to metaphysics, or in any way to the notions of an Absolute Good, causality, or metaphysical teleology.[8] *The Phenomenon*

---

[7] *PM*, 142.

[8] "Hominization," 1925, P. Teilhard de Chardin, *The Vision of the Past*, tr. J. Cohen, 51, hereafter cited as *VP*; "Esquisse d'un univers personnel," 1936, *OE* 6, 110–2; "Man's Place in the Universe," 1942, *VP*, 217; "La centrologie," 1944, *OE* 7, 105–6; "La pensée du Père Teilhard de Chardin," 1948, *Les études philosophiques* 10 (1955) 580. J. Russell, S.J., in his long article, "The Principle of Finality in the Philosophy of Aristotle and Teilhard de Chardin," *The Heythrop Journal* 3 (1962) 347–57; 4 (1963) 32–41, makes the serious error of attributing a philosophical and teleological point

of Man, written in 1940, is a presentation of his phenomenology of evolution insofar as he had formulated it at that time. In the preface, written in 1947, he writes:

If this book is to be properly understood, it must be read not as a work on metaphysics, still less as a sort of theological essay, but purely and simply as a scientific treatise. The title itself indicates that. This book deals with man *solely* as a phenomenon; but it also deals with the *whole* phenomenon of man.

In the first place, it deals with man *solely* as a phenomenon. . . . Put quite simply, what I have tried to do is this; I have chosen man as the center, and around him I have tried to establish a coherent order between antecedents and consequences. I have not tried to discover a system of ontological and causal relations between the elements of the universe, but only an experimental law of recurrence which would express their successive appearance in time. Beyond

---

of view to Teilhard. For example, Father Russell writes of Teilhard that "it is fundamental to him that the processes of nature are finalistic and teleological." (40.) As a matter of fact, it is fundamental to Teilhard's methodology to completely prescind from any finalistic or teleological perspectives or principles. Teilhard is sometimes criticized for presenting a personal vision instead of sticking to what can be definitely and definitively proven; this criticism is often based on a misunderstanding of Teilhard's methodology, which is to present hypotheses, not definitive and absolute proofs. A. Brunner, S.J., makes this criticism of Teilhard in an especially clear way in "Pierre Teilhard de Chardin," *Stimmen der Zeit* 165 (1959) 210–22. On Teilhard's methodology, see N. Luyten, O.P., "La méthode du Père Teilhard," *Teilhard de Chardin et la pensée catholique,* ed. C. Cuénot, 19–63; C. d'Armagnac, S.J., "Philosophie de la nature et méthode chez le Père Teilhard de Chardin," *Archives de philosophie* 20 (1957) 5–41. It should be remarked that Teilhard's scientific phenomenology has very little in common with the thought of the philosophical phenomenologists Martin Heidegger, Edmund Husserl, and Maurice Merleau-Ponty. Teilhard writes: "I recognize that my 'phenomenology' is not that of Husserl and Merleau-Ponty. But where can I find another word to define a *Weltanschauung* based on the development of the phenomenon?" (Letter of April 11, 1953, quoted in *Cuénot,* 255–6.) For a comparison of Teilhard's methodology with that of Heidegger, Husserl, and Merleau-Ponty, see N. Martin-Deslias, *Un aventurier de l'esprit: Teilhard de Chardin,* 13–27.

these first purely *scientific* reflections, there is obviously ample room for the most far-reaching speculations of the philosopher and the theologian. Of set purpose, I have at all times carefully avoided venturing into that field of the essence of being. . . .

But this book also deals with the *whole* phenomenon of man. Without contradicting what I have just said (however much it may appear to do so) it is this aspect which might possibly make my suggestions *look* like a philosophy. . . . It is impossible to attempt a general scientific interpretation of the universe without *giving the impression* of trying to explain it through and through. But look a little more closely and you will see that this "hyperphysics" is still not a metaphysic.[9]

[9] *PM*, 29–30. Fairly frequently, one finds expressed among current commentators on Teilhard's writings the opinion that his scientific phenomenology exceeds the bounds of science and enters the domain of philosophy. This opinion seems to be based on a misunderstanding of the nature of scientific hypothesis. There is a difference between a scientific hypothesis that is subject to verification under controlled conditions and a general scientific theory or hypothesis that is not subject to demonstration or verification under controlled conditions. *The Phenomenon of Man* is such a general hypothesis or theory. J. Donceel, for example, in "Teilhard de Chardin: Scientist or Philosopher?" *International Philosophical Quarterly* 5 (1965) 248–66, thinks that Teilhard himself doubted that *The Phenomenon of Man* is purely scientific because Teilhard admits that the notion that the universe has a direction is undemonstrable to science. (254.) See also P. Grenet, *Pierre Teilhard de Chardin, ou le Philosophe malgré lui*; the thesis of the entire work is that Teilhard's hyperphysics needs to be purified of its philosophical elements and, further, that it needs to be supported by a metaphysics. For somewhat similar opinions, see F. Russo, S.J., "La méthode du Père Teilhard de Chardin," *Recherches et débats* 40 (1962) 13–23; the title of this issue of *Recherches et débats* is *Essais sur Teilhard de Chardin*, and it contains other essays favoring the view that Teilhard was at least partially a philosopher. It seems correct to say, as does R. Francoeur in the epilogue to *The World of Teilhard*, ed. R. Francoeur, 187, that "Teilhardian phenomenology is not science in the strict sense of the word as used today by the experimental scientists. But it does seem to fall within the realm of science in a wider sense that is becoming more and more acceptable even to the strictest experimental scientist." There would be little point in undertaking here a long discussion

Teilhard's method is a generalized scientific method: the arrangement of the data to form a hypothesis, and the verification of that hypothesis. How can a hypothesis be verified? What is the test of a good hypothesis? "In science (and elsewhere) the great proof of truth is coherence and productiveness."[10] A theory is certain to the extent that it puts more order into our vision of the world (coherence), and to the extent that it directs and supports our efforts of research and of building the world (fecundity or productiveness). Like any hypothesis, Teilhard's hypothesis of evolution is open; a good hypothesis changes in a consistent direction according to further modifications and precisions. The hypothesis "is the aim, the soul, and true content of scientific theory; it is like life, changeable, fragile but progressive."[11] His scientific phenomenology, then, is just that; it is not a metaphysics. It is not deductive; it does not rest on eternal and self-evident principles; it does not claim final and absolute truth. It is inductive, based on the phenomena; it depends on observed data; it is tentative, open to revision and further precision. It is an effort to arrive at a more unified vision of the universe, a vision with a maximum of coherence and fecundity.

The Law of Complexity-consciousness

At the heart of Teilhard's theory of evolution is found a law of recurrence, an inductively formed law.[12] The law around which he

---

as to whether or not Teilhard really was a metaphysician without knowing it, or whether he was a metaphysician at all. He certainly did not think he was, and he was a philosopher only in the broad sense of one who takes a global view of reality.

[10] "Man's Place in the Universe," 1942, *VP*, 227. See "Esquisse d'un univers personnel," 1936, *OE* 6, 70–1; "Comment je vois," 1948, 1.

[11] "L'histoire naturelle du monde," 1925, *OE* 3, 156.

[12] In the formation of a law of recurrence, examples of some sequence or relationship are observed in several instances. After sufficient observation has shown that sequence or relationship to be apparently universal,

builds his hyperphysics he calls "the law of complexity-consciousness."[13] Up until now, science has considered only one axis in the universe, the axis that passes from the infinitely small (electrons, protons, and other particles) through bodies of "ordinary" size such as ourselves to the infinitely large (star systems, galaxies). Science, so far, has been interested only in these two "infinities," the very small and the very large. This is not sufficient. "In order to cover scientifically the totality of experience, it is necessary to consider one more infinity in the universe, one just as real as the other two: that of complexity. Around us, bodies are not merely small or large. They are also simple or complex."[14] There is, then, besides the infinities of the very small and the very large, a

---

the relationship is raised to the level of a law. All scientific laws are formed in this way; the process is called scientific induction. The classic case is the law of gravity. For clarity, Teilhard's law of complexity-consciousness, formed by scientific induction, might be contrasted with a metaphysical principle arrived at or grasped through philosophical induction. For example, the principle that the whole is greater than any of its parts or that every agent acts for some end can be understood in one or a few examples, and the mind immediately grasps both the principle and its universality.

[13] This law of complexity-consciousness has, over the years, an increasingly important place in Teilhard's theory of evolution. A comparison between the main text of *The Phenomenon of Man,* finished in 1940, and the "Summing Up or Postscript," pp. 300–10, written in 1948, is sufficient to indicate the progress of Teilhard's thought in the direction of a unification of his phenomenology of evolution around the central notion of the law of complexity-consciousness. The law of complexity-consciousness is treated by Teilhard in many places in his writings. Principal are: *MPN, passim* but especially Chapter I (this was written in 1949); "L'atomisme de l'esprit," 1941, *OE* 7, 29–63; "L'analyse de la vie," 1945, *OE* 7, 137–46; "Un sommaire de ma perspective 'phénoménologique' du monde," *Les études philosophiques* 10 (1955) 569–71. The most important of all, I believe, is "The Singularities of the Human Species," 1954, *AM,* 208–73. See also the references *infra.* An excellent brief statement of the law of complexity-consciousness can be found in the essay "Sur la nature du phénomène social humain et sur ses réactions cachées avec la gravité," 1948, *OE* 7, 173.

[14] "Comment je vois," 1948, I.

"third infinity" of organized complexity. Teilhard describes the complexity of a thing as that quality by which the thing is composed:

(a) of a larger number of elements, which are
(b) more tightly organized among themselves.

It is not simply a question of a multiplicity of elements, but of an *organized* multiplicity, "not simple complication, but *centrated* complication."[15] An atom is more complex than an electron; a molecule is more complex than an atom, a living cell is more complex than a molecule. In this sense, complexity is a dimension of the material world, like length or weight or duration.

Up until now, scientists have viewed the world as structured on one axis in space, an axis extending in a line from the infinitely small to the infinitely great. As a result of this limitation of perspective, science has been able to find no place in its schema for the larger molecules of organic chemistry, nor for the living cellular composites. However, the introduction of the dimension of complexity allows us to scientifically reconstruct the world not merely on a single axis in space, from small to large, but—at the same time—also on a second axis extending through time from the very simple to the extremely complex.[16] This is the axis of complexity. When we consider this axis of increasing organic complexity extending through the ages we are led to suspect that the phenomena of life and of consciousness, which were impossible to situate on an axis from the infinitesimal to the immense, might very well find their places on the axis of complexity.

Experimentally observable life and consciousness might well be nothing other than the properties of matter pushed to the very highest degrees of organization, to the highest degrees of arrange-

[15] "Life and the Planets," 1946, *FM*, 105.
[16] "The Planetization of Mankind," 1945, *FM*, 130; "Man's Place in the Universe," 1942, *VP*, 222–6.

ment and centration. The tiny particles studied by nuclear physics have their own special laws and properties; the immense bodies studied by astronomy show the special effects of relativity. At the levels of the infinitely small and the infinitely large we can see the phenomena that exist at all levels but that are observable only at the extremes. Why shouldn't this be true too of the extremely complex? The effects observable at the level of the very highly complex, then, would be life and, at the level of the very highest complexity, consciousness. For experimental science, life is seen as an effect of complexity, of a high degree of organization of matter; the level of life seems to depend on the degree of complexity of the living organism. This structural relationship between complexity and life or consciousness is experimentally incontestable.

But Teilhard goes further than this. Using the term "consciousness" in the broadest possible sense (life and intelligence, in this sense, would be two high forms of consciousness), he assumes as a postulate that the structural relationship that is observed between complexity and consciousness is a *universal law*. The "law of complexity-consciousness" is universal, applicable even where it cannot be observed; this is a basic assumption of Teilhard's phenomenology of evolution.[17] In other words, at every level of material being the degree of consciousness varies according to the degree of complexity. "Spiritual perfection (or conscious 'centreity') and material synthesis (or complexity) are but the two aspects or connected parts of one and the same phenomenon."[18]

In *The Phenomenon of Man*, Teilhard calls complexity the "without" of things, and consciousness the "within" of things. Since the law of complexity-consciousness is a universal law in his system, all things have both a "without" and a "within." That is, every material being has some structure, and so it also has the consciousness commensurate with the complexity of that structure.

[17] *PM*, 30, 300.
[18] *Ibid.*, 60–1.

At the lower levels of existence, in megamolecules and below, the structure is comparatively so simple as to make any consciousness imperceptible. Nevertheless, we are logically led to assume some sort of rudimentary and diffuse psyche even at the lowest levels of complexity. In Teilhard's perspective, purely inert matter, "brute matter," does not exist. Every element in the universe contains, at least in an infinitesimal degree, a germ of interiority, of spontaneity, of rudimentary consciousness. The smallest elements of the universe, the simplest and the most numerous, have the property of consciousness in such a diffuse way and at such a low level that their consciousness is imperceptible to us; it is as though they possessed no degree of consciousness at all. But consciousness increases as we go up in the order of complexity. At the level of the virus, which has a complexity—a centered arrangement—of about a million atoms, consciousness begins to be experimentally observable. It manifests itself at higher levels by successive leaps. Finally, after passing through a critical point of "reflection," it becomes—in man—intelligence; with man, consciousness dominates complexity.[19]

Teilhard's postulate concerning the law of complexity-consciousness does not just assume that this law is universal. It further states that matter presents itself to us as having the property of arranging itself in more and more complex groups with correspondingly higher levels of consciousness. This is not to postulate any teleological property or metaphysical finality in matter or in the universe as a whole. It is simply to state that, over long periods of time and through the various chance combinations that take place inevitably among very large populations, matter becomes arranged in more highly complex forms that have higher degrees of consciousness. In this perspective, life is seen as the outcome of a general physico-chemical process "in virtue of which cosmic mat-

---

[19] "Man's Place in the Universe," 1942, *VP*, 225.

ter, by its very existence and structure, . . . presents itself to our experience as actuated by a movement of qualitative infolding (or arrangement, if you prefer) upon itself."[20]

This "infolding arrangement" is in the direction of higher complexity; it results with the passage of time in cells, plants, animals. Life, far from being an oddity or an evolutionary aberration, is the result of millions of years of progress along the axis of complexity. "So as to overcome the improbability of arrangements leading to units of ever increasing complexity, the involuting universe, considered in its pre-reflective zones, proceeds step by step by dint of billion-fold trial and error."[21] This process of groping, together with the mechanism of reproduction and heredity, results in the various species of living things.

The appearance of life on the axis of complexity marks a critical point in evolution, a change of state analogous to the liquefaction of ice when it melts or the vaporization of water when it boils. Beyond the critical point of the appearance of life the lines of evolution branch out into species of bewildering diversity. These species tend to be grouped in bundles that are the "branches" of the "tree of life." Each bundle, or "phylum," contains several similar species. Is there some way that we can find a path through the jungle of species and phyla? Does evolution follow

[20] "Does Mankind Move Biologically upon Itself?" 1949, *FM*, 251. See "Comment je vois," 1948, 1–4; "The Phyletic Structure of the Human Group," 1951, *AM*, 139; "L'analyse de la vie," 1945, *OE* 7, 137–46.

[21] *PM*, 302. No scientist, I think, would deny the clearly observable structural correlation between complexity and consciousness. Perhaps few would object to the elevation of this correlation to the level of a universal law, at least as a hypothesis. On the other hand, many scientists would not admit that evolution has an even apparent direction along an axis of increasing complexity-consciousness, or any specific direction at all. See, for example, G. Simpson, *This View of Life*, 229–31. Simpson criticizes Teilhard for introducing "mysticism" into science. For a scientist's favorable view and elaboration of Teilhard's law of complexity-consciousness, see P. Chauchard, *Man and Cosmos*, tr. G. Courtright, 47–83.

some sort of central axis represented by one or more species or phyla? Or do the various phyla and species differ simply in their characteristics; after all, who is to say that, biologically speaking, a spider is less than a horse, or a bird less than a man? Teilhard finds a method of measurement, a guiding thread through the labyrinth of the different kinds of living creatures; it is the further application of the law of complexity-consciousness.

The more complex a being is, so our Scale of Complexity tells us, the more is it centered upon itself and therefore the more *aware* does it become. In other words, the higher the degree of complexity in a living creature, the higher its consciousness; and vice versa. The two properties vary in parallel and simultaneously. . . . So it comes to this, that when we have reached the point where complexity can no longer be reckoned in numbers of atoms we can nevertheless continue to measure it (and accurately) by noting the increase of consciousness in the living creature—in practical terms, the development of its nervous system.[22]

What this amounts to is using the factor of development of the brain, using the progress of cerebralization as a scale to measure the growth of complexity through the maze of diverse phyla. Using progress of cerebralization as a measure, we can see clearly that the main axis of complexity passes through the branch of the mammifers, and among the mammifers through the primates, and among the primates through the anthropoids.[23] The line of complexity-consciouness follows the evolutionary progress of the development of the brain, passing finally through the anthropoids. In this way, following the axis of complexity, we are led to another critical point; the thread of progressive cerebralization leads us along the axis of increasing complexity to the threshold of reflection.

[22] "Life and the Planets," 1946, *FM*, 111–2. See *MPN*, 55–8.
[23] *MPN*, 49–53.

Man's Place in Evolution

As to external appearances, man came into being in the world just like any other species of life. The traces of the earliest origin of man, like the traces of the origin of any species, are lost to our observation. Evolutionary beginnings are too tenuous to leave traces. Phenomenologically man appears in history as a population, spread out geographically, showing a certain diversity in its various groupings. And yet, man shows from the very beginning characteristics that mark his species as unique. Most important, by far, among these characteristics is the ability to reflect. Man not only knows, but *he knows that he knows*. This is more than consciousness; it is reflexive consciousness, "consciousness squared."

Following a "hominizing" cerebral mutation taking place among the Anthropoid group near the end of the Tertiary Period, psychic reflection (not simply "to know," but "to know that one knows,") erupted in the world and opened up an entirely new area of evolution. Under the appearances of a new zoological family more or less like the others, emerging man in fact marks the beginning of a *second kind of life*.[24]

[24] "Un sommaire de ma perspective phénoménologique du monde," *Les études philosophiques* 10 (1955) 570. The scientific phenomenology of human origins is treated in many places in Teilhard's writings. Perhaps especially important are: *PM*, 163–206, 302–4; *MPN*, 61–78; "The Singularities of the Human Species," 1954, *AM*, 230–44. It seems well to point out once more that Teilhard's hyperphysics of evolution is concerned only with phenomena. In his explanations he confines himself to the observable phenomena, to the experimental relations between consciousness and complexity, without any prejudice to the deeper causes. "It is only, it seems, *under the appearances* of a critical point that we can grasp experimentally the 'hominizing' (spiritualizing) step to reflection." (*PM*, 169, note 1.) Also, "What Should We Think of Transformism?" 1925, *VP*, 151: In a theory of evolution one must "not confuse the scientific plan (of empirical succession in time) with the philosophical plan (of an underlying causality)." Teilhard's hypothesis of evolution in no way denies some "creative operation"

The appearance of this "second kind of life," reflexive consciousness, is—like the appearance of life itself—a critical point in the process of evolution, an evolutionary change of state. Reflection is, "as the word indicates, the power acquired by a consciousness to turn in upon itself, to take possession of itself *as of an object* endowed with its own particular consistence and value."[25]

The consequences of a transformation from consciousness (to know) to reflexive consciousness (to know and to know oneself precisely as a knowing subject) are vast. A being that can know itself, that can be the object of its own reflection, becomes individualized, "centered," a person; and that being, further, has open to it the whole new world of the inner life: abstract thinking, art, invention, foresight, sentiment. Because man is reflective he is not just a separate species, but a whole new kind of life. It is not a simple increase in the degree of consciousness that separates man from the animals; it is a difference in nature resulting from a change in state. The difference is as great and as definite as the difference between living and nonliving; and both differences mark critical points in evolution.

Up to this point, Teilhard's effort to find a coherent unity in the universe has led him to consider the world as an organically unified complex, evolving in time along an axis of increasing complexity-consciousness. This axis, rising through time, passes through at least two critical points: the appearance of life in the world and the appearance of reflexive consciousness. The axis of evolution has a definite orientation; this orientation is in the direction of greater complexity and greater consciousness. The direction of evolution is toward the spiritual and the personal, and it

---

or "special intervention" on the part of God, an intervention taking place under a phenomenal veil and of course beyond the scope of a scientific phenomenology.

[25] *PM*, 165.

is in man that these are found.[26] Man is not an accident, nor is he just one species among many others; he is the unique but logical outcome of the long evolutionary rise of complexity and consciousness. He is at the forward point of the arrow of evolution. More, he is the key to the understanding of the whole process of Nature's "almost heart-rending effort towards light and consciousness."[27]

---

[26] See "Comment je crois," 1934, 6–9; "Esquisse d'un univers personnel," 1936, *OE* 6, 69–114; "Le phénomène spirituel," 1937, *OE* 6, 117–25. These essays were written before *The Phenomenon of Man* and well before the law of complexity-consciousness had been developed and given a central place in Teilhard's phenomenology. In the three above essays the emphasis is on evolution as a movement of spiritualization, as a process directed toward a higher degree of interiorization. Evolution is viewed as oriented toward "spirit" and "person." Although the personalism of Teilhard's theory of evolution is more apparent in these essays than elsewhere in his writings, he always presupposed the primacy of spirit over matter and he always considered evolution as oriented toward spirit and as achieving itself in man in the personal. At a stage of his thought even earlier than that represented by the above essays (1934–1937), in a series of essays written between 1928 and 1931, Teilhard, in order to point up evolution's direction toward greater life, consciousness, spirit, opposes evolution and entropy. Entropy is taken in its sense of the gradual long-term degradation of energy in the universe, a degradation that increasingly approaches an ultimate uniform state. Evolution is seen as a countercurrent compensating for the energy loss by a corresponding increase in the level of consciousness in the universe. ("The Movements of Life," 1926, *VP*, 149–50; "Le phénomène humain," 1928, *OE* 9, 125–6; "The Phenomenon of Man," 1930, *VP*, 167–9.) Finally, see "Comment je crois," 1934, 1; "Le coeur de la matière," 1950, 12: "I believe the Universe is an Evolution. I believe that the Evolution goes toward Spirit. I believe that the Spirit achieves itself in man in the Personal."

[27] Letter of August 5–6, 1915, *MM*, 62. The similarity between Teilhard's idea of evolution as moving toward always greater spiritualization and the philosophy of Sri Aurobindo has been remarked on by A. Monestier, "Teilhard et Aurobindo," *Revue Teilhard de Chardin* 4, no. 14 (1963) 11–3, and by P. Sorokin, "Discussion," *American Catholic Sociological Review* 33 (1962) 330–5. Although Teilhard and Aurobindo share the general idea of spirit mounting through evolution toward God, the differ-

The objection is sometimes made that Teilhard's theory rests on the *assumption*—unproven—that consciousness is superior to unconsciousness, that spirit is superior to matter. The objection is a perfectly valid statement, but it is no objection. Teilhard admits that the primacy of spirit is a postulate, an assumption (although certainly well-founded). "It is better at any price to be more conscious rather than less conscious. This principle seems to me to be a required condition for the very existence of the world."[28] In the preface to *The Phenomenon of Man,* Teilhard points out that his first assumption is "the primacy accorded to the psychic and to thought in . . . the universe."[29] For Teilhard the truth of his hypothesis of evolution does not depend on "proving" any of its underlying assumptions; the truth of a hypothesis depends on how much sense it makes when confronted with reality. A similar objection is made to Teilhard's anthropocentrism; it is sometimes argued that in assuming the primacy of the spirit Teilhard presupposes, at least implicitly, that the direction of evolution is toward man—who is, after all, the most highly spiritual creature on earth. Again, the objection is true, but it is no objection. There surely is an at least implicit presupposition in Teilhard's system that evolution is oriented toward man. The question is not, "Can the presupposition be scientifically proven?" but, "Does the universe make more sense in the light of this presupposition?"

Truth is nothing other than the total coherence of the Universe with respect to each part of itself. Why should we suggest or underestimate that coherence because we ourselves are the observers? Some vaguely defined "anthropocentric illusion" is continually being opposed to some equally vaguely defined "objective reality." This distinction

---

ences between their ideas would seem to be much greater than any similarity.

[28] "Comment je crois," 1934, 9.

[29] *PM*, 30. See "L'union créatrice," 1917, *Ecrits*, 175.

does not exist. The truth for Man is the truth of the Universe as that Universe is seen by Man; and this, quite simply, is what truth is.[30]

The Noosphere

This consideration of the critical point of reflection and the appearance of man leads us immediately into the second part of Teilhard's phenomenology of evolution. There is no reason to suppose that evolution stops when it reaches man, any more than to think it stopped at the appearance of life. The evolutionary process, having pushed beyond the critical point of the appearance on earth of life, continued to function and to produce ever greater complexity and consciousness in the sphere of living things, in the "living envelope" that covers the earth, in the "biosphere." Now, having passed through the critical point of the appearance on earth of reflexive consciousness, evolution continues in the "thinking envelope" that covers the earth through its human population. Teilhard calls this "thinking envelope" or terrestrial sphere of reflexive consciousness the "noosphere" (from the Greek *noos*, "mind").

Every species of living things shows the tendency, over a large span of time, to split (under the statistical effect of genetic mutations) into branches that are varieties and subspecies; some of these branches eventually become true species, and the cycle repeats itself. "Until the coming of man the pattern of the Tree of Life was always that of a fan, a spread of morphological radiations diverging more and more, each radiation culminating in a new 'knot' and breaking into a fan of its own." But in the case of man this tendency to "branch" has been overcome and, consequently, the law of development has been radically changed. By the power of reflexive consciousness, men "become capable (and indeed are under an irresistible compulsion) of drawing close to one another,

[30] "Esquisse d'un univers personnel," 1936, *OE* 6, 71.

of communicating, finally of uniting."[31] The result is that the fundamental divergent tendency of the evolutionary radiations is overcome by a stronger force, toward conscious union, that induces them to converge. In other words, any living species has a tendency to diverge over a long period of time into separate and different branches which in turn become new species. But in the case of man no new human species has developed. The tendency to diverge into new species is overcome by the intense intraspecies cohesion that comes from the socializing force of reflexive consciousness. Instead of branching out, mankind tends to fold in upon itself; human groups tend to merge and interpenetrate to a greater extent than they tend to separate.

Furthermore, because of the biological advantage gained by this greater cohesion, mankind spread until, after several hundred thousand years, it covered the face of the earth. It has taken about ten thousand years more for earth's human envelope to consolidate itself. Finally, today, the powers of industry and science have given the noosphere a new force of cohesion. It is in this highly specialized layer of the earth, in the noosphere, despite its comparatively small mass and its extreme thinness, that the world continues to evolve. The world continues to evolve, but now, in man, evolution has become conscious. Evolution continues to follow the axis of complexity-consciousness, but with the difference and the complications that come from the fact that the critical point of reflection has been passed.

Any human society,

[31] "The Formation of the Noosphere," 1947, *FM*, 158. Teilhard's analysis of human evolution, of the evolution of the noosphere, really dates from 1939, just after he finished writing *The Phenomenon of Man*. Consequently, this important part of his thought is not at all adequately contained in that book. "The Formation of the Noosphere" is Teilhard's most important essay on the subject. See also all the works cited in regard to socialization in reference 36 *infra*.

whenever left to itself, immediately starts spontaneously to arrange itself at a social level into an organized system of ends and means, in which two basic components are always present: First, a material component, or "increase in complexity," which includes both the various types of implements and techniques necessary to the gathering or the production of all kinds of food or supplies and the various rules or laws which provide the best conditions for an optimum birth rate or for a satisfactory circulation of goods and resources within the limits of the population under consideration. Second, a spiritual component, or "increase in consciousness," namely, some particular outlook on the world and life (an approach which is at once philosophical, ethical, aesthetic, and religious), the function of which is to impart a meaning, a direction, and an incentive or stimulus to the material activities and development of the community.[32]

In other words, evolution in the noosphere "conforms to the general law of recurrence which leads to the heightening of consciousness in the universe as a function of complexity";[33] the "new evolution" of the noosphere is a true evolution. And just as evolution at prereflective levels takes place by means of the mechanism of heredity and of adaptation or invention, so does the evolution of the noosphere take place by means of a new and more efficient heredity and a new and more efficient invention.[34]

The automatic chromosomic heredity that exists at all levels of life is, in the noosphere, duplicated in the zone of conscious activ-

[32] "The Antiquity and World Expansion of Human Culture," *Man's Role in Changing the Face of the Earth*, ed. W. L. Thomas, Jr. (Chicago, University of Chicago Press, 1956), 106–7.

[33] "The Formation of the Noosphere," 1947, *FM*, 174. See "Transformations et prolongements en l'homme du méchanisme de l'évolution," 1951, *OE* 7, 313–23.

[34] "The Formation of the Noosphere," 1947, *FM*, 107; "L'énergie d'évolution," 1953, *OE* 7, 384. See "Zoological Evolution and Invention," 1947, *VP*, 234–6; "Social Heredity and Progress," 1938, *FM*, 25–36.

ity by social heredity. Through language, education at various levels, and modern mass media, an immense number of complex ideas and techniques "accumulate continuously, and organize themselves permanently, in the unlimited capacity of human memory."[35] An ever growing culture is transmitted to each successive generation of mankind through social heredity. Parallel to the growth of culture is the growth of the means to store, increase, and pass on that culture; man has increasingly improved systems of libraries, schools, communications. Complexity and consciousness increase together.

Since life began it has never ceased to adapt itself in myriad ways by "inventing" new organic devices that improve on the old ones. This adaptation through invention has taken place through a sort of "groping," that is, the utilization of the chance opportunities for evolutionary progress that are inevitably provided in populations of very large numbers. But man can have a purpose in mind; he can plan. With man, the more or less automatic mechanism of invention becomes a conscious power. This power of planning permits man, through plans based on research and discovery, to help shape his own future through technology. Man is still subject to many limitations; he remains an organic substance and, as such, will always be limited. But the area of man's freedom in controlling his future through "invention" is gradually expanding.

The most important mechanism of human evolution and the one to which Teilhard gives by far the most attention is "socialization." Unlike the prereflective living species, the human species does not split and branch into separate species. On the contrary, it folds in upon itself and forms one increasingly cohesive species. This process of "infolding" and increasing cohesion is the phenomenon of socialization.[36]

---

[35] "The Antiquity and World Expansion of Human Culture," *op. cit.*, 108.
[36] This is not to claim that socialization is a purely human phenomenon. In fact, from all evidence socialization is "an expression of a primary,

He considers the socialization process as having two phases: a phase of expansion and a phase of compression. The expansion phase of socialization extended from the appearance of man on earth up to recent times; it was a period of population growth and of the gradual occupation of the earth. During this long period of expansion mankind progressed, civilizations and cultures developed, there was a long-term increase in social complexity and the growth of a rudimentary technology. With this gradually increasing complexity went an increasing consciousness or growth in culture and in knowledge and vision of the world. Sometime near

---

universal, property of vitalized matter. For a convincing proof of this all one needs to do is to observe how much each animal lineage, once it has attained its own specific maturity, demonstrates . . . a tendency to group . . . into supra-individual complexes. At these prereflective levels, however (and particularly with insects), the ray of socialization, however advanced that state may be, is still extremely weak, stopping short, for example, at the family group. . . . With man a new chapter opens for zoology, since for the first time in the history of life it is no longer a matter of a few isolated leaves: we now see a complete phylum—and, what matters even more, an ubiquitous phylum—suddenly and as one whole, giving evidence of becoming totalized. . . ." (*MPN*, 80.) The idea of socialization is one of the great themes of Teilhard's thought. However, nowhere in his writings is there a full and developed treatment of socialization. The most important sources are all published. In *FM*, see "The Grand Option," 1939, 37–60; "Life and the Planets," 1945, 97–123; "A Great Event Foreshadowed: The Planetization of Mankind," 1945, 124–39; "The Formation of the Noosphere," 1947, 155–84; "The Human Rebound of Evolution and Its Consequences," 1947, 196–213; "Turmoil or Genesis?" 1947, 214–26; "The Directions and Conditions of the Future," 1948, 227–37; "Does Mankind Move Biologically upon Itself?" 1949, 244–59; "How May We Conceive and Hope that Human Unanimization Will Be Realized on Earth?" 1950, 281–8. See also "L'atomisme de l'esprit," 1941, *OE* 7, 29–63; "La montée de l'autre," 1942, *OE* 7, 67–81; "La place de la technique dans une biologie générale de l'humanité," 1947, *OE* 7, 161–9; "Note-mémento sur la structure biologique de l'humanité," 1948, *OE* 9, 267–9; the postscript to *The Phenomenon of Man*, 1948, 303–8; *MPN*, 79–121; "The Phyletic Structure of the Human Group," 1951, *AM*, 132–71; "La réflexion de l'énergie," 1952, *OE* 7, 335–53; "The Singularities of the Human Species," 1954, *AM*, 208–73.

the end of the nineteenth-century the expansion phase ended; the globe was sufficiently covered by man, and the compression phase of socialization began.

Teilhard often uses an image to describe the progression of socialization: the image of a pulsation going from one pole of a sphere to the other pole. Imagine a wave or pulsation beginning from the south pole of a sphere and advancing toward the north pole, spreading out on the surface along an advancing front, moving to the equator, and then contracting along the still advancing front. This wave converges from the beginning, and its degree of convergence is continuously increasing; but its progress is in two parts: an expansive phase until it reaches the equator, followed by a phase of contraction. The image illustrates what has happened to mankind. For many thousands of years man spread over the face of the globe, branching out into races, peoples, and nations and empires. This was the long expansive phase of socialization. Near the end of the last century the habitable surface of the earth was more or less covered; the pulsation of mankind, to follow our image, had reached the equator, and the phase of contraction or compression began. Mankind, then, entered the compressive phase of socialization less than one hundred years ago. This very recent beginning of the compressive phase of socialization—it can be said to be even now still in its beginning—has come at the same time as a sharp increase in world population and an almost incredible progress in human intercommunication. The result has been a sudden and increasing acceleration in socialization.

Despite the havoc of war, the population on the limited surface of this planet which bears us is increasing in almost geometrical progression; while at the same time the scope of each human molecule, in terms of movement, information and influence, is becoming rapidly co-extensive with the whole surface of the globe. A state of tightening compression, in short; but even more, thanks to the biological intermingling developed to its uttermost extent by the growth of Reflection, a state of organised interpenetration, in which each element is linked with every other. No one can deny that a network (a world network) of economic and psychic affiliations is being woven at ever increasing speed which envelops and constantly penetrates more deeply within each of us. With every day that passes it becomes a little more impossible for us to act or think otherwise than collectively.[37]

There seems to be no doubt that mankind is going through a process of increasing collectivization. We can see the process in many contemporary phenomena: the increasing centralization of governments, the formation of associations and super-associations at all levels. What does this mean in terms of the law of complexity-consciousness? It means that mankind is rapidly becoming more socially organized; it means a sharp increase in complexity and a corresponding increase in collective human consciousness.

Person and Community

Will the increasing collectivization of mankind necessarily lead to some Orwellian world welfare state, to a universal totalitarianism? Teilhard foresees the question:

All this, you may say to me, sounds splendid: but is there not another side to the picture? You tell us that this new phase of human evolution will bring about an extension and deepening of terrestrial consciousness. But do not the facts contradict your argument? What is actually happening in the world today? Can we really detect any heightening of human consciousness even in the most highly collectivised nations? Does it not appear, on the contrary, that social totalisation leads directly to spiritual retrogression and greater materialism?[38]

[37] "The Formation of the Noosphere," 1947, *FM*, 170–1.
[38] "Life and the Planets," 1945, *FM*, 118.

His answer is that insofar as modern attempts at collectivization seem to result in the subhuman state of the anthill, "it is not the principle of totalization that is at fault, but the clumsy and incomplete way in which it has been applied."[39] The fact that so much of the contemporary force of socialization has gone into movements like Nazism, Fascism, and Communism should not discourage us but, rather, lead us to an examination of what has gone wrong. "Monstrous as it is, is not modern totalitarianism really the distortion of something magnificent, and thus quite near to the truth?"[40] To calm our fears of a totalitarian future, we have only to look at the process of increasingly complex human organization in a sufficiently broad perspective. The modern phenomenon of accelerating socialization is not an isolated phenomenon. On the contrary, it is the extension in the noosphere of the universal curve or axis of complexity-consciousness. Human socialization is a part, an extension, of the same universal evolutionary process that has produced living things and, eventually, man himself. The universe is, as it were, continually searching—along the axis of complexity-consciousness—for more complex arrangements of matter and correspondingly higher states of consciousness. Human socialization is part of this search, of this evolutionary process. So, as mankind becomes more highly organized, develops greater "complexity," we should expect an accompanying rise in the level of "conscious-

[39] *Ibid.*, 119.

[40] *PM*, 257. For a Marxist's judicious comparison of Teilhard's ideas with those of Marxism, see R. Garaudy, *Perspectives de l'homme: existentialisme, pensée catholique, marxisme*, 170–203. See the treatment of this question, a treatment based on a review of Garaudy's book, by G. Morel, S.J., "Karl Marx et le P. Teilhard de Chardin," *Etudes* 304 (1960) 80–7. Also, M. Barthélemy-Madaule, "Teilhard de Chardin, Marxism, Existentialism," *International Philosophical Quarterly* I (1961) 648–67. The periodical *Europe* 43, no. 431–2 (1965), has three comparative studies on Teilhard and Marxism: I. Varga, "Teilhard, Marx et le progrès social," 152–8; C. Cuénot, "Teilhard et le marxisme," 164–85; R. Garaudy, "Le Père Teilhard, le Concile et les marxistes," 185–208.

ness" of mankind as a whole. But Teilhard insists, it is not through "anthill" organization that real socialization takes place; efforts like modern Communism are travesties of true socialization.

We have to take into account what is required by the law of complexity if Mankind is to achieve spiritual growth through collectivisation. The first essential is that the human units involved in the process shall draw closer together, not merely under the pressure of *external* forces, or solely by the performance of material acts, but directly, center to center, through *internal* attraction. Not through coercion, or enslavement to a common task, but through *unanimity* in a common spirit. The construction of molecules ensues through atomic affinity. Similarly, on a higher level, it is through sympathy, and this alone, that the human elements in a personalised universe may hope to rise to the level of a higher synthesis.[41]

It is at this point in his hyperphysics of evolution that Teilhard introduces the formula "union differentiates." "True union, the union of heart and spirit, does not enslave, nor does it neutralize the individuals which it brings together. It super-personalizes them."[42] More generally, true union "does not suffocate nor does

[41] "Life and the Planets," 1945, *FM*, 119. For two studies of Teilhard's idea of socialization, see F. Russo, S.J., "La socialisation," *Teilhard de Chardin et la pensée catholique*, ed. C. Cuénot, 171–87, and the remarks of N. Wildier, S.J., following Russo's article, 188–90, 199–200. See also R. Frank, "Social Evolution and the Human Species," *American Catholic Sociological Review* 33 (1962) 291–337.

[42] "Life and the Planets," 1945, *FM*, 119. For Teilhard's thought on the principle that union differentiates, see especially "Esquisse d'un univers personnel," 1936, *OE* 6, 79–105; "Quelques vues générales sur l'essence du Christianisme," 1939, 1–3; "The Formation of the Noosphere," 1947, *FM*, 182–4; *MPN*, 114–5. See also "Panthéisme et Christianisme," 1923, 10; "Mon univers," 1924, *OE* 9, 72–7; "Introduction à la vie chrétienne," 1944, 13. Probably the best consideration of differentiating union in the context of socialization is "The Grand Option," 1939, *FM*, 52–7. Although the formulation and application of the principle that union differentiates are

it confuse the elements; it super-differentiates them within the unity."[43] In any domain of life, he writes in *The Phenomenon of Man,* whether we speak about the cells of a body, the members of a society, or the elements of any synthesis, *union differentiates.*[44] We sometimes fail to see this fact, he goes on, because we confuse *person* with *individual*; this is the fatal error of all forms of egoism.

In trying to separate itself as much as possible from others, the element individualises itself; but in doing so it becomes retrograde and seeks to drag the world backwards towards plurality and into matter. In fact it diminishes itself and loses itself. To be fully ourselves it is in the opposite direction, in the direction of convergence with all the rest, that we must advance—towards the "other." The goal of ourselves, the acme of our originality, is not our individuality but our person; and according to the evolutionary structure of the world, we can only find our person by uniting together. There is no mind without synthesis. The same law holds good from top to bottom. The true ego grows in inverse proportion to "egoism."[45]

It is not *union* of persons that is the source of retrogression and materialism and subhuman states; true union of persons is personalizing. It is egoism that is retrogressive; self-seeking ends, fi-

---

original with Teilhard, the principle itself is not. It is, for example, as A. Jeannière, S.J., remarks, "at the base of all theological analyses of the Persons of the Trinity." See A. Jeannière, S.J., "Sur le mal, l'union et le point Oméga," *Esprit* 32 (1964) 361–6.

[43] "L'esprit de la terre," 1931, *OE* 6, 52.

[44] *PM*, 263.

[45] *Ibid.* See "Esquisse d'un univers personnel," 1936, *OE* 6, 81–2: "The source of our repugnance for the collective is found in the illusion that makes us stubbornly identify 'personal' with 'individual.' This confusion and its consequences should disappear if the fundamental law of being is really . . . that 'union differentiates.' In virtue of this rule, we cannot achieve our true self except in organic association with everything else."

nally, in the reduction of self. Paradoxically, man finds himself in the "other." Union differentiates, personalizes, develops the persons united.

But what of the freedom of the individual? Is it not true that a man becomes less free by uniting with other men? According to Teilhard, this is basically the same error as the identification of person and individual. He insists that union makes a man freer, not less free. In a world that is more and more socialized, more and more highly organized, and where people are more and more united, what remains, he asks, of our freedom of choice and action? He answers that freedom appears everywhere and is everywhere increased:

I know very well that by a kind of innate obsession we cannot rid ourselves of the idea that we become most masters of ourselves by being as isolated as possible. But is not this the reverse of the truth? We must not forget that in each of us, by our very nature, everything is in an elemental state, including our freedom of action. We can only achieve a wider degree of freedom by joining and associating with others in an appropriate way. This is, to be sure, a dangerous operation, since, whether it be a case of disorderly intermingling, or of some simple form of co-ordination, like the meshing of gear-wheels, our activities tend to cancel one another out or to become mechanical —we find this only too often in practice. Yet it is also salutary, since the approach of spirit to spirit in a common vision or a shared passion undoubtedly enriches all; in the case of a team, for example, or of two lovers. Achieved with sympathy, union does not restrict but exalts the possibilities of our being. We see this everywhere and every day on a limited scale. Why should it not be worth correspondingly more on a vast and all-embracing scale, if the law applies to the very structure of things?[46]

[46] "The Formation of the Noosphere," 1947, *FM*, 182–3. See "Some Reflections on the Rights of Man," 1947, *FM*, 193–5.

True union, then, does not suppress differences; it exalts them; it differentiates to an even higher degree the members of the union. And when the members of the union are persons, the differentiation is a further personalization. We can see evidence of this all around us. In teams in sports, in industry, and in research a close degree of teamwork, of union, is joined to a high degree of specialization, or differentiation, of each team member. Teamwork and the specialization of each team member go together. In human society in general, as that society becomes more organized, specialization increases. We see the same thing in interpersonal relationships, particularly in close friendships and in marriage, where a high degree of union brings out the best in both persons, helps them to develop more as persons. In every practical sphere true union does not confound; it differentiates. "True union, the union of heart and spirit, does not enslave, nor does it neutralize the individuals which it brings together. It *super-personalizes* them."[47]

What makes man a personal being, a person, is that he has reflexive consciousness; he can know himself precisely as a knowing subject. He can, therefore, by virtue of his power of reflexive consciousness, form associations of common consciousness in which the differentiation born of union reacts primarily on man *as conscious,* as a *person.* Man can form unions that personalize. What is important is that these unions be between persons precisely insofar as they are persons, that the unions be between the "withins" of persons. That is, what matters is that union of persons be a union informed with love. Without love, without an attraction and a cohesion that come from the interior, there can be no real human association, no true union. Without *interior* bonds of union, without love, we are left with organization imposed from the outside, the totalitarian society of the beehive and the anthill.

[47] "Life and the Planets," 1946, *FM*, 119.

It is not difficult to see in Teilhard's principle that "union differentiates" simply an application, almost a restatement, of the law of complexity-consciousness, the law of recurrence that is the thread running through and holding together his whole phenomenology of evolution. Every true union is an increase in complexity. And every true union differentiates the members of the union; that is, the union (or increase in complexity) gives rise to a corresponding increase in consciousness. In a union of persons, this rise in common consciousness is, from the point of view of each of the persons involved, an increase in personalization. What is happening to mankind today is that men are being forced into closer association and so being urged to greater union with one another. The result is, increasingly, personalization and socialization, both simultaneously and in necessary interdependence. For Teilhard, "person" and "community" are not opposed concepts; they are correlative, complementary; person and community grow and deepen together.

So far, we have outlined Teilhard's phenomenology of evolution insofar as it describes evolution, including human evolution, up to the present time. He himself summarizes his thought up to the point we have reached in three propositions:

1. In the material world, the essential phenomenon is life.

2. In the living world, the essential phenomenon is man.

3. In the human world, the essential phenomenon is the gradual collectivization, totalization, socialization of mankind.[48]

In these three propositions we have traced the central axis of evolution as that axis was found by following the path of increasing complexity-consciousness. We can see that the central

---

[48] "Comment je vois," 1948, 7. See "Turmoil or Genesis?" 1947, *FM*, 214–5, where Teilhard states these three propositions in somewhat different words as three successive theorems or approximations, each of which "clarifies and substantiates the one preceding it on a single line of experience and thought."

axis of evolution coincides with the socialization of mankind. Can we extend the axis of evolution by a kind of extrapolation from the present time into the future? Can we see ahead along the axis of evolution?

Evolution as Converging

Evolution, moving forward in time, arrives at always more complex arrangements of matter and always higher levels of consciousness, of spirit. The evolutionary process has passed through the critical points of the emergence of life and the birth of thought; it continues in man through increasing socialization. Is there perhaps another critical point in the future? Is there some limit to evolution's progress in the direction of increasing complexity-consciousness?

For Teilhard,

two things, at least, seem certain. The first is that, following the state of collective organisation we have already achieved, the process of planetisation can only advance ever further in the direction of growing unanimity. And the second is that this growth of unanimity, being of its nature convergent, cannot continue indefinitely without reaching the natural limit of its course. Every cone has an apex. . . . What will finally crown and limit collective humanity at the ultimate stage of its evolution, is and must be, by reason of continuity and homogeneity, the establishment of a sort of focal point at the heart of the reflective apparatus as a whole.

If we concede this the whole of human history appears as a progress between two critical points: from the lowest point of elementary consciousness to the ultimate, noospherical point of Reflection. In biological terms, humanity will have completed itself and fully achieved its internal equilibrium only when it is physically centered upon itself (which may yet take several million years).[49]

[49] "The Formation of the Noosphere," 1947, *FM*, 178–9.

In the first place, socialization can advance only "in the direction of a growing unanimity." Mankind, in the compressive phase of socialization, is forced to arrange itself on the shrinking globe as well as possible, to make more and more progress in the invention and use of economic, social, and technological systems. Mankind, that is, is compelled to reflect and so, ultimately, to become more human. Man, in a world growing ever smaller, is obliged more and more to adjust himself to the situation. The geographical curvature of the earth, the fact that a growing mankind must adjust to a limited surface area, accounts for a part of the pressure on man, pressure in the direction of further organization and unanimity. But this, Teilhard states in an essay on human unanimity, is not all. To this geographical force of compression there is added a tightening effect "due this time to the emergence and influence of a curvature which is not mechanical but *mental*. . . . The reflective psychic environment which surrounds us is so constituted that we cannot remain in it without moving forward; and we cannot advance except by drawing closer and rubbing shoulders with one another."[50]

In sum, mankind is forced, today more than ever, by two irresistible factors, the curvature of the globe and the curvature of our converging minds, to move toward undreamt-of degrees of organized complexity and of reflexive consciousness. These higher degrees of socialization demand and create the condition for an ever increasing interior "oneness," a unanimity of all men.

Furthermore, this growing socialization and unification of mankind, because it is convergent, cannot go on forever. To return briefly to the image of the globe, socialization has "passed the equator" and is in its compressional phase, moving toward the opposite pole from which it began its phase of expansion. This "pole of convergence" of socialization represents for Teilhard a

[50] "How May We Conceive and Hope that Human Unanimization Will Be Realized on Earth?" 1950, *FM*, 283.

future critical point of evolution. He sees the whole socialization process as tending to center mankind on itself, as converging to some hypothetical future maximum point of socialization, of centration of the Noosphere as a whole upon itself. If we extend the curve of evolution into the future, "the technical-social-mental convergence of mankind upon itself demands that we foresee a paroxysm of co-reflection at some *finite* distance ahead of us in time."[51]

Teilhard sees this "paroxysm of co-reflection" as a critical point of evolution; he calls it a point of "ultra-reflection." At this stage of his generalized physics, then, he introduces into his hypothesis of evolution the future existence of some critical point of social ultra-reflection; this point is the limit point of evolution, the focus of its convergence. At this hypothetical focal point of convergent evolution, mankind will have reached a maximum both of unity of the species and—union differentiates—of personalization of the individual.

Teilhard calls this future focal point of union and of personalization the "Omega point." Omega is the limit point of the socialization process, and so of evolution itself. At this particular stage of his phenomenology of evolution, Omega is seen as a future state of mankind; it is really a future activity or action of mankind, a paroxysm of social reflexive consciousness. Since it is precisely the limit point of evolution and thus not itself subject to evolution to some further state, Omega is somehow outside the evolutionary process. Yet, because it *is* the limit point of evolution, Omega is also somehow a part, the terminal point, of evolution. So far, Omega is a vague and shadowy concept. But this does not prevent us from making statements concerning certain required properties that it should have. Teilhard does not stop his analysis of the Omega point here. He makes a further and crucial consideration,

[51] "Un sommaire de ma perspective 'phénoménologique' du monde," *Les études philosophiques* 10 (1955) 570.

and in so doing he passes from a view of Omega as a future action of mankind to a view of Omega as an independent and already existing personal center.[52]

The Omega Point

Can we be certain of arriving at the Omega point? Is there any guarantee that mankind will finally attain the highest degree of solidarity and of personalization? There is no guarantee apparent within the framework of a generalized physics of evolution; it is one thing that the world, through man, is evolving toward a future focal point, and it is another thing to be sure that evolution will reach that focal point. What, Teilhard asks, are the conditions upon which the attainment of the Omega point depends?[53] There are external conditions: the chances of some cosmic catastrophe or the death of the human race by some nuclear accident seem negligible; there is, however, the possibility that sufficient food will be lacking in the future, or necessary metals. It is possible that the solution of some grave future problem of survival will be beyond the human skill and wisdom of the time. The human race could fail to reach Omega; it could cease evolving and disappear before arriving at Omega because of some exterior difficulty. But there is an *interior* condition of attaining the Omega point which is much more important than any exterior condition of survival. That interior condition is the *will* of mankind to continue.

In inanimate beings and even in animals the "tendency to survive" is a constant; in man this is not necessarily true. Man can *foresee,* and unless man foresees a future consonant with his own being and nature, he will lose the "tendency to survive"; he will

---

[52] For a particularly scientific presentation of Teilhard's reasoning concerning the Omega point, see *MPN*, 115–21.

[53] See especially *MPN*, 118–21; "The Directions and Conditions of the Future," 1948, *FM*, 227–37.

lose what Teilhard calls "the taste for life."[54] Mankind needs a guarantee that evolution will have an outcome, that there is a way out of this apparently closed universe. Mankind, if it is overcome by a "sickness of the dead end," by the anguish of feeling trapped in a closed universe, by the fear of its own total death, will not have the will to go on. Even if the exterior conditions are ideal, it is from the interior that human endeavor must be nourished.

The evolutionary vigour of Mankind can wither away although it be surrounded by mountains of coal, oceans of petroleum and limitless stocks of wheat; it can do so as surely as in a desert of ice, if Man should lose his impulse, or worse, develop a distaste for ever-increased growth "in complexity and consciousness." With all respect to the materialist school, which still refuses to examine *human* biology, it is undeniable that in Man the external drive of Life tends to be transformed and turn inward to become an *ardour* for Life. Try to get productive work out of a workman, an engineer or a scientist who is "browned off"! So in the first place, if Evolution is to continue, it is this impetus which must be maintained in the heart of Man and encouraged to grow at all costs.[55]

In man, then, the instinct for survival takes the form of a "taste for life," and the taste for life can be lost. What would happen, Teilhard asks, if mankind were to find that the universe is closed, that there is no way out, that the conjectural Omega point is a dead end, the point beyond which the human race can no longer exist? It seems clear, he answers, that immediately and on the spot men, like miners discovering that the tunnel is blocked ahead of them, would lose the heart to act. The human will and drive to move ahead would be completely deflated by discouragement.[56]

[54] See "Le goût de vivre," 1950, *OE* 7, 239–51. Also, "Du cosmos à la cosmogénèse," 1951, *OE* 7, 273–5.

[55] "The Human Rebound of Evolution," 1947, *FM*, 205.

[56] "La biologie, poussée à fond, peut-elle nous conduire à émerger dans le transcendant?" 1951, *OE* 9, 279.

In man, he points out again, evolution has become conscious; it can see ahead.

From the moment when Evolution begins to *think itself* it can no longer live with or further itself except by knowing itself to be *irreversible*—that is to say, immortal. For what point can there be in living with eyes fixed constantly and laboriously upon the future, if this future, even though it take the form of a Noosphere, must finally become a zero? Better surely to give up and die at once. In terms of this Absolute it is sacrifice, not egotism, that becomes odious and absurd.[57]

This reasoning leads Teilhard to the following proposition: If the pole of convergence toward which evolution is tending were nothing other than an impersonal massed grouping of reflective elements, temporary and "reversible" (not lasting, precarious), then —if that were so—evolution would slow down and stop in the measure that, in progressing, evolution (conscious in man) became aware of the dead end toward which it was heading.[58] In other words, Omega must somehow exist *now* and it must be a guarantee of irreversibility. It is necessary, he goes on, to conceive Omega as the meeting point of (1) the universe having come to its maximum point of centration and (2) some other Center that is self-subsistent and the ultimate principle of unity and personalization. What is more, Omega must somehow provide a guarantee for mankind of a "way out"; Omega must be the ultimate principle of irreversibility so that mankind, in joining to Omega, passes a critical point and somehow enters into a permanent and irreversible existence.

This is not the only reason that Teilhard makes the Omega point, considered as a self-subsistent Center and already existing

---

[57] "The Human Rebound of Evolution," 1947, *FM*, 206.
[58] *MPN*, 120–1.

focal point of converging evolution, a part of his hypothesis. In 1948, he writes that "even under the irresistible compulsion of the pressures causing it to unite, Mankind will only find and shape itself if men can learn to love one another in the very act of drawing closer."[59] But, he continues, he is less disposed than before to think that the tightening of the human mass is sufficient by itself to lead to the unanimity required for the process of social-ization to reach Omega. He is more than ever convinced, however, of the

hidden existence and eventual release of forces of attraction between men which are as powerful in their own way as nuclear energy appears to be. . . . And surely it is this kind of attraction, the neces-sary condition of our unity, which must be linked at its roots with the radiations of some ultimate Center (at once transcendent and immanent) of psychic congregation: the same Center as that whose existence, opening for human endeavor a door to the Irreversible, seems indispensable (the supreme condition of the future!), for the preservation of the *will* to advance, in defiance of death, upon an evolutionary path become reflective, conscious of the future.[60]

The Omega point, then, is a self-subsistent Center that is exist-ing now; it is irreversible. And, although the end-point of the evolutionary process, it escapes that process and its conditions of space and time; it is transcendent. Autonomy, present existence, irreversibility, and transcendence are the four attributes of Omega.[61]

To sum up, Teilhard's analysis of Omega begins with an initial hypothesis of an Omega point which would be the product of evolution, the highest and last point on the curve of complexity-consciousness, a conjectured and probable point in the future, an

[59] "The Directions and Conditions of the Future," 1948, *FM*, 235.
[60] *Ibid.*, 236.
[61] *PM*, 268–72.

action (of co-reflection) of mankind. In analyzing the necessary conditions for the *future* existence of this probable Omega, he is led to posit the *actual* existence here and now of an Omega point that is independent of mankind, self-subsistent. Rather than the natural product of evolution, Omega is now seen as transcending the evolutionary process, although in some mysterious way a part of that process; yet, it is evolution that depends on Omega rather than Omega on evolution. It may seem that his argument for an autonomous, existing, irreversible, transcendent Omega is a circular argument, and in a way it is. He makes an existing Omega point a part of his hypothesis of evolution because it makes the hypothesis more coherent, because the hypothesis makes more sense that way. His real argument for the existence of Omega is that, if life has meaning, Omega has to exist. He makes this especially clear in *The Phenomenon of Man*.

Either nature is closed to our demands for futurity, in which case thought, the fruit of millions of years of effort, is stifled, stillborn in a self-abortive and absurd universe. Or else an opening exists—that of the super-soul above our souls; but in that case the way out, if we are to agree to embark on it, must open out freely onto limitless psychic spaces in a universe to which we can unhesitatingly entrust ourselves. . . .

In last analysis the best guarantee that a thing should happen is that it appears to us as vitally necessary.[62]

Teilhard de Chardin's phenomenology of evolution is an attempt to give the basis for a coherent view of reality, but it is not a closed system. Far from being closed, his phenomenology of evolution is the foundation of his religious thought; it is open to the whole question of a God who reveals Himself in history. The fact that his hypothesis of evolution contains the existence of an autonomous,

[62] *Ibid.*, 233–4.

transcendent, irreversible Center of converging evolution means that the hypothesis poses the further questions of the precise relation of the universe to Omega and of the nature of Omega. Ultimately, it leads to questions about revelation and about the phenomenon of Christianity.[63] Teilhard's hypothesis of evolution provides at least the basis for a coherent view of the universe. But a good hypothesis possesses fecundity as well as coherence, and his phenomenology of evolution points to further and more profound questions at deeper levels of reality. This is as it should be, for a vision of the universe that will give real meaning to human existence and human effort demands elements that can be pointed to, but not supplied, by a scientific phenomenology.

[63] For Teilhard's own outline and analysis of the way in which his phenomenology of evolution leads through a consideration of Omega to the notion of a Divine Creator who reveals Himself, then to a phenomenological evaluation of Christianity, and finally—moving into the realm of the clearly supernatural—to a theology of Christ, see "Esquisse d'une dialectique de l'esprit," 1946, *OE* 7, 149–58.

3 · THE UNIVERSE AS MEANINGFUL

ALTHOUGH anxiety is as old as mankind, contemporary man suffers from an anxiety that is specific to our age and that is somehow bound up with the rapid rate of human progress. Conscious or not, a fundamental anguish of being, a general anxiety of existence, strikes deep inside all men today. "Something threatens us, something more than ever is lacking, but without our being able to say exactly what."[1]

In Teilhard de Chardin's analysis of contemporary anxiety he claims that the root cause of that anxiety is what he calls "the sickness of the dead end—the anguish of feeling shut in"; it is, more than fear of the future or fear of the death of the individual, the fear that there will ultimately be no future, the fear of the total

[1] *PM*, 227. See Chapter I, references 23–30.

death of mankind. What distinguishes modern man, what makes him specifically modern, is his consciousness of evolution. What causes his anxiety is not being sure "that there is an outcome—*a suitable outcome*—to that evolution."[2] The universe seems closed; there seems to be no "way out" of the universe for mankind.

Toward the end of his life Teilhard writes that the more the years pass, "the more I recognize in myself and around me the great secret preoccupation of modern man; it is not so much to dispute possession of the world as to find some means to escape from it. The anguish of feeling, inside this bubble of the universe, not just spatially but ontologically shut in!"[3] "Fear of being lost in a world so vast . . . that man seems to have lost all significance. Fear of being reduced to immobility. Fear of being unable to find a way out."[4] A universe that is closed, hermetically sealed, is a universe that is meaningless for man, bewildering and menacing and finally stifling of enthusiasm for life and for action. A world that is closed and meaningless is a world in which human endeavor has no lasting value. And man needs to be sure that something of his endeavor is lasting, that something in all that he does has some truly permanent value.

For Teilhard de Chardin modern man's most pressing psychological need is an assurance that some successful outcome exists for that progress on earth for which he knows himself to be responsible. Unless such a guarantee is given, that is to say, unless the prospect of a total death ahead can be eliminated, then there is serious

---

[2] *Ibid.*, 229.

[3] "Le coeur de la matière," 1950, 32.

[4] "The Singularities of the Human Species," 1954, *AM*, 208–9. For a study of the interaction of this cosmic anxiety and his Christian faith in the personal life of Teilhard and how this problem of his own life is reflected in his writings, see C. Mooney, S.J., *Teilhard de Chardin and the Mystery of Christ*, 13–33.

danger that progress will flounder and the whole human enterprise come to a halt.[5]

Teilhard tries to show to the man of this age that there is such a guarantee, that the world around him is meaningful, and that human endeavor does have a lasting value. He does this at two levels, at the level of an objective study of the phenomena (with the selection and arrangement of data to form an ordered series of increasingly comprehensive general hypotheses) and at the level of theological reflection. The first step in his effort to give his contemporaries a vision that is an assurance that the world is meaningful and that man's endeavor has a lasting value is his generalized physics, or scientific phenomenology of evolution.

At the heart of Teilhard's phenomenology of evolution is a law that he finds constantly recurring in the world of our experience, the law of complexity-consciousness. According to this law the universe is in movement, in evolution, toward ever more complex material arrangements and correspondingly higher degrees of consciousness. Having passed through the critical points of the appearance of life and the dawn of reflexive consciousness, evolution continues in man, advancing to still more complex arrangements through technical achievements and socialization and to still higher degrees of psychic tension, of consciousness. In this perspective, evolution is seen to be convergent; that is, it has an upper limit, an interior point of maximum development of complexity and consciousness. Evolution, then, has become conscious in man; it continues in and through man in the direction of a focus of convergence that Teilhard calls the Omega point.

Since evolution is reflective and free in man, Teilhard argues that it must be not only convergent but also irreversible; evolution —now conscious—could not continue without some assurance of

[5] C. Mooney, S.J., *Teilhard de Chardin and the Mystery of Christ*, 67.

escaping annihilation or total death. The demand for irreversibility implies the existence of an Omega point that is a transcendent center of unification. This, in summary form,[6] is Teilhard's phenomenology of evolution, a kind of generalized physics of the universe in process. It is a general hypothesis of the evolutionary structure of the universe, a dynamic hypothesis in the sense that it opens out to further investigation, to further refinement.

This further investigation takes the form of an apologetics, an *apologia* for Christianity, in the sense that it is a logical presentation of reasons for believing in Christ and His Church, a rational invitation to supernatural faith. Ultimately this *apologia* leads to an identification of the Omega point with the risen Christ. In this way Teilhard's apologetics approaches a theology of Christ. Nevertheless, he never *confuses* his apologetics with a theology of Christ. His apologetics remains at the level of scientific phenomenology even though it is conceived with revelation in mind. Like any good apologetics, it does not depend intrinsically on revelation, but leads to a recognition of revelation. Speaking of his apologetics, he writes in an unpublished letter:

I confine myself to describing a psychological advance in the order of causes of credibility (the effort to find God through reason: first session of the Vatican Council). At this preliminary stage, subordinate to supernatural adherence to what is revealed, the act of theological faith is not denied, for it has not yet come up for consideration.[7]

---

[6] The summary here follows Teilhard's own summary of his thought, written in 1948 and published under the title "La pensée du Père Teilhard de Chardin," *Les études philosophiques* 10 (1955) 580–1.

[7] Quoted in H. de Lubac, S.J., *Teilhard de Chardin, the Man and His Meaning*, tr. R. Hague (copyright © 1965 by Burns & Oates Ltd., published by Hawthorn Books Inc., New York), 187. The second section of Father de Lubac's book, 133–203, is devoted to an explanation of Teilhard's apologetics with emphasis on a defense of Teilhard's method.

Teilhard's apologetics is a presentation of a line of reasoning that indicates that Christianity should be accepted, believed in; it is a setting forth of evidence of the credibility of his faith. As Father de Lubac puts it:

> The formal cause of divine or supernatural faith is the testimony given to us by God about himself. Père Teilhard was perfectly aware of this. But in addressing the unbeliever, he is speaking of something quite different. He sets out various "reasons for belief" by which he hopes to lead him, starting from some human faith they both have in common, to the threshold of supernatural faith. We need dwell no further on that approach, which is that of any sound apologist.[8]

Taking his theory of evolution, including the existence of an Omega point, as a foundation and primary phase of his apologetics, Teilhard moves into a second phase where, reasoning from the existence and nature of the Omega point, he tries to show the high degree of probability that some divine revelation has been made to mankind. From there, in a third phase, he moves to an objective and phenomenological investigation of the fact and the credentials of Christianity, for Christianity claims to possess just such a revelation.

The Probability of a Revelation and the Phenomenon of Christianity

We can consider the total process of evolution to be in the form of a cone; the evolutionary process, then, is moving, converging, to the summit of the cone, the Omega point. The Omega point, according to Teilhard's analysis, is the final point in the evolutionary process and so necessarily a part of that process, somehow within

[8] *Ibid.,* 171.

it. On the other hand, the Omega point is autonomous and transcendent, somehow divine. For Teilhard the Omega point, insofar as it is transcendent of evolution, is God.[9] Omega is not, in this view, a simple future point of convergence but a now-existing God. This modifies our conception of evolution. Before, all that was evident was a seemingly spontaneous progress of evolution toward higher levels of consciousness; the cause of evolution's progress along the curve of complexity-consciousness was not at all apparent. We can see now that the universe makes evolutionary progress because it is *drawn* by a transcendent God.

From this point on in his apologetics Teilhard considers it sufficiently shown that the universe is moved from ahead by a God-Omega who attracts all things as their First Mover, and this not only in the physical and the biological orders but (especially) in the order of human consciousness. Teilhard reasons that if God is First Mover "by attraction from ahead" in the order of what is most human, in the order of intelligence and love and freedom, then it seems natural to grant the theoretical probability that God has somehow spoken to mankind, that God has communicated some revelation of Himself and His plan for men. That is, if God-Omega is the ultimate mover of evolution and so the ultimate principle of consciousness and personalization, it seems reasonable to suppose that God has somehow manifested Himself to men in a way that is commensurate with their nature and with His own, in a personal way, by some sort of "word" or "speech." Some divine revelation by God-as-personal to man-as-person seems probable.[10] In an epilogue to *The Phenomenon of Man* Teilhard sums

[9] In "Esquisse d'une dialectique de l'esprit," 1946, *OE* 7, 149–58, Teilhard identifies "the transcendent face of Omega" with God (152). The entire essay is essential to an understanding of Teilhard's thought and especially of his apologetics. This chapter, for the most part, follows the plan of Teilhard's essay and relies on it heavily.

[10] *Ibid.*, 155. Also, "Introduction à la vie chrétienne," 1944, 6.

up his argument for the probable existence of such a supernatural revelation:

If Omega were only a remote and ideal focus destined to emerge at the end of time from the convergence of terrestrial consciousness, nothing could make it known to us in anticipation of this convergence. At the present time no other energy of a personal nature could be detected on earth save that represented by the sum of human persons.

If, on the other hand, Omega is, as we have admitted, already in existence and operative at the very core of the thinking mass, then it would seem inevitable that its existence should be manifested to us here and now through some traces. To animate evolution in its lower stages, the conscious pole of the world could of course only act in an impersonal form and under the veil of biology. Upon the thinking entity that we have become. . . . it is now possible for it to radiate from the one center to all centers—personally. Would it seem likely that it should not do so?[11]

At this point Teilhard turns to an examination of Christianity considered simply as a phenomenon. "The Christian fact stands before us. It has its place among the other realities of the world."[12] Although he now proposes investigating a matter of religion, let it be stressed that we are still on the methodological level of a strict scientific phenomenology; his reasoning in this last stage of his apologetics is still independent of revelation as a source.

As a preliminary to his analysis of Christianity, Teilhard considers and compares the great religions of the world. From the point of view of his apologetics, he is looking for a probably existing revelation; the question is where to look, and he considers

11 *PM*, 291–2.
12 *Ibid.*, 292.

all the great religions before settling on Christianity as by far the most suitable religion in which to search for a divine revelation.[13] What is his criterion in his comparison of the world's great religions? Whereas most systematic apologetics of the past have relied heavily on miracles as proofs of the credibility of Christianity, miracles in Teilhard's apologetics, while remaining criteria of truth, have a subordinated and secondary place. His principal criteria are coherence and fecundity. That is, the truth of a religion can be seen in how much it gives us a meaningful vision of reality and in how much it motivates us to act in a meaningful way. "To the eyes of modern man," he writes,

the finally decisive criterion of the truth of a religion must be the capacity shown by that religion to give a global meaningfulness to the universe that we are discovering around us. The contemporary point of view is that if the "true" religion exists it should be recognizable . . . by this sign: that under its influence and by its light the world as a totality takes on a maximum of coherence and a maximum of interest for our taste for action.[14]

What this means ultimately in Teilhard's apologetics is that the criterion of the truth of a religion is how well that religion harmonizes with the view of a universe that is progressing along a path of increasing complexity-consciousness toward an autonomous and transcendent Center of convergence.[15] The religion that best fits this perspective, the "truest" religion, will be the religion the most relevant to human existence and to human endeavor, the religion that gives a maximum of meaning to life and to action.

---

[13] This preliminary step does not seem to be essential to Teilhard's apologetics. He leaves it out in most outlines of his thought; cf., however, "Comment je crois," 1934, 17–22.

[14] "Introduction à la vie chrétienne," 1944, 2.

[15] "Comment je crois," 1934, 18–9. See "Le Christianisme dans le monde," 1933, *OE* 9, 142–3; "Introduction à la vie chrétienne," 1944, 2.

Teilhard finds inadequate the oriental religions and the modern neo-humanist "religions of progress" (including Communism). Very briefly, neither of these two groups of religions is really *activating;* neither adequately activates man in the direction of evolution, toward God-Omega. The oriental religions tend to remove man from an active participation in evolution; they tend not to encourage human endeavor but to discourage and even eliminate it.[16] Neither are the "religions of progress" really activating in the long run; they leave no "way out" for the universe. They are closed systems and regard the universe as a closed system; they do not give assurance against the possibility of total death for mankind. The "religions of progress" are hollow with the "sickness of the dead end," and so—finally—they too, in spite of their claims, discourage human endeavor.

It is Christianity which best fits Teilhard's criterion, which is the religion that most encourages human effort and participation in evolution, and which—still from the point of view of a scientific phenomenology—is the superior religion and will survive all the others.

From the . . . viewpoint which I have adopted, it may be said that the historic rivalry of mysticisms and creeds, each striving to conquer the earth, represents nothing but a prolonged groping of the human soul in search of a conception of the world in which it will feel itself to be more sensitised, more free and active. This surely means that the faith which finally triumphs must be the one which shows itself to be more capable than any other of inspiring Man to action. And it is here, irrespective of all philosophical or theological considerations, that Christianity decisively takes the lead with its extraordinary power of immortalising and personalising in

[16] See E. Tomlin, *The Oriental Philosophers*, 23: "We can act only in a world that we believe to be both real and worth inhabiting. Now characteristics such as reality and value are precisely those which Eastern thought, with certain exceptions, refuses to ascribe to the natural world."

Christ, to the extent of making it lovable, the time-space totality of Evolution.[17]

Looking at Christianity objectively and empirically, Teilhard argues, we find it to be "a religious current characterized by the following group of properties: intense vitality; a strange adaptability that permits it, contrary to other religions, to develop best and chiefly in the zone of growth of the noosphere; finally, a remarkable similarity . . . with all that a study of the human phenomenon has taught us."[18] Christianity appears as a central phylum of human evolution and as conscious of finding itself in intimate relation with a spiritual and transcendent pole of universal convergence.[19] Why not then accept the hypothesis that the Christian religion contains the revelation that is to be looked for? The purpose of Teilhard's apologetics has been just this: to bring the unbeliever to accept at least the reasonable probability, the hypothesis, that the living thought of the Church is the reflection (adapted to our state) of the divine thought, to bring the unbeliever to accept as a hypothesis that Christianity contains the personal divine revelation that should be sought and that gives meaning to human life and action.[20]

Christian Faith and Theological Method

Up to now, up to and including the acceptance of the Christian message as a hypothesis, Teilhard has never left the order of rea-

[17] "The Human Rebound of Evolution," 1947, *FM*, 208–9.

[18] "Comment je vois," 1948, 15.

[19] *PM*, 292–9. See "L'énergie humaine," 1937, *OE* 6, 193–5.

[20] Teilhard writes to a friend that he intends to begin an essay entitled "The Place of Christianity in the Universe" in which he wants to show that "religion fills a basic and continually growing need in the process of universal evolution," and that "at present the only viable form of religion is Christianity." It seems, however, that he never wrote the essay. (Letter of April 3, 1930, *Lettres à Léontine Zanta*, 114.)

son and of scientific phenomenology. He has studied phenomena objectively and, with the facts accumulated and ordered, formed a hypothesis. A central part of the hypothesis is the truth (accepted as at least hypothetical) of Christianity. Teilhard with his apologetics has led the unbeliever right up to the supernatural act of faith. Strictly speaking, this is the endpoint of his scientific phenomenology and of his apologetics. He makes this perfectly clear when he states that up until now

we have progressed . . . only by the way of reason; our successive intuitions have been kept within the scientific bounds of the hypothesis. As soon as we accept the reality of an answer coming from on high, we in some way enter the order of certainty. But this comes about not, as before, as a function of mere confrontation of subject and object, but of contact between two centers of consciousness. Now it is not simply an act of knowing, but an act of *recognition*: the whole complex interplay of two beings who freely open and give themselves to one another—the emergence, under the influence of grace, of theological faith.[21]

The theological faith that Teilhard is talking about in the above passage is supernatural faith in Christ, in the incarnate God. It is a faith that *"really* has God as its principal Agent, source, and milieu of its development."[22] For Teilhard, Christian faith is the

---

[21] "Esquisse d'une dialectique de l'esprit," 1946, *OE* 7, 155.

[22] "La foi que opère," 1918, *Ecrits*, 325. See also "Forma Christi," 1918, *Ecrits*, 342–4. On the strict supernaturality of Christian faith, see Teilhard's letter of December 29, 1919, to Maurice Blondel: "We must exclude in an exact formula anything that might give the impression of naturalism, or humanism, or of a Christian Emersonianism. I would like to find a definition of the divinizing transformation of our being which would clearly distinguish it in its very mechanism from every other kind of transformation or *natural* division (like the divisions that separate matter from life and life from thought). But I ask myself if the world's structure itself is not opposed to this effort. The great division of the supernatural is preceded

acceptance of the fact of the Incarnation, not by inference or as part of a hypothesis, but by adherence to an affirmation received from God. From now on, he will use revelation as a source; from now on, his thought is theological, a reflection on and an explanation of Christian revelation. The fact that he retains the framework of his scientific phenomenology and integrates that phenomenology with divine revelation to form a synthesis does not make his thought any less theological.

It is true that his theological thought is not *metaphysical;* it is not based on an ontology or on any *a priori* set of abstractions. It is a theology that has as its sources not divine revelation and a *philosophy* (as, for example, the theology of Saint Thomas is based on revelation and Aristotelian philosophy) but divine revelation and a *scientific phenomenology.* As early as 1919 he foresaw opposition because his theology was not philosophical; he writes in a letter, in the context of his own theological research, that in discussion with his friends he has

come to realize the turn of my mind that divides me from them. I'm less concerned than they are with the metaphysical side of things, with what might have been or might not have been, with the abstract conditions of existence: all that seems to me inevitably misleading or shaky. I realize that, to the very marrow of my bones, I'm sensitive to the real, to what is made of it. My concern is to discover the conditions for such progress as is open to us, and not, starting from first principles, some theoretical development of the universe. This bias means that I'll always be a philistine to the professional

---

by other little ones." (H. de Lubac, S.J., "Maurice Blondel et le Père Teilhard de Chardin, mémoires échangés en décembre 1919, présentés par H. de Lubac," *Archives de philosophie* 24 (1961) 123–56, hereafter cited as *Archives.* See Philippe de la Trinité, O.C.D., *Rome et Teilhard de Chardin,* 78–9: "It must be stated clearly: . . . knowledge of the supernatural order of the Incarnation and of grace can never be reduced objectively, even indirectly, to reason alone nor to natural intuition alone."

philosophers; but I feel that my strength lies in the fidelity with which I obey it. So I'll continue to advance along those lines. Others can bring me into line with the principles if they can.[23]

There is in Teilhard's thought a single epistemological line that goes from the observed phenomena, through the formation of a hypothesis (according to the law of complexity-consciousness) that includes a transcendent Omega, and that finally terminates after a consideration of the Christian phenomenon. Here, just before the theoretical point of the supernatural act of faith, the line breaks off. A new epistemological line begins on the other side, so to speak, of the act of faith. This new line is theological; Christian revelation, now accepted in Christian faith, becomes the source (together with Teilhard's hyperphysics of evolution) of a reflection on that revelation.[24]

[23] *MM*, 302. It is true that Teilhard sometimes speaks of his "philosophy," but he is using the term loosely. Occasionally he uses the term "metaphysics" to describe his theology. See, for example, the second section of "Comment je vois," 17–21; the three sections of this work are entitled "Physics (phenomenology)," "Metaphysics," "Mystique." But Teilhard's "metaphysics" is no real metaphysics; it is a theology that is based on his hyperphysics of evolution as well as on revelation. For his own ideas on theological methodology, see "Note sur le Christ-Universel," 1920, *OE* 9, 1, 6; "Action et activation," 1945, *OE* 9, 222, 227–9.

[24] See C. Mooney, S.J., *Teilhard de Chardin and the Mystery of Christ*, 58–66. Father Mooney points out the differences in Teilhard's methodologies in the formation of the hypothesis of an existing Omega and in the identification of Omega with Christ. On Teilhard's methodology in general, see N. Luyten, O.P., "La méthode du Père Teilhard," in *Teilhard de Chardin et la pensée catholique*, ed. C. Cuénot, 19–63; C. d'Armagnac, S.J., "Philosophie de la nature et méthode chez le Père Teilhard de Chardin," *Archives de philosophie* 20 (1957) 5–41. For a particularly severe criticism of Teilhard's methodology, see M. Guérard des Lauriers, O.P., "La démarche du P. Teilhard de Chardin, réflexions d'ordre épistemologique," *Divinitas* 3 (1959) 221–68. P. Chauchard, a scientist who has written extensively on the thought of Teilhard, insists that Teilhard is not a theologian in any way and that in none of his writings does he leave the domain of science. See his *Man and Cosmos*, tr. Courtright, 114, 118.

In a true sense, however, one can say that Teilhard's method is always the same; the real difference between his pretheological thought and his theological reflection is that his theology (like any Christian theology) uses revelation as a source. Even in his theological reflection his method is to arrange the data so as to form a hypothesis that has a maximum of coherence and productiveness.[25] He tries to explain certain central parts of the Christian message so as to give a vision of reality that is as ordered and coherent as possible, and a vision that directs us always more deeply into the heart of the total Christian mystery. In other words, he forms a general theological hypothesis that is true, verified, because (and to the extent that) it is coherent and that it leads more profoundly into the mystery of Christianity. The data of his theological hypotheses are not, of course, of uniform certainty. The truths of revelation have the certainty of faith; the law of complexity-consciousness has the certainty of an inductively formed scientific law; the theory that evolution is converging has the certainty of a scientific theory, and so on. But he uses both the data of revelation and the data of his hyperphysics. He is not interested in the relative degrees of certainty of the data but in the formation of a Christian vision with a maximum of meaningfulness for contemporary man.

Teilhard, then, uses two sources for his theology, Christian revelation and his own phenomenology of evolution (up to and including his treatment of the Christian phenomenon). Because he uses two sources to form one theological synthesis, it sometimes appears in his writings that he is confusing the two sources, either deducing the contents of revelation from his theory of evolution or using revelation to give a scientific explanation of the universe. Nothing could be further from the truth.[26] There is no attempt

[25] "Man's Place in the Universe," 1942, *VP*, 227; "Esquisse d'un univers personnel," 1936, *OE* 6, 70–1; "Comment je vois," 1948, 1.

[26] "Science et Christ," 1921, *OE* 9, 59–60.

whatever at a concordism that would mix and confuse the findings of science (or his own hypothesis of evolution) with the facts known only from revelation or that would try to make either depend on the other. He met with criticism on this very point, that his thought was a "generalized concordism." To the criticism he replies that

one should not confuse concordism with coherence. Religion and science obviously represent two different meridians on the mental sphere; it would be false not to keep them separate (the concordist error). But these different meridians must necessarily meet somewhere at a pole of common vision (this is the meaning of coherence); otherwise our whole intellectual quest for knowledge falls apart.[27]

The two meridians of scientific knowledge and strictly religious knowledge are and must be separate "at the equator," separate because guided by different principles, using different sources and so differing methods. But, presupposing that reality makes sense, that the universe is coherent, these two meridians must meet at some pole of the ultimate convergence of truth.[28] Teilhard, while remaining at the equator, looks ahead to that ultimate pole. His presupposition of a coherent universe makes him expect the meridians to meet there; his discovery is that they meet so well.

The above considerations do not mean to imply that his theology has no apologetic purpose. On the contrary, its purpose is precisely to show contemporary man the meaningfulness of Christianity for him. Modern man, Teilhard observes, is looking for something to give meaning to his world and value to his activity. The only religion that, from now on, mankind wants and can

---

[27] "La pensée du Père Teilhard de Chardin," 1948, *Les études philoso-phiques* 10 (1955) 581.
[28] "Comment je vois," 1948, 1.

accept is a religion that is capable of giving life and meaning to the cosmic progress that can be discerned in mankind's upward movement.[29]

The Living Church

Once the fact of the Incarnation is accepted on ground of supernatural faith, Teilhard can return to the Christian phenomenon, now not merely to consider it as a phenomenon but to see it through the eyes of faith and to penetrate more deeply into its nature using the data of revelation. In his earlier analysis of the Christian phenomenon he found Christianity to appear to be a central phylum of human evolution; the main axis of evolution would seem to pass through Christianity. But now he is going to consider the Church as phylum or main stem of evolution in the light of Christian faith. Before proceeding to this consideration, let us pause to describe the nature and development of a phylum of evolution. For Teilhard, "phylum" is an analogous term; for our purposes it is enough to say that a phylum is a "bundle" of lines of evolutionary development. It is a collective reality; it could be a species or a group of species. A phylum behaves like a living thing; it grows and flourishes.[30] Teilhard compares the growth of a phylum to the successive stages undergone by a human invention.

We know those stages well from having seen them for about a century constantly around us. Roughly the idea first takes the shape of a theory or a provisional mechanism. Then follows a period of rapid modification. The rough model is continually touched up and adjusted until it is practically completed. On the attainment of this stage, the new creation enters its phase of expansion and equilibrium. As regards

29 "Introduction à la vie chrétienne," 1944, 2.
30 *PM*, 114–5.

quality it now only undergoes minor changes; it has reached its ceiling. But quantitatively it spreads out and reaches full consistence. It is the same story with all modern inventions, from the bicycle to the aeroplane, from photography to the cinema and radio.

In just this way the naturalist sees the curve of growth followed by the branches of life. At the outset the phylum corresponds to the "discovery," by groping, of a new type of organism that is both viable and advantageous. But this new type will not attain its most economical or efficient form all at once. For a certain period of time it devotes all its strength, so to speak, to groping about within itself. Try-out follows try-out, without being finally adopted. Then at last perfection comes within sight, and from that moment the rhythm of change slows down. The new invention, having reached the limit of its potentialities, enters its phase of conquest. Stronger now than its less perfected neighbours, the newly born group spreads and at the same time consolidates. It multiplies, but without further diversification. It has now entered its fully-grown period and at the same time its period of stability.[31]

Mankind itself is a phylum. In his consideration of the Christian phenomenon Teilhard observed Christianity to behave like a central phylum within the human phylum; that is to say, the principal axis of evolution passes not only through mankind but, more exactly, through Christianity. Human evolutionary progress takes place along the axis of complexity-consciousness and chiefly through socialization. This progress is convergent, moving toward a critical point of maturation, the Omega point. And the central axis of mankind's evolutionary progress appears to be Christianity.

Using Christian revelation as a further source, Teilhard confirms this observation with much greater certainty than could be had simply by inspection of phenomena. He makes a firm structural part of his theology the fact that "the Christian phylum is not an accessory or divergent shoot in the human social organism, but

[31] *Ibid.,* 116.

constitutes the axis itself of socialization."[32] For the Christian, the terminal point of human evolution is the Parousia, the second coming of Christ at the end of time. Teilhard identifies the Parousia with the end point of the socialization process, the maximum point of complexity-consciousness of the total organism of mankind. Evolution, then, is proceeding along the axis of the Church-phylum toward the Parousia. "To the Christian . . . the whole process of hominization is merely a paving of the way for the ultimate Parousia."[33]

It seems well to point out that when Teilhard speaks of the "Church-phylum" he means the Catholic Church. To say that the Roman Catholic Church is the only authentic expression of Christianity is, to Teilhard, not an unjustifiable pretension; on the contrary, the Catholic Church's claimed prerogative answers an inevitable organic need. Christianity is definitely not a fixed system, not just a collection of truths given once and for all to be literally conserved. It is founded on a revealed nucleus, but it is in continuous development. Biologically, Christianity behaves like a phylum of evolution. Consequently and by biological necessity it should have the structure of a phylum; it should form an organized and progressive system of collectively associated spiritual elements.[34] It is only Catholicism that has these characteristics. To say that the Church is infallible is simply to recognize that the Church is a phylum and so, like any phylum, can find its way through innumerable gropings to maturity and fulfillment; it is simply to say that the Church is a phylum that is extraordinarily alive. Furthermore, to localize the organ of this phyletic infallibility in the Councils or in the Pope (formulating and expressing not his own per-

---

[32] "Turmoil or Genesis?" 1947, *FM*, 215. See *DM*, 117: the light of Christianity "radiates from *an historical center* and is transmitted along *a traditional and solidly defined axis.*"

[33] "Turmoil or Genesis?" 1947, *FM*, 224–5.

[34] "Introduction à la vie chrétienne," 1944, 2.

sonal ideas but the thought of the Church) is entirely in conformity with the law of "cephalization" that dominates all biological evolution.[35] Teilhard knows very well that there are many non-Catholic Christians who know and love Christ and who are united to Him as well as or better than Catholics. But these individuals are not grouped together in the living organic reality of a *body* that reacts as an organized totality and in a living way. It is only in Catholicism that new dogmas continue to be born and that new attitudes are formed in a continuous synthesis of the traditionally held truths of Christianity and the views that emerge in the process of developing human consciousness. If Christianity is truly to be the religion of the future, then—judging by all the evidence—it can measure up to the advance of human progress only through the living and organized axis of Roman Catholicism. "To be a Catholic is the only way to be fully and most profoundly a Christian."[36]

Christ-Omega

It is only after all the above successive stages of Teilhard's thought that he finally identifies Omega with the risen Christ. At the end of a somewhat long dialectical process, he is able to assert that the already existing Omega of his general hypothesis of evolution is identical to the risen Christ. Following his own outline we can schematize his thought in four successive phases of movement from what is known to what is less known.[37]

	known	*less known*
phase 1	the human phenomenon (1)	a transcendent and autonomous Omega (2)

[35] *Ibid.*, 2–3.

[36] *Ibid.*, 11. See "Christianisme et évolution," 1945, 10; "Le coeur de la matière," 1950, 10; "Le goût de vivre," 1950, *OE* 7, 249, note 1.

[37] "Esquisse d'une dialectique de l'esprit," 1946, *OE* 7, 157.

phase 2	evolutionary creation (3)	a God who is Mover and Revealer (4)
phase 3	the Christian phenomenon (5)	God incarnate (6)
phase 4	the living Church (7)	Christ-Omega (8)

The act of Christian faith is placed between step (5) and step (6). "It is under the illuminative influence of grace that our mind recognizes, in the unitive character of the Christian phenomenon, a manifestation (reflection) of Omega on human consciousness, and it identifies the Omega of reason with the Universal Christ of revelation."[38] Notice that it is Christian faith, not rational deduction, that discovers Christ and Omega to be the same. Teilhard could not be more clear on this.[39]

Teilhard has taken us far beyond the level of scientific phenomenology to the basic principle of his theology of Christ: the identification of Christ and Omega. This identification is, in fact, the keystone of Teilhard's whole vision of reality. The Omega of his generalized physics of evolution and the Christ of Christian revelation are one and the same; it is this that, for him, gives meaning to the universe and a direction to human effort.

In Teilhard's pretheological analysis of evolution and the Omega point, Omega remains part of a general hypothesis, part of a theory of the evolutionary structure of the world. It is hardly a guarantee of the meaningfulness of life and action; it cannot, by itself, be the assurance that the modern world desperately needs. The Omega-God of the hypothesis is a faceless God and, at best, vague. Furthermore, a God whose existence is not a certainty can hardly be a guarantee. In the final analysis, the Omega of Teilhard's theory of evolution is posited by extrapolation; by its nature it remains a conjecture, an assumption. "It nourishes our hope on

---

[38] "La pensée du Père Teilhard de Chardin," 1948, *Les études philosophiques* 10 (1955) 581.

[39] See "Science et Christ," 1921, *OE* 9, 59–60.

traits that are vague and ethereal."[40] What is more, the characteristics and nature of the Omega of Teilhard's hypothesis of evolution stretch our imagination to the point where it "becomes necessary to support our confusing extrapolations with some positive facts."[41] These positive facts come from Christian revelation.

Christ has precisely the same characteristics as the Omega foreseen by Teilhard's theory, provided He is seen in the full realism of His Incarnation, and He tends to produce exactly the spiritual totalization that is awaited.[42] No matter how we look at things, the universe cannot have two heads. Christian revelation calls for a supernatural operation of ultimate synthesis by Christ; it is inconceivable that this event would take place in divergence from the natural convergence of the world. When all is said and done, the universal Christic center demanded by Christianity and the universal cosmic center postulated by Teilhard's phenomenology of evolution must coincide or at least overlap.[43] Christ could not be the only mover and the only salvation of the world if the world could somehow find its cohesion (even to an inferior degree) outside of Him. "It is in fact toward Christ that we turn our eyes when, with no matter what degree of approximation, we look ahead to a superior pole of humanization and personalization."[44] For the Christian believer, then, the final success of evolution is positively guaranteed, with a guarantee whose basis goes beyond the plane of phenomena, by the resurrecting power of God incarnate in His creation.

For a Christian, provided his Christology accepts the fact that the collective consummation of earthly Mankind is not a meaningless

[40] "Le Christique," 1955, 7.
[41] "Mon univers," 1924, *OE* 9, 81.
[42] "L'énergie humaine," 1937, *OE* 6, 192.
[43] "Super-humanité, super-Christ, super-charité," 1943, *OE* 9, 209–10.
[44] *Ibid.*, 210.

and still less a hostile event, but a precondition (necessary, but not sufficient in itself) of the final, "parousiac" establishment of the Kingdom of God—for such a Christian the eventual biological success of Man on Earth is not merely a probability but a certainty; since Christ (and in Him virtually the World) is already risen. But this certainty, born as it is of a "supernatural" act of faith, is of its nature supra-phenomenal.[45]

It is Christ-Omega who is not only the guarantee of the outcome of evolution but who gives evolution its order and meaning.

To the Christian humanist—faithful in this to the most sure theology of the Incarnation—there is neither separation nor discordance, but coherent subordination, between the genesis of Mankind in the World and the genesis of Christ in Mankind through His Church. The two processes are inevitably linked in their structure, the second requiring the first as the matter upon which it descends in order to super-animate it. This view entirely respects the progressive effective concentration of human thought in an increasingly acute consciousness of its unitary destiny. But instead of the vague center of convergence envisaged as the ultimate end of this process of evolution, the personal and defined reality of the Word Incarnate, in which everything acquires substance, appears and takes its place.[46]

If we accept the evidence that the Christ of revelation and the Omega of evolution are the same, then a way out begins to shine through in the distant future. "In a world certainly open at its summit in Christ Jesus we no longer risk dying of suffocation."[47]

Ultimately, the world has meaning, takes on a real coherence, only when seen as converging on Christ. But it must be kept in mind that Teilhard in identifying the Omega of his theory of evolu-

---

[45] "The Directions and Conditions of the Future," 1948, *FM*, 237.
[46] "Social Heredity and Progress," 1938, *FM*, 34.
[47] "Le Christique," 1955, 7.

tion and the Christ of divine revelation is in no way confusing the natural and the supernatural. That Omega, in his reasoning, is first an extrapolation from natural evolution and finally (in the light of faith) is seen to be Christ does not mean that the natural and the supernatural are for him confused or identified. Failure to understand this important point has caused no end of misunderstanding of his views.[48] In the epilogue to *The Phenomenon of Man* Teilhard asks, "To confirm the presence at the summit of the world of what we have called the Omega point, do we not find here the very cross check we have been waiting for?" In a footnote he adds:

To be more exact, "to confirm the presence at the summit of the world of something in line with, but still more elevated than, the Omega point." This is in deference to the theological concept of the "supernatural" according to which the binding contact between God and the world, *hic et nunc* inchoate, attains to a superintimacy (which is thus outside all logic) of which man can have no inkling and to which he can lay no claim by virtue of his "nature" alone.[49]

[48] George Gaylord Simpson is a good example of a scientist who strongly criticizes Teilhard for mixing science and religion; he writes: "Teilhard's beliefs as to the course and the causes of evolution are not scientifically acceptable, because they are not in truth based on scientific premises. . . . Teilhard's mystic vision is not thereby invalidated, because it does not in truth derive from his beliefs on evolution—quite the contrary. There is no possible way of validating or of testing Teilhard's mystic vision of Omega. Any assurance about it must itself be an unsupported act of mystic faith. . . . The attempt to build an evolutionary theology mingling mysticism and science has only tended to vitiate the science. I strongly suspect that it has been equally damaging on the religious side, but here I am less qualified to judge." (*This View of Life* [New York, Harcourt, Brace & World, Inc., 1964], 232.) Teilhard would strongly agree that any real assurance about his "mystic vision of Omega" can come only from an act of supernatural faith; this is a key point in his thought rather than a criticism of that thought. And certainly Teilhard was careful to avoid any confusion of science and religion.

[49] *PM*, 298.

It is true that Christ is not the center that creation could *by nature* aspire to be joined to. That the evolving universe (and all that is in it) is moving toward, converging on, Christ is an undeserved and gratuitous favor of the Creator. But it is also true that Christ *is* the center toward which all things are converging. By His Incarnation He has so steeped the world in the supernatural that we can hardly imagine toward what other center the world might have been destined to gravitate if God's plan had been different and if there had been no Incarnation. We can really know nothing about some natural center or Omega point that might have existed in a different order of things.[50] The fact, however, that we cannot imagine some natural Omega that might have existed does nothing to diminish the gratuity of God's gift in centering the existing universe on Christ. What makes the supernatural gratuitous is that God gives Himself. In any hypothesis, the world must have some center in order to be thinkable. The presence of some Omega has nothing to do necessarily with a "supernatural elevation." What makes the present order gratuitous is precisely that "the place of the universal Center has not been given to some supreme intermediary between God and the universe, but taken by the Divinity itself."[51]

The Christ of History as Center of the Universe

In 1924, when Teilhard begins to clarify his position on Christ as the center of the universe, he writes that the affirmations by St. John and especially by St. Paul of Christ's physical supremacy over the universe are sufficient demonstration of the proposition that the revealed Christ is none other than Omega.[52] He goes on

[50] "L'union créatrice," 1917, *Ecrits*, 195–6. See "Du cosmos à la cosmogénèse," 1951, *OE* 7, 272.

[51] "Mon univers," 1924, *OE* 9, 84.

[52] *Ibid.*, 82. Teilhard refers in a footnote to the following texts: *Rom.* 8:81ff, 14:7–9; I *Cor.* 4:22, 6:15ff, 10:16, 12:12ff, 15:23–9, 39ff; II *Cor.*

to say that everything is summed up in two essential affirmations: "In Him all things hold together" (Col. 1:17) and "in Him all things find their completion" (Col. 2:10; see Eph. 4:9) in such a way that "Christ is all things and in all" (Col. 3:11).[53] Teilhard is not claiming that St. Paul's epistles contain Teilhard's own cosmology; he would be the last to claim that St. Paul wrote in contemporary scientific categories or that Paul's theology is based on the modern concept of evolution. He is simply using St. Paul as a source while at the same time using as a second source his own phenomenology of evolution.[54] Relying on both sources, he contends that *the historical Jesus, the Christ of the Gospels, is the personal and physical center of the universe and the focus of the converging evolution of the universe.*

In reading Teilhard's works, especially *The Phenomenon of Man*, it is possible to lose sight of the all-important fact that Christ-Omega, the center of the universe and the focus and terminus of evolution, is the historical Jesus of Nazareth risen from the dead. Teilhard's evolutionary perspective makes him more interested in the terminus of growth than in its beginnings; in an evolutionary system of thought it is natural that growth and development and their end-result receive more consideration than origins. "There is nothing in our progressively changing world that is truly understandable as long as it has not reached its terminus. . . . So if we want to have an accurate idea of the Incarnation it is not at its beginnings (Annunciation, Nativity, even the Passion) that we must place ourselves, but—insofar as possible—at its definitive

---

3:18, 5:11, 5:4, 19; *Gal.* 3:27–8; *Eph.* 1:10, 19–23, 2:5, 10, 13–4, 3:6, 18, 4:9, 12:3–16; *Phil.* 2:10, 3:10–1, 20–1; *Col.* 1:15–20, 28, 2:9–10, 12, 19, 3:10; *I Thes.* 4:17; *Heb.* 2:7–8.

[53] "Mon univers," 1924, *loc. cit.*

[54] See the discussion of Teilhard's use of the Pauline texts in the light of modern exegesis in C. Mooney, S.J., *Teilhard de Chardin and the Mystery of Christ*, 67–103.

terminus."[55] The Incarnation as an historical fact is a beginning, and Teilhard always attached more importance to endings than to beginnings; nonetheless, it is the historical Christ, history's Jesus of Nazareth, who is the Omega of Teilhard's theological vision. The point is essential to any understanding of his theology: the Jesus of the beginning is identical with Omega, the same Person. "If it is really by Christ-Omega that the universe is held in movement, then . . . it is from His concrete source, the Man of Nazareth, that Christ-Omega draws (theoretically and historically) His whole solidity."[56]

The mystical Christ, the universal Christ of St. Paul, has neither meaning nor value in our eyes except as an expansion of the Christ who was born of Mary and who died on the cross. The former essentially draws his fundamental quality of undeniability and concreteness from the latter. However far we may be drawn into the divine spaces opened up to us by Christian mysticism, we never depart from the Jesus of the Gospels.[57]

Teilhard's own personal faith in Christ found satisfaction in the conception of Christ-Omega, Center of the universe; but this conception, he writes, "is nothing other than an authentic expression of the Christ of the Gospels."[58] Christ-Omega then is far from being simply a symbol of humanity in some future state or some kind of ideal for mankind. Christ-Omega is Jesus of Nazareth risen from the dead, the same Person with a cosmic function that is central to the existence and the development of the universe.

The Christ who is Omega is not only divine but human, not only transcendent of the world but a part of it. By His Incarnation

---

[55] "Panthéisme et Christianisme," 1923, 8.
[56] "Christianisme et évolution," 1945, 7.
[57] *DM*, 117.
[58] "Comment je crois," 1934, 24.

THE UNIVERSE AS MEANINGFUL 99

Christ has entered the world, "shouldered and assimilated it by experiencing it Himself."[59] This leads Teilhard to hold that Christ, as Omega, is not simply a personal center of a universe in a state of converging evolution, but the *physical* center. It follows logically from all that has gone before that in Teilhard's theology Christ should be considered the organic and physical Center of the universe. In Teilhard's system of thought the universe possesses a solidarity in space and time, a solidarity that is organic. It is natural, then, that the already existing center and focus of this universe be an organic center. Teilhard's insistence on the organicity of the place of Christ in the cosmic structure may be startling but it is perfectly consistent with his thought as a whole. It is precisely on this conception of Christ as the personal and organic center of a converging universe that Teilhard is going to build his theological synthesis between Christianity and the contemporary spirit, between faith in Christ and faith in human endeavor, between Christian detachment and involvement in human progress, between the kingdom of God and human achievement.

The universe is in evolution, in a state of becoming, of genesis; by identifying the focus of this convergent genesis with Christ, Teilhard provides himself with the necessary synthetic principle to reformulate the theology of Christ in terms of the genesis of the cosmos, or cosmogenesis. More exactly, since Christ is Omega, Teilhard can combine the evolutionary conception of cosmogenesis with revealed data and so rethink cosmogenesis in terms of *Christogenesis*. At the same time, he can develop the main elements of a Christian mystique of human endeavor, a human endeavor which is above all a participation in the universal process of Christogenesis. In a universe that is in motion and has a direction and a purpose, in a universe that is coherent and meaningful, man too—because he is evolution become conscious of itself—has a direction

[59] *DM*, 103.

and a purpose. It is easy to see the immense advantages when cosmogenesis is recognized as identical with Christogenesis. In Teilhard's words, "Finished . . . are the anxieties of an unsatisfied and divided adoration. Finished too the anguish of a conscious awakening to a blind and closed world. And, in place of the darkness, a great light."[60] For if Christ and Omega are one and the same, then

by this conjunction Christian cosmology, harmonized and effectively articulated at its peak with human cosmology, shows itself to be fundamentally and in real values homogeneous with the latter. Thus dogma is no mere flowering of the imagination, but something born of history; and it is in literal not metaphorical terms that the Christian believer can illumine and further the genesis of the universe around him in the form of a Christogenesis. . . . It is above all Christ who invests Himself with the whole reality of the Universe; but at the same time it is the Universe which is illumined with all the warmth and immortality of Christ. So that finally (the point cannot be too strongly stressed) a new impulse becomes possible and is now beginning to take shape in human consciousness. Born of the psychic combination of two kinds of faith—in the transcendent action of a personal God and the innate perfectibility of a world in progress—it is an impulse (or better a spirit of love) that is truly evolutionary.[61]

Faith in God and faith in the world find their principle of synthesis in the fact of Christ-Omega, the center and focus of a world that derives its meaning and coherence from Him.[62]

[60] "Réflexions sur la probabilité scientifique," 1951, *OE* 7, 290.

[61] "Turmoil or Genesis?" 1948, *FM,* 224.

[62] See the Second Vatican Council's *Constitution on the Church in the Modern World,* "Introductory Statement," section 10: "The Church . . . holds that in her most benign Lord and Master can be found the key, the focal point and the goal of all human history."

4 · CREATION, HUMAN EFFORT, AND THE EUCHARIST

IN ONE of his early essays, written while serving with the French forces during the First World War, Teilhard states the problem of the twentieth-century Christian as he himself understands it.[1] Far more than an abstract problem for the theologians, it is a problem at the center of everyday Christian living. It is the problem of the Christian's unification of effort. At the heart of the practical life of today's Christian there is an appearance of duality. The Christian who wants to really live his religion comes up against a dualism of effort: how can he reconcile the renunciation of the world (necessary to living as a Christian) and interest in the affairs of the world (an interest that is indispensable for the activation of human

[1] "Mon univers," 1918, *Ecrits*, 278. See Chapter I, 10–20, for a broader treatment of Teilhard's understanding of this problem.

effort)? In *The Divine Milieu* Teilhard describes this duality in terms of the "Christian problem of the sanctification of action."[2]

It is quite certain from the constant teaching of the Church beginning with the New Testament that human effort and action can be sanctified; the Church has always taught that the totality of life should be holy, should be a life "in Christ," including all that is most "natural." "The general influence and practice of the Church has always been to dignify, ennoble and transfigure in God the duties inherent in one's station in life, the search for natural truth, and the development of human action."[3] The Church's teaching is a fact; but the logical coherence of this teaching with the general perspectives of Christianity is not immediately evident and the problem remains, as the following statement brings out:

How is it that the perspectives opened up by the kingdom of God do not, by their very presence, shatter the distribution and balance of our activities? How can the man who believes in heaven and the Cross continue to believe seriously in the value of worldly occupations? How can the believer, in the name of everything that is most Christian in him, carry out his duty as man to the fullest extent and as whole-heartedly and freely as if he were on the direct road to God? That is what is not altogether clear at first sight; and in fact disturbs more minds than one thinks.[4]

[2] *DM*, 50–3.

[3] *Ibid.*, 50–1.

[4] *Ibid.* From Teilhard's very statement of the problem it is clear that he does not want to set modern secular attitudes within the context of some "theology of terrestrial realities" that would bring up to date the medieval synthesis. Nor does he wish modern secularity assimilated directly into Christianity. The contemporary "religion of the world" is, for Teilhard, not something contrary to a Christian understanding of the world and so to be overcome by Christianity. The contemporary and secular "religion of the world" is, on the contrary, an integral element of a complete Christian perspective. On this whole problem, see J. Metz, "A Believer's Look at the World," tr. H. Wansbrough, O.S.B., *The Christian and the World*, 68–100. For a consideration of Teilhard's attitude toward secularity, see M. Murray, *The Thought of Teilhard de Chardin*, 114–22.

There is much more here than simply a problem of the "theology of work" or a question of the "theology of terrestrial values." It is a question of the inner reconciliation of the two components of man's whole dynamic drive. The human being does not merely exist; he acts. Since he is one being, his effort of action, his dynamism of being, should be in one direction, unified. But the Christian is caught by forces that seem to be pulling him in two directions. His religion, with its stress on renunciation of the world and the vanity and the transiency of things here below, and with its emphasis on the transcendence of God and the primacy of laying up a treasure in heaven, pulls him up. The modern spirit, the spirit of involvement in the world, of science and technology, of social progress, of building the earth, pulls him forward.

The Christian is torn in two directions; both seem good and right and deserving of all his effort, but they seem to be two different directions. So some Christians follow chiefly the "upward" direction of prayer and mortification and living only for God and the hereafter. Others put their main energies into the "forward" direction of human progress, of the daily human task. But the great majority, despairing of ever really working out a solution, a synthesis of "the Upward" and "the Forward," make a kind of compromise and spend their lives not wholly Christian and not wholly human, divided in their loyalties and wavering in their inner direction, half given to the things of God and half given to the things of the world.

We are interested here in Teilhard's theological solution of the problem; the problem is a practical one, but its roots are in theology. Teilhard's earliest theological essays were read by his close friends, mostly fellow Jesuit priests. The ideas of Teilhard, he himself reports in 1918, gave rise among some who read his essays to "astonishment and a certain inquietude."[5] As a result, he wrote

---

[5] "Mon univers," 1918, *Ecrits*, 267. The essays that caused astonishment were written in 1916, 1917, and early 1918. They certainly include "La vie

another paper in the effort to explain and clarify what he had previously written. His religious and theological ideas, he writes, come from a fundamental experience that is the support of his whole religious life, an experience that is the most general condition of his interior equilibrium. This experience can be expressed as the desire to be able to admit a certain coextension of Christ with the universe, such that (1) Christ takes on the power and the grandeur of the universe, and (2) meritorious action can be performed with the consciousness of acting in union with the whole universe. He adds that only to this, among all his ideas, does he attach the very greatest importance.[6] Teilhard's lifetime work was to rethink certain aspects or parts of Christian theology, remaining always faithful to the teaching of the Church, so as to formulate this "experience" and "general condition." A large part of this work touches directly the relation between Christianity and human effort.

How does he resolve the components of "the Upward" toward God and "the Forward" of human progress? How does he unify in one direction the apparently diverging directions of Christian and human effort? His solution follows a double line. First, he considers human effort as a participation in God's continuous creative action, an action aimed at the organization of the Pleroma, of the establishment of all things in Christ. An important part of this line of thought is his reflection on the relation between the universe and the Eucharist. Secondly, he considers human effort as a participation in the redemptive action of Christ. His view of human effort as redemptive will be taken up in the next chapter. In this chapter, we will outline his theology of human activity as sharing in God's creative action of bringing all things to the fullness of Christ, and

---

cosmique," 1916, *Ecrits*, 1–61, and "La lutte contre la multitude," 1916, *Ecrits*, 108–32.

6 "Mon univers," 1918, *Ecrits*, 272–3.

we will briefly present the complementary idea of the relation of the world to the Eucharist. Before we do this, however, we will try to describe in summary form Teilhard's conception of creation.

Human Effort and Theology of Creation

With regard to a Christian theology of creation, Teilhard's purpose, as always, is to construct a theory that will have a maximum of coherence, of meaningfulness, that will make as much sense as possible in the light of all the data available. What is more, he wants a theory, a coherent understanding of creation, that will provide a maximum of interest and motivation for human effort. For him the criterion of truth for any understanding or theory of creation is this: to what extent does the theory give us a coherent and meaningful vision of creation and at the same time somehow activate us? In particular, any understanding of creation that would undermine human effort must be reexamined.

Teilhard's objection to the theology of creation that has been dominant since the Middle Ages is that it seems to discourage human effort. The problem of any theology of creation, and the problem that medieval scholastic theology tried to solve, is this: it would seem that God cannot be thought of except pantheistically, as Himself constituting all being; thus either the world would be only a mirage or else it would be a part or an aspect or a phase of God. To solve the problem, scholastic metaphysics developed the notion of "participated being," an inferior or secondary form of being gratuitously drawn out of nothing by a special act of God's transcendent causality, the *"creatio ex nihilo"* or "creation out of nothing." The ontological distinction between the Creator and the creature is, of course, absolutely necessary, and Teilhard finds no fault with scholasticism on this point; on the contrary, he strongly reaffirms the distinction. But from the point of view of human action and effort, he finds difficulty with the scholastic theology of creation. The idea that creation is entirely gratuitous, a gesture of pure good will whose only object is that God share his plenitude with a ring of "participants" of whom he has absolutely no need whatever—this idea, when imposed on the contemporary world view, tends to make the whole great complex of creation look like a sort of game whose sole purpose is to beatify men. It tends to diminish the dignity of human existence and to diminish reverence for the Creator.[7]

The contemporary Christian realizes that, in himself and of himself, he is nothing without God; to be fully himself, he has a psychological need of this realization. But if the Christian were to think that in a general manner of speaking he is obliged to serve God without any reciprocal giving on God's part, without God giving anything of Himself, then the very mainsprings of that Christian's effort and action would be broken. An understanding of creation that insists on the complete self-sufficiency of God and consequently on the utter contingency and even arbitrariness of His creation risks making the Christian lose all his taste for and his interest in the world; it risks conveying a strong depreciation of God's creation, and it tends to discourage the necessary human effort to work and to contribute to the world's progress.

Rigorously deduced from a specific metaphysics of act and potency, this thesis of the complete gratuity of a static universe where the creature would have nothing other to do but to accept himself and

---

[7] "Action et activation," 1945, *OE* 9, 227-8. The theology of creation that Teilhard is criticizing can be found in almost any seminary textbook. In L. Ott's widely used compendium, *Fundamentals of Catholic Dogma*, the following theses are presented and defended: "All that exists outside God was, in its whole substance, produced out of nothing by God." (79.) "The world was created for the glorification of God." (81.) "God created the world free from exterior compulsion and inner necessity." (83.) "God was free to create this world or any other." (84.) Teilhard, of course, does not object to these or similar propositions (except perhaps the last); he objects to the general impression that this type of theology creates.

save himself—this thesis remains inoffensive within the framework of Thomism. However, it becomes dangerous and virulent (because discouraging) in a system of cosmogenesis when the "participated being" that each of us is begins to ask himself if the radically contingent condition to which the theologians have reduced him really justifies the effort it takes him to evolve. How could a revelation that is said to be made to man, the revelation of his radical uselessness, fail to create in that man a distaste for action?[8]

A theology of creation that stresses God's goodness and the goodness and lovableness of His creation is all right as far as it goes. But it does not go far enough. And if that theology seems to detract from the value of man's effort of progress in the world and even to make that effort despised, then the theology is positively dangerous. So, in reaction to the theology of creation that he learned as a seminarian, in reaction to a scholasticism perhaps more rigid and "closed" than the teaching of many Thomist theologians today, Teilhard tries to rethink the idea of creation in terms of his own system of thought.

Creative Union

In his first essay devoted to creation, written in 1917, Teilhard states a principle of his thinking that many of his critics might not accept and that all of them seem to overlook. The principle is this: it is much better to present *tentatively* a mixture of truth and error than to mutilate reality in trying to separate before the proper time the wheat from the chaff. Teilhard follows this rule, the rule of every intellectual effort and of all scientific progress, without hesitation.[9] His ideas are tentative, and his theological reflections consist of proposed theological hypotheses, quite open to further

---

[8] "Contingence de l'univers et goût humain de survivre," 1953, 3.
[9] "L'union créatrice," 1917, *Ecrits*, 175–6.

development and refinement or, for that matter, rejection. This is true of nothing so much as of his theology of creation. He is proposing a way of considering, of looking at, creation; he is not at all setting up an opinion baptized as a dogma.

He calls his theory of creation the theory of "creative union" (*l'union créatrice*). " 'Creative union' is not exactly a metaphysical doctrine. It is much better described as a sort of empirical and pragmatic explanation of the universe."[10] It is true that he sometimes refers to his theory as a metaphysics, particularly in the essay "How I See" of 1948, the most developed treatment of his theology of creation among his later writings.[11] But a careful reading makes quite clear that his "metaphysics" is really still an "empirical and pragmatic explanation"; it is a kind of deductive hypothesis of creation, containing elements from both sources of his theology, his scientific phenomenology of evolution and the revealed data of Christianity. It is important to keep in mind that his theology of creation is not metaphysical, particularly since many authors insist on thinking that it is.[12]

He does not consider creation strictly in terms of being, as would be the case if his approach were traditionally metaphysical. Rather, he describes being in terms of union. For him, being in its active sense means "to unite oneself or to unite others"; in its passive sense, being means "to be united or unified by another."[13]

---

[10] "Mon univers," 1924, *OE* 9, 72. On creation and evolution in Teilhard, see M. Barthélemy-Madaule, *Bergson et Teilhard de Chardin*, 45–61, 599–618. See also the long review of this book by P. Grenet in *L'ami du clergé* 76 (1966) 38–42, especially 40–2.

[11] "Comment je vois," 1948, 17–21.

[12] See M. Guérard des Lauriers, O.P., "La démarche du P. Teilhard de Chardin, réflexions d'ordre épistemologique," *Divinitas* 3 (1959) 227–8; R. North, S.J., "Teilhard de Chardin and the Problem of Creation," *Theological Studies* 24 (1963) 557–601.

[13] "Comment je vois," 1948, 17. See "Mon univers," 1924, *OE* 9, 73.

As we shall see, "to create" means "to unite," and "to be created" means "to be united." It seems well to point out too that he does not think of creation "as an instantaneous act, but in the manner of a process or synthesizing action."[14] This will become clearer as we proceed through the four steps of his theory of creative union.[15]

In a first step, Teilhard supposes as accepted the existence of a divine and self-sufficient First Being. This First Being or First Cause is in some way identified with the personal Omega that we have described at the end of Chapter II and at the beginning of Chapter III. The second step is the recognition according to the revelation of God as Trinity that the existence of this First Being, of this divine Center, consists in the act of opposing and uniting Himself in a Trinitarian manner. It is in the third and fourth steps that Teilhard describes creative union. In the third step, God, in the very act by which He opposes and unifies Himself in His unique existence,

[14] "Christologie et évolution," 1933, 6.

[15] We will follow Teilhard's most important text on creation, the only fairly complete consideration of creation among his mature writings. The text is in "Comment je vois," 1948, 17–21. The reflections on creation that are found in his early writings, especially in "La lutte contre la multitude," 1917, Ecrits, 109–32; "L'union créatrice," 1917, Ecrits, 169–97; "Les noms de la matière," 1919, Ecrits, 415–32, are not only difficult and somewhat obscure, but they are filled with his confusing early gropings for an adequate vocabulary. The ideas in these early essays are sometimes as inadequate as the vocabulary. For example, the section on the "Positive Void" in "L'union créatrice" (Ecrits, 184–6) is explicitly admitted to be a modest and inadequate attempt to explain the notion of infinite multiplicity. But its inadequacies are large, and the explanatory footnotes only make matters worse. It would be unfair to take this sort of reflection, written in the unlikely circumstances of army service during World War I and in which the wheat and the chaff seem to be in almost equal proportions, as Teilhard's theory of creation and to ignore his more developed and much clearer and more acceptable later thought on creative union.

ipso facto causes another type of opposition to arise, not within Himself but at His antipodes. . . . There is a self-subsistent unity at the pole of being and, as a necessary consequence, there is a multiplicity all around at the periphery; be it well understood that this is a pure multiplicity, a "creatable void" which is nothing, and which nevertheless, by its passive potency for arrangement, for union, is a possibility and an appeal for being. And it is here, at these depths, that our intelligence is quite definitely incapable of distinguishing supreme necessity from supreme freedom. What happens to this pure multiplicity happens as though God were not able to resist.[16]

Teilhard is saying that correlative to God's existence is a void. He describes or pictures this void as an infinite multiplicity with the possibility of being united. And in the fourth step he will describe creation as union. There is a problem here: his statement that there is necessarily an infinite multiplicity antecedent to any creative act. This could seem to mean that something exists besides God that is not created by God, a sort of eternal matter out of which God creates. But this is not at all what he means. The infinite multiplicity is *nothing*. An infinite quantity or an infinite number of things cannot exist in the real order; an infinite quantity is a quantity beyond all bounds, and so an indefinite quantity— and because indefinite, not really existing. Teilhard's "infinite multiplicity" is not to be thought of as a multiplicity that exists in the real order. It does not really exist; it is nothing. Remember that he is constructing a pragmatic explanation, a deductive hypothesis. For purposes of his hypothesis, it is suitable to *think* of a pre-creation void as an infinite multiplicity. He is in no way denying creation from nothing; he is affirming it, but he is picturing that "nothing" as an infinite multiplicity.[17]

16 "Comment je vois," 1948, 19.

17 See H. de Lubac, S.J., *La pensée religieuse du Père Teilhard de Chardin*, 282–9. The reader is referred to Father de Lubac's thorough and enlightening discussion of creative union, much fuller than anything we could attempt in this short outline of Teilhard's theory.

In the fourth step of the theory of creative union, Teilhard explains the advantages of considering creation as a unitive process. Creation can now be seen to be the result, in a manner of speaking, of a reflection of God, although this reflection is outside God rather than within the divine essence. Creation can be seen to be the building up of the pleroma, a "pleromization," a giving of reality to participated being by arrangement and totalization. "Creation somehow fills a void. It finds a place for itself. And, at the same time, it becomes expressible in the very terms that we used to define being. To create means to unite."[18]

To create means to unite, to bring together previously disunited elements, and creation itself is a *process* the expression of which is evolution. Evolution "is the expression of creation, for our experience, in time and space."[19] As we saw in Chapter II, evolution has a direction; evolution follows an axis of increasing complexity-consciousness. According to the law of complexity-consciousness, the degree of consciousness of a material being varies according to that being's complexity of structure, and this law is valid universally, even in cases that we cannot verify by observation. To say that evolution proceeds along an axis of increasing complexity-consciousness means that the universe is evolving not only in the direction of greater spirituality or consciousness but, at the same time and correlatively, in the direction of greater unity. In the light of this we can say that evolution is the expression of God's continuous creation by which He more and more unifies the world.

---

[18] "Comment je vois," 1948, 18–9.

[19] "Man's Place in the Universe," 1942, *VP*, 231. This is one point in which the theory of creative union differs from Bergson's "creative evolution." For Teilhard, evolution is not creative, but the expression of God's creative activity. When we say that creation is a *process*, we are referring to creation "taken passively," as seen in its result. The creative *act* of God, of course, is not a process, but one indivisible act. "The creative act is not split up. . . . Its term is the universe taken in all its extension and in all its duration." ("Mon univers," 1924, *OE* 9, 107.)

"God creates by uniting."[20] Teilhard habitually considers creation in its result, creation "taken passively," and—considering it this way—he understands creation as a process.

Creation has never ceased. Its act is a great continuous movement spread out over the totality of time. It is still going on; incessantly but imperceptibly the world emerges more and more from nothingness. The operation that creation gives rise to and that it forms is infinitely refracted in creatures in which the work of creation is materialized and accumulated.[21]

The creative act of God, of course, is not split up; it is one indivisible act. But the term of that creative act is the entire universe in all its extension and in all its duration. Creation began, then, with an infinite multiplicity of elements, and by a gradual process of unification of elements it is approaching a point of maximum unity. This point, of course, is the Parousia, the point of maximum union with Christ-Omega.

Creation in Christ

God creates by uniting. The process of creation is expressed in the evolution of the universe, and this process of creation by unification is pointed toward Christ-Omega. The key to Teilhard's theory of creation is the relation of the whole creative process to Christ. Now we can see that Teilhard's theory of creation, far from being a merely rational speculation, depends on revelation and is intrinsically theological. His theology of creation does not prescind from the fact of the Incarnation; it is constructed with the Incarnation in mind. More exactly, it is built around a keystone, and that keystone is Christ-Omega.

20 "Mon univers," 1924, *OE* 9, 72.
21 "Le milieu mystique," 1917, *Ecrits*, 149.

The whole theology of creative union is thought out in the light of the fact that Christ is the Head of creation. "The Incarnation is the renewal and the restoral of *all* the forces and the powers of the universe; Christ is the instrument, the Center, the Term of *all* creation . . . ; by Him, everything is created, sanctified, vivified."[22] "All things find their coherence in Christ."[23] "He is the First and He is the Head. In Him everything was begun and everything holds together and everything is consummated."[24] "God willed His Christ, and to have His Christ He had to create the world of the spirit—man in particular—in which Christ would germinate; and, to have man, He had to launch the enormous movement of organic life—and that this be born, the whole tumult of the cosmos was necessary."[25] "In the actual world there is only one dynamism: that which leads everything to Jesus . . . ; in Him, the 'Plenitude of the Universe,' everything is created because in Him everything is united."[26] Christ is "the Alpha and the Omega, the beginning and the end, the foundation stone and the keystone."[27] Christ is He "in whom everything is created and He in whom the entire world in all its depth, its length, its breadth, its grandeur, its physical and its spiritual, comes to be and takes on consistence. . . . The world is above all a work of continuous creation in Christ."[28] In 1919

[22] "La vie cosmique," 1916, *Ecrits*, 48.

[23] "Forma Christi," 1918, *Ecrits*, 338. C. Mooney, S.J., in *Teilhard de Chardin and the Mystery of Christ*, 170, points out that in strict theological terminology the object of the theory of creative union is not "creation" but "elevation," or creation in Christ.

[24] "Christologie et évolution," 1933, 10.

[25] "Mon univers," 1924, *OE* 9, 108.

[26] "L'union créatrice," 1917, *Ecrits*, 196.

[27] "Science et Christ," 1921, *OE* 9, 60.

[28] "Intégration de l'homme dans l'univers," 1930, lecture 4, 12–3. Teilhard's idea of creation in Christ includes the conception of a "mysterious pre-existence of Christ" in the sense that everything is created in Him "not only in the order of intention, but also in the order of nature." ("Mon univers," 1924, *OE* 9, 89.) That is, God's creative act is with Christ primarily in view; Christ is "first in the order of intention." And, also, all

Teilhard writes that he has occasionally thought of attenuating this conception, at first sight so unlikely, of the creation of the entire world, natural as well as supernatural, in Christ. One might think of

a world outside of Christ, a world that would have primal existence of its own and be self-sufficient; this would be the natural order, the sphere of human progress. Only those who held fast to Jesus Christ by faith and good intention would go beyond this first circle . . . and enter the field of Christ's divinizing power. In this way there would be in the objective order two *distinct* compartments in the universe: the created world and the world of Christ, the latter gradually absorbing the former. . . . But it seems to me that this attenuation would be illogical, not in accord with the identity of God the Creator and God the Redeemer and incompatible with the elevation of the whole natural order. . . . For grace does not enter into

---

creation depends on Christ "in the order of nature"; all creation from the beginning has depended and depends on the Incarnate Word, and if this is true (and for Teilhard it is), then Christ must somehow have a mysterious *real* pre-existence both according to His divinity and according to His humanity. Such a pre-existence of Christ is, of course, necessary to Teilhard's idea of Christ-Omega as the real and physical focal Center of the universe *from its beginning*. Teilhard gives no explanation of how this pre-existence of Christ is possible. His view of Christ's pre-existence is, however, coherent with the rest of his thought, and even a necessary element in that thought because of his idea of a Christ-Omega who is co-extensive in duration to the entire universe. In fact, this view of the pre-existence of Christ is inevitable, granted Teilhard's cosmology. For if the cosmos is an organically united space-time system, with a beginning and an end, and if Christ by His resurrection has truly transcended our space-time system, then He must be transcendent to both the duration and the space of the cosmos, and so if not pre-existent, at least transcendent in the sense of being simultaneously present to each element of the universe in space and in time.

Teilhard depends on St. Paul for his view. Some modern exegetes do hold that whenever St. Paul mentions the pre-existence of Christ he means the pre-existence of the historical God-man. See, for example: J. Bonsirven, S.J., *The Theology of the New Testament*, tr. S. Tye, 254; F. X. Durrwell,

man from another universe. It makes its entrance through an extension of our own universe.[29]

Teilhard's theology of creative union is not a theology of some possible world, not an abstract reconstruction of the metaphysical mechanics of what God's creative act is "in itself." Teilhard is concerned with *this* world, the world that God *has* created; and this world is created in Christ; it is a world in which God has concretely involved Himself. Teilhard wants not only to reaffirm the primacy of Christ over all creation; he also wants to dispel the notion of the arbitrariness of the creation of this world. He stresses instead the mutual complementarity of the Creator and His creation. "Truly it is not the notion of the contingency of the created, but the sense of the mutual completion of God and the world that makes Christianity live."[30] "God is entirely self-sufficient, and

---

C.SS.R., "Le Christ, premier et dernier," *Bible et vie chrétienne* 9 (1963) 16–28; J. Huby, S.J., *Les épîtres de la captivité*, 40. Teilhard's notion of Christ's pre-existence has been compared to the Scotist idea of the Incarnation as God's primary motive in creating the world. Teilhard, however, seems to go much further than the Scotist theory of the Incarnation as first in the order of God's intention in creating the world; Teilhard holds that Christ is first not only in the order of intention but also in the order of nature. See N. Wildier, *Teilhard de Chardin*, 92–5. Teilhard's position is similar in some points to that of G. M. Hopkins who, though working within the traditional Scotist categories that bear little resemblance to Teilhard's evolutionary framework of thought, goes further than the usual Scotist opinion in holding Christ's physical and incarnate pre-existence to the creation of the cosmos. See *The Sermons and Devotional Writings of Gerard Manley Hopkins*, ed. C. Devlin, S.J., 111–5. On the classic Scotist position regarding Christ and creation, that Christ is the first willed by God of all His creation and predestined—independently of original sin and the need for redemption—to be the Head of creation, see the article on John Duns Scotus by P. Raymond in the *Dictionnaire de théologie catholique*, vol. 4, 1896; see also A. Bertoni, *Jean Duns Scot*, 300–4. Teilhard mentions Scotus only once in his writings: "Esquisse d'une dialectique de l'esprit," 1946, *OE* 7, 158.

[29] Letter of December 29, 1919, *Archives*, 154.

[30] "Contingence de l'univers et goût humain de survivre," 1953, 4.

nevertheless creation brings to Him something vitally necessary."[31] The object of God's creative act can be understood as "a
mysterious product of completion and fulfillment for the Absolute
Being Himself."[32]

Teilhard is saying that, in the concrete and for God as well as
for us, creation is creation in Christ. God, therefore, by His own
free willing of a total plan of creation that includes His Incarnation, has freely immersed Himself in His creation, has freely willed
a real mutual complementarity between Himself and the world. In
our understanding of the actual world in which we find ourselves,
it appears to us that God is inevitably led to immerse Himself in
the Many so as to unite it to Himself.[33] God, therefore, should not
be thought of as personally independent of the present world that
He has created in Christ.

On the one hand, in virtue of the Incarnation, God cannot—at least
in the present order and from now on—do without the Many in
which he has immersed Himself. And on the other hand, the reality
of "God plus the Many" in Jesus Christ seems, in Christian practice
and in Pauline spirituality, to represent a perfection which—no matter
how qualified it is as extrinsic to God—carries with it a real completion in the balance of universal Being.[34]

The present world with its supernatural order is not something that
God can just do without. It is not an utterly contingent world and
its creation is not an arbitrary act. The world is not superfluous to
God. God is not indifferent to the world that He has created; He is
personally involved in it.[35]

[31] "Christianisme et évolution," 1945, 4. See "Action et activation," 1945,
OE 9, 229.
[32] "Le coeur de la matière," 1950, 30.
[33] "Comment je vois," 1948, 19.
[34] "La route de l'ouest," 1932, 20.
[35] See C. Mooney, S.J., Teilhard de Chardin and the Mystery of Christ,
174–6.

Teilhard's theology of creative union does not *explain* God's freedom in creating. This is because it is a theology of the existing *de facto* world, in which God, as a matter of fact, has willed to deeply involve Himself. From all eternity God has willed to immerse Himself in this world by the Incarnation; from all eternity He has willed to create the world in Christ. And the perfection of God's plan is such that, in the concrete, it appears to us as having a certain necessity. At the level of Teilhard's theory of creation the mystery of God's freedom in creating remains hidden in the ineffable Act that He Himself is, and supreme necessity and supreme freedom cannot be distinguished except by recognizing the presence of freedom in the "infallible sign of an accompanying love."[36] We can say that creation occurs *as if* God were constrained to create. This is in no way a denial of the Creator's sovereign freedom.

Nor does Teilhard want to weaken in any way the abstract idea of the additional gratuity—over and above the gratuity of creation —of the Incarnation. The concept of God's freedom in willing the Incarnation remains intact in Teilhard's theology. Teilhard affirms not only the gratuity of the "natural order" of creation but also the gratuity of the "supernatural order" including the Incarnation.[37] The theology of creative union "in no way detracts from the fundamental dogma of the gratuity of the supernatural."[38] But in

[36] "Comment je vois," 1948, 18.
[37] See the works cited in footnotes 49 and 50, Chapter III.
[38] "Forma Christi," 1918, *Ecrits*, 336. C. Journet, however, in "La vision teilhardienne du monde," *Divinitas* 3 (1959) 330–44, holds that Teilhard's vision of reality is strictly naturalistic and applies to Teilhard the statement that "any vision of the world that presents the present condition of mankind as *natural*, as *naturally* convergent toward its ultimate goal, is radically aberrant." (340.) Teilhard's vision of Christianity is "thoroughly and absolutely naturalistic." (341.) Cardinal Journet is an aggressive critic of Teilhard's ideas; see also his "L'effort théologique du P. Teilhard de Chardin," *Nova et vetera* 39 (1964) 305–10, where he attacks Teilhard

the mind of God as well as in reality the order of salvation is one; the theory of creative union stresses this oneness. Because of the organic unity of God's plan, the Incarnation appears to us as inevitable.[39]

Teilhard, then, understands God's continuous creation as a process of unification, of building up the universe in the direction of increasing unity. The entire process of creation in Christ is toward the Pleroma, the final state of the world, the consummation of all things in Christ. God's continuous creation is directed to "the quantitative repletion and the qualitative consummation of all things . . . , the mysterious Pleroma in which the substantial *One* and the created *many* fuse without confusion into a *whole* which, without adding anything essential to God, will nevertheless be a sort of triumph and generalization of Being."[40] The final result of God's creation will be the Pleroma. Teilhard's idea of the Pleroma is the traditional one: not an absorption of creatures into God that involves a loss of identity for the creatures, but an absorption of creatures that is a maximum union with God. Since "union differentiates" the individualities of the elements united, the Pleroma— while being the state of minimum separation between God and His creatures—will be the state of maximum union and so without any confusion of identities. Creative union is a continuous process whose expression is the converging evolution of the world and whose term is the fullness of the Pleroma.

The Universal Christ

The Pleroma, "the mysterious synthesis of the Uncreated and the created, the great fulfillment—both quantitative and qualitative

---

for altering the doctrines of the faith, transposing revealed doctrine to fit the discoveries of man.

[39] "Action et activation," 1945, *OE* 9, 271–2.
[40] *DM*, 122.

—of the universe in God . . . finds its physical principle, its expression, and its stability in the figure of Christ-Omega, the Universal Christ."[41] Creative union is the gradual formation of the Pleroma; this "pleromization" is directed toward Christ-Omega, toward "Jesus, the Center toward whom all moves."[42] Creation, for Teilhard, is accomplished not "from behind" by a causality analogous to efficient causality, but "from up ahead" by the unifying influence of Christ. "All energies hold together, are welded deep down into a single whole, and what the humanity of Our Lord does is to take them up again and re-weld them in a transcendent and personal unity."[43] "Christ gives Himself to us through a world which is to reach completion even on a natural level by reason of its relationship to Him."[44]

The notion of Christ's universal influence over all creation is present in Teilhard's early essays. A few years before writing *The Divine Milieu,* this universal influence begins to be expressed by him as a universal *presence* of Christ. "The presence of the Incarnate Word penetrates everything like a universal element. It shines at the heart of all things."[45] This "pan-christism" has nothing in common with a false pantheism where all things are identified with God and fuse into Him to the loss of their own indentity. The universal influence of Christ, "far from disassociating things, consolidates them; far from confusing things, it differentiates them."[46] A central theme of *The Divine Milieu* is the universal presence and influence of Christ; it is developed explicitly near the end of the

---

[41] "La parole attendue," 1940, *Cahiers Pierre Teilhard de Chardin, 4, La parole attendue,* 26–7.
[42] "La vie cosmique," 1916, *Ecrits,* 60.
[43] Letter of February 2, 1916, *MM,* 93.
[44] Letter of December 12, 1919, *Archives,* 154.
[45] "Mon univers," 1924, *OE* 9, 87.
[46] *Ibid.*

book in terms of the divine milieu and the Universal Christ.[47] Teilhard identifies Christ's omnipresence and the divine milieu:

Let us examine step by step how we can validate to ourselves this prodigious identification of the Son of Man and the divine milieu.

A first step, unquestionably, is to see the divine omnipresence in which we find ourselves plunged as *an omnipresence of action*. God enfloods us and penetrates us by creating and preserving us.

Now let us go a little further. Under what form, and with what end in view, has the Creator given us, and still preserves in us, the gift of participated being? Under the form of an essential aspiration towards Him—and with a view to the unhoped-for cleaving which is to make us one and the same complex thing with Him. The action by which God maintains us in the field of His presence is *a unitive transformation*.

Let us go further still. What is the supreme and complex reality for which the divine operation moulds us? It is revealed to us by St. Paul and St. John. It is the quantitative repletion and the qualitative consummation of all things: it is the mysterious Pleroma, in which the substantial *one* and the created *many* fuse without confusion in a *whole* which, without adding anything essential to God, will nevertheless be a sort of triumph and generalisation of being.

At last we are nearing our goal. What is the active center, the living link, the organising soul of the Pleroma? St. Paul, again, proclaims it with all his resounding voice: it is He in whom everything is reunited, and in whom all things are consummated—through whom the whole created edifice receives its consistence—Christ dead and risen *qui replet omnia, in quo omnia constant.*

And now let us link the first and last terms of this long series of identities. We shall then see with a wave of joy that *the divine omnipresence* translates itself within our universe by the network of the organising forces of the total Christ. God exerts pressure, in us and upon us—through the intermediary of all the powers of heaven, earth and hell—only in the act of forming and consummating

[47] *DM*, 121–32.

Christ who saves and sur-animates the world. And since, in the course of this operation, Christ himself does not act as a dead or passive point of convergence, but as a center of radiation for the energies which lead the universe back to God through His humanity, the layers of divine action finally come to us impregnated with His organic energies.[48]

The Universal Christ is Christ in His cosmic role as Omega. Teilhard sometimes uses as synonyms for "Universal Christ" the expressions "total Christ" and "cosmic Christ." These expressions designate Christ in His cosmic role, not some ideal or archetypal image of humanity or of the world, but the same Jesus of Nazareth who by His resurrection "has become co-extensive with the physical immensities of duration and space without losing the preciseness of His humanity."[49] The point is worth making that "Universal Christ," "cosmic Christ," and "total Christ" are expressions that refer to the *individual Incarnate Person* of Christ insofar as He has the role and function of Omega. These expressions refer to the Body-Person of Christ in His role of uniting mankind and all the universe to Himself by His creative and redemptive power.[50]

Teilhard sums up in a few sentences his theology of the Universal Christ. If Christ and the Omega of evolution are the same, then all evolution, all becoming or genesis, is directed toward the fullness of Christ and is animated by Christ's influence. The evolutionary process, then, is not simply cosmogenesis, biogenesis, and

[48] *Ibid.*, 122–3.
[49] "Esquisse d'un univers personnel," 1936, *OE* 6, 113.
[50] See C. Mooney, S.J., *op. cit.*, 178. Teilhard's language in speaking of Christ in His cosmic role can be confusing and, to the careless reader, misleading. Some expressions, even when accompanied by explanations, are unfortunate; "Super-Christ," "the Universal Element," and "the Soul of the World," are used infrequently to designate the Universal Christ, but they might well have been omitted altogether. Of all these expressions, "Universal Christ" is by far the most common.

noogenesis. It is, ultimately and most globally, Christogenesis.[51]
Finally, then, creative union and the gradual formation of the
Pleroma are seen to be Christogenesis. Teilhard's aim has been to
reformulate the theology of creation in terms of a genesis, a "becoming" of the universe, in Christ. The word he finally makes up
after years of reflection is "Christogenesis," an awkward word
perhaps, but a word that sums up the evolutive structure of the
universe as Teilhard sees it: a dynamic movement directed to the
final unity of all things in Christ, directed to Christ in the fullness
of the Pleroma.

Union of the Christian with God's Creative Action

Creative union is directed to the Pleroma, and it finds its expression in time and space in the progress of the world's evolution, an
evolution that converges on Christ-Omega. Since evolution has, so
to speak, become conscious of itself in man, man can help the
progress of evolution toward the Pleroma. Man himself is called
upon to cooperate with God, to adhere to God's creative action in
the gradual formation of the Pleroma. The world takes on a new
significance to the man "who gives himself to the tasks of his daily
life not egotistically but *religiously,* with the consciousness of pursuing, in God and for God, the great work of creation and sanctification."[52] "The creative operation of God does not simply mold

[51] "Le Christique," 1955, 8. Teilhard never really did find an adequate
vocabulary for these ideas. Even in this essay written just before his death
he is still groping for words and uses a very poor expression: "this third
nature of Christ—a nature that is neither human nor divine, but cosmic."
(8; in "Comment je crois," 1948, 21, Teilhard also uses the expression
"third nature" of Christ.) His idea, of course, is fairly clear but his
vocabulary is still inadequate and even at times bizarre. For a positive
appreciation of Teilhard's vocabulary and language in general, as well as
of his style and thought patterns, see the short but excellent analysis by
E. Rideau, S.J., *La pensée du Père Teilhard de Chardin,* 566–82.
[52] "La nostalgie du front," 1917, *Ecrits,* 213.

us like soft clay. It is a Fire that animates all it touches, a spirit that gives life. So it is *in living* that we should give ourselves to that creative action, imitate it, identify with it"; the Christian who is *actively* obedient to God's creative will "becomes a more perfect instrument the more he steeps himself in God's creative action,"[53] the more he unites his "freedom to the creative and unifying action of God."[54] These quotations are from the early essays of the First World War. They are an example of the beginnings of Teilhard's reflection on the Christian's adhesion to God's creative action.

This reflection reaches its most developed formulation in 1927 in *The Divine Milieu*. In his action the Christian adheres to the creative power of God so that one may say he "coincides" with that creative power; he becomes "not only its instrument, but its living extension." The Christian is caught up in and joined to God's creative operation; "the will to succeed" in what he does and "a certain enthusiastic delight in the work to be done" form an integral part of his creaturely fidelity. *What* we do, therefore, is important; it is a cooperation with God creating. "God does not deflect our gaze prematurely from the work He Himself has given us, since He presents Himself to us as attainable through that very work."[55] In *The Divine Milieu* the idea of man's union with God's creative action has become well integrated with the idea of building the Pleroma.

It is through the collaboration which he stimulates in us that Christ, starting from *all* created things, is consummated and attains his plenitude. . . . We may, perhaps, imagine that the creation was finished long ago. But that would be quite wrong. It continues still more magnificently, and at the highest levels of the world. . . . And we serve to complete it, even by the humblest work of our hands. That is, ultimately, the meaning and value of our acts. Owing to the in-

[53] "Le milieu mystique," 1917, *Ecrits*, 152–4.
[54] "Forma Christi," 1918, *Ecrits*, 342.
[55] *DM*, 64.

terrelation between matter, soul and Christ, we bring part of the being which he desires back to God *in whatever we do*. With each one of our *works*, we labour—in individual separation, but no less really—to build the Pleroma; that is to say, we bring to Christ a little fulfillment.[56]

From 1927 on, the two ideas of the Christian's union with God creating and the Christian's endeavor as a contribution to the Pleroma are treated as one single idea. There is no more direct elaboration of the simple notion of man's adherence to God's creative operation, although the notion remains basic. "My whole spiritual life," Teilhard writes in 1941, "consists more and more in abandoning myself (actively) to the presence and action of God. To be in communion with Becoming has become the formula of my whole life."[57] But as he develops more and more the idea of creation, unification, taking place by the attractive influence of Christ-Omega, an influence that comes "from up ahead," he puts more emphasis on human endeavor as contributing to the Pleroma, to the plenitude of Christ.

Human Activity and the Fullness of Christ

From the very beginning, in his first wartime essay, Teilhard is struggling to express his conviction that the work we do, our daily human activity, somehow contributes something permanent to the plenitude of Christ. Some of the expressions are ill-chosen, but the central idea of human activity as helping to bring about the plenitude of Christ is there. By His Incarnation Christ became not only a part of mankind but a part of the universe. And He is not only part of the universe; He is its directive principle. Christ has a "cosmic body" that fills the whole universe. And the cosmic

[56] *DM*, 62.
[57] Letter of May 19, 1941, *LT*, 283.

Christ has not finished forming Himself. "The world is still being created, and it is Christ who is coming to fulfillment. . . . That the kingdom of God arrive, it is necessary that man conquer the earth." Therefore, "among the workers for a greater world the Christian, by reason of his beliefs, has the right to claim a place."[58] A little more than a year after finishing this essay he writes, "I believe more and more that there is a sacred *human work.*"[59]

In later essays of the same period he is concerned with the value of human endeavor, with the actual result of the work as distinguished from the good intention with which it is performed. "It is my whole being" that Christ wants, "the tree with the fruit, . . . the product as well as the labor"; Christ needs the results of our labor so that He can reach His plenitude.[60] It is not only a good and merit-gaining intention that makes man's efforts valuable, but his very works "appear to be susceptible of being integrated in the absolute Term of the world: Jesus Christ."[61] There is "an earthly work to be done" that is an integral part of the whole development of the supernaturalized world; this development, for Teilhard, has the form of a vast movement of unification that converges toward Christ.[62]

Finally, in a short paper written in 1919, Teilhard reviews his thinking during the preceding years. He was led to search some "universal element" that would sum up the meaning of the universe and the value of human activity in their relation to God. He was led from a consideration of "the will of God" to a view that the creative action of God was this universal element. Still unsatisfied, he reflected further and at last succeeded in giving an ade-

---

[58] "La vie cosmique," 1916, *Ecrits,* 47, 51, 42, 54.

[59] Letter of July 26, 1917, in H. de Lubac, S.J., *La pensée religieuse du Père Teilhard de Chardin,* 353.

[60] "Le prêtre," 1918, *Ecrits,* 296.

[61] "Note pour l'évangélisation des temps nouveaux," 1919, *Ecrits,* 374.

[62] "Terre promise," 1919, *Ecrits,* 395; "Mon univers," 1918, *Ecrits,* 276.

quate name to the universal element that he had already been conscious of for a long time: "the cosmic influence of Christ." Teilhard speaks of what he has referred to before as "the cosmic Body of Christ" as being a way of describing all things insofar as they converge toward Christ, under His attraction, to be fulfilled in Him in the Pleroma.[63] About the same time he writes in a letter directed to Maurice Blondel that "it is not only by fidelity to obedience but also by the work being done that we are building up to the fullness of Christ by preparing the more or less proximate matter of the Pleroma."[64]

Teilhard's theological reflection on the importance of man's earthly activity continues during the next decade. In an essay on the Universal Christ written in 1920, he reasons that if Christ is really universal then it follows that His kingdom goes essentially beyond the domain of what is called strictly supernatural life. All human activity can be referred to Christ, can cooperate toward the fullness of Christ.[65] A few years later he writes of "the marvelous grace communicated to every human activity, no matter how material, to efficaciously cooperate by its physical result in the building up of the Body of Christ."[66] In 1924, he formulates the basic theology that lies behind the beautiful treatment of human endeavor in *The Divine Milieu* of 1927, "Around us Christ acts physically."[67]

[63] "L'élément universel," 1919, *Ecrits*, 405–8.

[64] Letter of December 12, 1919, *Archives*, 140.

[65] "Note sur le Christ universel," 1920, *OE* 9, 41. Teilhard adds that human effort can be divinized *in opere* and not only *in operatione*.

[66] "Panthéisme et Christianisme," 1923, 12.

[67] "Mon univers," 1924, *OE* 9, 87–8. Just precisely what Teilhard means here by "physically" is somewhat vague. He often refers to Christ as *physical* center of the universe and to Christ's influence as *physical*. The French "physique" is a much broader term than the English "physical" that is used to translate "physique." The French word does not mean "material"; it often has the sense of "really existing," and this is probably the best understanding of Teilhard's use of the word. Teilhard was strongly

The whole movement of the world, and all the parts and lines of development of that movement, are animated by Christ. The forward impetus of each thing in the universe comes from Christ drawing all things to Himself. He does not, however, disturb the world's normal processes; this natural dynamism itself comes from Christ's action on the world. What is more, Christ benefits physically from all the movements of the world. Everything in the universe that is good, that goes into the effort of unification, is received by Christ and transformed and divinized.

If Christ is Omega, then everything can be directed to the building up of His universal body. Any action that is performed in the direction of unification, no matter how humble and hidden that action, adds something to reality; "and what is best in this is immediately and forever assimilated by the total Christ. . . . Christ waits for the result of my work . . . not only for the intention of my action, but also for the tangible result of my work."[68]

Teilhard's most extensive discussion of the importance and the worth of human activity is found in *The Divine Milieu*. The world and man's labor in it have a highly religious value. "By virtue of the Creation and, still more, of the Incarnation, *nothing* here below *is profane* for those who know how to see."[69] The Christian's faith imposes on him the "right and the duty" to throw himself "into the things of the earth."[70]

---

opposed to any language that would seem to make the relation of the universe to Christ merely moral or juridical. "Physique," as used by Teilhard, is never opposed to "metaphysical" or to "supernatural." See H. de Lubac, S.J., *Teilhard de Chardin, the Man and His Meaning*, tr. R. Hague, 35, footnote. See especially C. Mooney, S.J., *Teilhard de Chardin and the Mystery of Christ*, 77–84; Father Mooney has a thorough discussion of Teilhard's idea of Christ as *physical* center of the universe.

[68] "Mon univers," 1924, *OE* 9, 96.

[69] *DM*, 66.

[70] *Ibid.*, 69.

Christianity is not, as it is sometimes presented and sometimes practiced, an additional burden of observances and obligations to weigh down and increase the already heavy load, or to multiply the already paralyzing ties of our life in society. It is, in fact, a soul of immense power which bestows significance and beauty and a new lightness on what we were already doing.[71]

In his writings after *The Divine Milieu* Teilhard often emphasizes that God is served and adored actively through creatures, in and through man's earthly activity itself. "Up until now, to adore has meant to prefer God to things by referring them to Him and by sacrificing them to Him. Now adoration means the giving of our body and soul to creative activity, joining that activity to Him to bring the world to fulfillment by effort and research."[72] The things of earth should no longer simply be considered as "instruments to be used" to give God glory, but as "co-elements" of the universe, to be integrated into the gradually forming unity of the world, integrated by mankind in the progress of its work in the formation of the Pleroma. The apparent opposition between earth and heaven is resolved in a new formula: to heaven by the building up of the earth.[73]

In a last essay just before his death, Teilhard puts man's earthly activity in the context of Christogenesis. The Christian finds himself more and more consciously identified with Christogenesis.[74] Teilhard speaks of a "third way" of union with God. In the diverse religions of the world man has heretofore sought union with the Divinity either in flight from the things of earth or in a pantheistic immersion in things so as to be lost in union with the "all." But the Christian religion contains a "third way."[75] With a Christified

71 *Ibid.*, 70.
72 "Christologie et évolution," 1933, 12.
73 "Recherche, travail et adoration," *OE* 9, 289.
74 "Le Christique," 1955, 6.
75 *Ibid.*

universe an evolutive super-milieu appears: the divine milieu. In this divine milieu that has Christ as its center and is filled with His presence, every activity, whether rising from man or descending from Christ, is ultimately both "pan-humanizing and pan-christifying."[76]

The Mass on the World

We can approach the whole question of the importance of human activity and of that activity as an extension of God's creative operation from a different point of view, that of Teilhard's theology of the Eucharist. Teilhard's Eucharistic theology not only throws much light on his theology of creative union and of human effort in bringing about the fullness of the Pleroma, but it is an integral part of Teilhard's view of the double influence of Christ and of human activity in the gradual transformation of the world, a transformation directed to the unity of all things in Christ. Teilhard has by no means a complete theology of the Eucharist. He does not, for example, treat specifically the problem of the mode of Christ's real presence in the Eucharist; he simply takes the Real Presence completely for granted. Nor does he consider the specific relation between the sacrifice of the Mass and the sacrifice of the Cross, although these two find their theological place in Teilhard's

[76] *Ibid.*, 9. See the excellent pages on "Labor and Man's Final Fulfillment" in P. Schoonenberg, S.J., *God's World in the Making* (Pittsburgh, Duquesne University Press, 1964), 179–84. Father Schoonenberg writes, for example, that labor "is not a pastime but a fulfillment of life. It is even the building of our life in relation to the final fulfillment. We cooperate in the construction of the final community of love by the work we are doing now. And then we shall behold what we are now in the process of building." (184.) See also M. van Caster, S.J., "Human and Christian Meaning of Work," *Lumen Vitae* 22 (1965) 283–306. For a perceptive analysis of the development of Teilhard's ideas on the significance of human action, see M. Barthélemy-Madaule, "La perspective teilhardienne et l'action," *Europe* 43, no. 431–2 (1965) 70–88.

thought in his conception of Christogenesis. For Teilhard, these are abstract problems; he is more interested in the concrete problem of the relation of man, the universe, and man's activity in the universe to Christ, and it is in terms of this problem that the development of his theology of the Eucharist takes place.

The Eucharist is sometimes mentioned in the speculative essays of the first period of Teilhard's writings, from 1916 to 1919, and two of Teilhard's three mystical reflections on the Eucharist belong to this period: "Christ in the World of Matter," written in 1916, and "The Priest," written in 1918. Both of these are highly poetic rather than theological, but they contain the seeds of Teilhard's later and clearer idea of the relation between the world and the Eucharistic Christ.

In the poetic imagery of "Christ in the World of Matter," the universe is described as vibrant with Christ's influence. A second poetic image describes the Eucharistic Host as expanding so as to encompass the whole world, transforming the world and giving it life. In a third and complex image, the Host symbolizes the fact "that the multiplicity of evolutions into which the world-process seems to us to be split up is in fact fundamentally the working out of one single great mystery."[77]

"The Priest" was written at the front and is in the form of a meditative prayer. It begins: "Since, Lord, I your priest have today neither bread nor wine nor altar, I will extend my hands over the totality of the universe and take its immensity as the material for my sacrifice. Is not the infinite circle of things the final Host that you want to transform?"[78] For Christ prolongs the movement of His Incarnation "when He descends to replace the bread," and "His action is not limited to the material particle that His brief

[77] P. Teilhard de Chardin, *Hymn of the Universe*, tr. S. Bartholomew, 50, hereafter cited as *HU*. See the letter of July 14, 1916, written just a few months before "Christ in the World of Matter," *MM*, 112.

[78] "Le prêtre," 1918, *Ecrits*, 285.

presence volatizes. The transubstantiation is aureoled with a real divinization of the whole universe."[79] Teilhard prays: "In this moment, All-powerful Father, . . . looking further than the white host, and depending on it, . . . I will say over every development and every substance: 'This is my body.' "[80] Teilhard's sacrifice has the whole world for its matter, for "there is not an atom, no matter how humble or how evil, that should not cooperate, at least by its repulsion or its reflection, to the fullness of Jesus."[81] Thus the whole world, under the influence of the Host, secretly becomes the Body and Blood of Christ. "The small inert Host has become to my eyes as big as the world. . . . The universal consecration ends in an inexhaustible and universal Communion."[82] Because the universe is the Body of Christ, "the work that men do is sacred, sacred in the will with which they submit it to God and sacred in the great work of which it is a part."[83]

A year earlier, Teilhard had written: "Ever since You said, Lord, 'This is my Body,' not only the Bread of the altar, but—in a certain measure—*everything* in the universe that nourishes the soul for the life of spirit and grace has become *Yours* and *divine,* divinized, divinizing, and divinizable."[84] The words of "The Priest" might disturb some, as they did Teilhard's provincial superior when he read the copy Teilhard sent him,[85] by an apparent pantheism. But it should be remembered that the language and the imagery of "The Priest" is the language and imagery of prayer, and that it was not written for the general public. It was primarily Teilhard's way of praying when he could not say Mass because of the conditions of wartime service.

[79] *Ibid.*, 287.
[80] *Ibid.*
[81] *Ibid.*, 288.
[82] *Ibid.*, 294.
[83] *Ibid.*, 299. See "La vie cosmique," 1916, *Ecrits*, 40–1.
[84] "Le milieu mystique," 1917, *Ecrits*, 164–5.
[85] Letter of October 3, 1918, *MM*, 243–4.

Six years later, on a scientific expedition in the desert and again unable to say Mass, Teilhard wrote "a new edition, much changed, of . . . 'The Priest,' which I had written during the war."[86] This is "The Mass on the World."[87]

Since once again, Lord—though this time not in the forests of Aisne but in the steppes of Asia—I have neither bread nor wine nor altar, I will raise myself beyond these symbols, up to the pure majesty of the real itself; I, your priest, will make the whole earth my altar and on it will offer you all the labours and sufferings of the world. . . .

This bread, our toil, is of itself, I know, but an immense fragmentation; this wine, our pain, is no more, I know, than a draught that dissolves. Yet in the very depths of this formless mass You have implanted—and this I am sure of, for I sense it—a desire, irresistible, hallowing, which makes us cry out, believer and unbeliever alike: "Lord, make us *one*."[88]

Teilhard offers to the Father "the sacrament of the world."[89] For Christ is, "by power and by right, incarnate in the world . . ."[90] At the end of his Mass on the world, Teilhard prays:

For me, my God, all joy and all achievement, the very purpose of my being and all my love of life, all depend on this one basic vision of the union between yourself and the universe. . . .

It is to Your Body in this its fullest extension—that is, to the world become through your power and my faith the glorious living crucible in which everything melts away in order to be born anew—it is to this that I dedicate myself with all the resources which your

[86] Letter of December 30, 1923, quoted in *Ecrits*, 285, editor's footnote. Teilhard adds immediately that this new edition of "The Priest" is *"ad usum privatum*, as it should be."

[87] *HU*, 19–37.

[88] *Ibid.*, 19–20.

[89] *Ibid.*, 26.

[90] *Ibid.*, 28.

creative magnetism has brought forth in me: with the all too feeble resources of my scientific knowledge, with my religious vows, with my priesthood, . . . with my deepest human convictions. It is in this dedication, Lord Jesus, that I desire to live, in this that I desire to die.[91]

Father de Lubac reports that "it was perhaps in the mystery of His Eucharist that Jesus Christ was most often the subject" of Teilhard's personal meditative prayer.[92] Teilhard's theology of the Eucharist and the world comes from his prayerful reflection.

The Eucharist and the Universe

In two essays of 1923 and 1924, Teilhard approaches the relation between the Eucharist and the world in a somewhat less mystical manner. The universe is viewed as an extension of the Eucharist. When Christ says through the priest, "This is my Body," these words go far beyond the bread over which they are pronounced. Beyond the Host, the priestly action extends to the cosmos itself which gradually, with the passing centuries, is transformed. In an extended but nevertheless real sense, "the total Host is the universe which Christ penetrates and vivifies."[93] The extensions of Christ's Eucharistic presence are real. The Host is first, above all, and in its primary sense, a fragment of matter where by transubstantiation the presence of Christ enters into the human zone of the universe. In the Host is fixed the center of Christ's personal energy. And, just as we refer to the local center of our own personal and spiritual influence as "our body," so in this sense the Body of Christ is limited by the appearances of the

[91] *Ibid.*, 37.
[92] *Teilhard de Chardin, the Man and His Meaning*, 56. Father de Lubac, when he wrote this, had access to Teilhard's meditation notebooks.
[93] "Panthéisme et Christianisme," 1923, 12.

bread and wine. It is also true that, when the words "This is my Body" are pronounced, "this" refers primarily (*primario*) to the bread. But in an extended, secondary sense, the matter of the sacrament is the world itself, in which the presence of the Universal Christ expands—to bring it to fullness.[94] Teilhard sees in the Eucharist the prolongation of Christ's redemptive and unitive act, and it is through the Eucharist, understood in its universal power and realism, that "the influence of the Universal Christ is transmitted to us here and now."[95]

It is not the universe considered as a static cosmos that is the subject of the "universal consecration," but the universe in action, evolving and developing. Human activity, therefore, is included in the consecration of the universe; human effort is consecrated and, furthermore—again in an extended sense—consecrating. There is a phrase that explains all God's creative activity and that permits us to be united to God in everything we do and in everything we undergo. "He for whom the universe appears as the universal 'species' where—according to infinitely diverse but real modes—Christ becomes incarnate by the combined action of determinisms, freedom and grace, hears this phrase. It is: 'This is my Body.' "[96]

It is in *The Divine Milieu* that Teilhard brings together in a synthesis the ideas of the organization of the Pleroma and Christ's presence in the Eucharist.

When the priest says the words "This is my Body," his words fall directly on the bread and directly transform it into the individual reality of Christ. But the great sacramental operation does not cease

[94] "Mon univers," 1924, *OE* 9, 94.

[95] *Ibid.*, 93. It might be pointed out that whenever Teilhard speaks of the universe as the Body of Christ it is invariably in the context of the Eucharist, and in a derived (but real) sense.

[96] "Note sur l'évangelisation des temps nouveaux," 1919, *Ecrits*, 374–5. See the letter of December 29, 1919, *Archives*, 151.

at that local and momentary event. Even children are taught that throughout the life of each man and the life of the Church and the history of the world there is only one Mass and one Communion.

Individual communions "are only the diversely central points in which the continuity of a unique act is split up and fixed in space and time for our experience." Throughout history, "a single event has been developing in the world: the Incarnation, realized in each individual through the Eucharist."[97] The Communions of all men form one great Communion by which Christ assimilates men to Himself. But the universe is one organic cosmos, and all its parts and levels and all the things in it are inextricably linked together. What is most spiritual in the world, the souls of men, forms "in some manner, the incandescent surface of matter plunged in God." Or, to use another image, man is the forwardmost and most spiritual point in the universe's evolution, and all creation is somehow continuous with him and summed up in him. So, since it is impossible to draw a hard and fast line between man and his cosmic environment, the Eucharist, in its influence on man, necessarily extends that influence "into the less luminous regions that sustain us."

As our humanity assimilates the material world, and as the Host assimilates our humanity, the eucharistic transformation goes beyond and completes the transubstantiation of the bread on the altar. Step by step, it irresistibly invades the universe. . . . In a secondary and generalized sense, but in a true sense, the sacramental Species are formed by the totality of the world, and the duration of the creation is the time needed for its consecration.[98]

[97] *DM*, 123–4.
[98] *Ibid.*, 125–6. See W. Durig, "The Eucharist as Symbol of the Consecration of the World," tr. L. Connolly, *The Christian and the World*, ed. at Canisianum, Innsbruck, 120–9.

"At every moment the Eucharistic Christ controls—from the point of view of the organization of the Pleroma (which is the only true point of view from which the world can be understood)—the whole movement of the universe: Christ, through whom, Lord, You create, vivify, and bestow on us all things."[99]

These texts from *The Divine Milieu* mark the end of a developing reflection on the Eucharist and the world; the line of Teilhard's thought begins in 1916 with the poetry of "Christ in the World of Matter" and ends in 1927 with the poetic intuitions expressed in the form of a cosmic theology of the Eucharist. Teilhard has succeeded in integrating his devotion to the Eucharist into his theological world-view. He writes only twice more about the Eucharist, in 1944 and just before his death in 1955; both times he treats of the Eucharist in the context of Christogenesis. The Eucharist is not only "first" among the sacraments; it is *the* sacrament, and all the others are in reference to it. This is because through the Eucharist passes directly the axis of the Incaration, that is to say of creation. In the first place, when we receive Christ in Communion we come personally into physiological contact with His assimilative power. But all our Communions are the successive instants of the one long Communion of our life, of "one process of Christification." This is true of all the Communions of all Christians, so that all the Communions in history form, in their organic unity, one vast Communion. For the Eucharist, considered in its total function, is really the manifestation of the unifying divine energy applied in detail to each spiritual unit of the universe. When he goes to Communion, the Christian touches the very heart of evolution, because to receive the Eucharistic Christ is to be incorporated— a little more each time—into the process of Christogenesis. What is more, just as the heart of evolution is touched in Communion,

---

[99] *DM*, 125.

so—to really "touch the heart of the Host— . . . it is indispensable to be in communion with the body of the world in evolution."[100]

If Christ is the same as the Omega of evolution, then we should think of Him as radiating physically over all things, penetrating them and activating them. As the Prime Mover of the creative unification of the universe, Christ has a real omnipresence of transformation. "And here it is precisely the Eucharistic mystery itself . . . which is extended to infinity in a truly universal 'transubstantiation' where the words of consecration fall not only upon the sacrificial bread and wine, but also upon the totality of joys and sufferings occasioned in the course of its progress by the convergence of the world."[101]

[100] "Introduction à la vie chrétienne," 1944, 9–10.
[101] "Le Christique," 1955, 8–9.

5 · THE VICTORY OVER EVIL

THE NEW TESTAMENT theology of the Redemption has a two-fold point of view corresponding to what might be called the negative and the positive aspects of the Redemption. The negative aspect of the Redemption is Christ's atonement for the sins of the world, "that Christ died for our sins in accordance with the scriptures."[1] The positive aspect lies in the fact that the Redemption is a victory over the powers of evil. "During our minority we were slaves to the elemental spirits of the universe, but when the term was completed God sent His own Son, born of a woman, born under the law to purchase freedom for the subjects of the law in order that we might attain the status of sons."[2] "Bearing the human

[1] I Cor. 15:3.
[2] Gal. 4:3–5.

likeness, revealed in human shape, He humbled Himself and in obedience accepted even death—death on a cross. Therefore God raised Him to the heights and bestowed on Him the name above all names, that at the name of Jesus every knee should bow—in heaven, on earth, and in the depths—and every tongue confess, 'Jesus Christ is Lord,' to the glory of the Father."[3] Since the end of the age of the Fathers of the Church, Christian theology of the Redemption has paid more attention to the negative aspect than to the positive. Teilhard de Chardin in his reflections on Christ's Redemption of the world, while not neglecting the ideas of reparation and expiation for sin, stresses the positive aspect.

Teilhard tries to formulate the beginnings of a theology of the Redemption that he feels is in the direction of answering the questions and the needs of contemporary man. His theological reflection emphasizes the constructive side of the Redemption, the victory over the forces of evil, and it allows more room than most past theology for man's place in the redemptive process, more room for active as well as passive human participation in the redemption of the world. He sees past views as giving great stress to the dark side, the negative aspect of the Redemption; he himself tentatively suggests a point of view that gives more stress to the positive aspect.

Concerning the dogma of the Redemption, Christian thought and piety have up to now emphasized above all, for obvious historical reasons, the idea of expiating reparation. Christ has been regarded above all as the Lamb burdened with the sins of the world, and the world above all as a fallen mass. But from the very beginning there was another side of the picture, another element—a positive one— of reconstruction or re-creation. A new heaven and a new earth:

[3] Phil. 2:8–11. R. Schnackenburg mentions that "Paul's soteriology, which embraces the whole world, needs clarification on more than one point—on the question of its cosmic import (Cf. Col. 1:20), for example." (*New Testament Theology Today*, tr. D. Askew, 75.)

these were, even for Augustine, the result and the reward of the Sacrifice of the Cross.

Is it not conceivable—even more, is it not coming about in conformity with . . . the evolution of dogma, that these two aspects of Christ's power, the positive aspect and the negative aspect, reverse their respective importance and even their natural order in the outlook and the piety of the faithful, who are guided by the Spirit of God?

Under the pressure of modern events and discoveries, the tangible world and its influence are in our time certainly taking on a growing interest for the followers of the Gospel. And so there is a "humanistic" renewal in religion, a renewal which—without in any way rejecting the dark side of things—prefers nevertheless to emphasize the luminous side of creation. At this moment we are witnessing and participating in the irresistible rise of a Christian optimism.

How does this optimism react on the form that our adoration takes?

In the first place, Christ seems to attract us more and more as Leader and as King as well as and as much as Reparator of the world. Purification, of course, but at the same time vitalization: these two functions, although still thought of as independent, already appeal to our heart as joined together and having equal force.

But this seems to be only an intermediary position. . . . The religious expansion and élan that we are all more or less consciously waiting for—should not it come from a renewed Christology where the idea of reparation, no matter how integrally preserved, would pass to the second place "in the order of nature" in the Incarnate Word's work of salvation? *Primario*, to lead creation to its fulfillment in union with the divine, and for this purpose *secundario* to eliminate the evil forces of regression and dispersion. No longer first to expiate and in addition to restore, but first to create—or to re-create more perfectly—and for this purpose, in inevitable consequence, to fight against and to compensate for evil.

With this approach, . . . the Cross would appear as symbolizing not just the expiation of sin, but the upward and laborious rise of all creation; . . . the Lamb of God would appear to us as carrying, with the weight of sin, the weight of the world's progress; the ideas of pardon and sacrifice would be enriched with the aspects of fulfillment and of conquest.[4]

This long quotation from Teilhard gives an idea of what he is trying to do in his theology of the Redemption. He sees the Redemption primarily as a creative effort, as a positive victory over the forces of evil. With his general point of view in mind, we can turn to a short outline of his thought on the nature and the problem of evil.

The Problem of Evil

In classic Thomist philosophy, evil is considered as a privation of being, as "non-being," as a certain lack of that "being" that a creature should have. Teilhard, on the other hand, sees evil as an incompleteness of the creature, the incompleteness of organization of a creature that is progressing toward a higher state of unity. In the static cosmos of the medieval philosophers it was impossible to give any kind of a really satisfactory answer to the problem of evil, to the question, "Why is there evil in the world?" Evil could be described in terms of "non-being," but not really justified. But now that the universe is seen to be in evolution, evil is at least to some extent explainable.

In a universe in process of evolution, "for implacable statistical reasons, and at every level—pre-living, living, reflectively conscious—it is impossible that there not be some disorder or lack of organization in a multiplicity that is *progressively* moving toward a higher degree of organization."[5] For in an evolutionary system it

---

[4] "Le Christ Evoluteur," 1942, *Cahiers de la fondation Teilhard de Chardin, 5, Le Christ Evoluteur, Socialisation et Religion*, 24–6.

[5] "Du cosmos à la cosmogénèse," 1951, *OE* 7, 268. In "La pensée du Teilhard de Chardin," 1948, *Les études philosophiques* 10 (1955) 581,

is inevitable that each advance in organization, in order, be paid for by failures and discords. Evil is a secondary effect, an inevitable byproduct of the forward progress of a universe in evolution. This is basically Teilhard's position on the problem of evil, stated generally and abstractly. Let us take a closer look at this position in order to see some of its implications for a theology of the Redemption.

As we saw in Chapter IV, God's creative act is best understood as a gradual process of unification. That is, to create is to unite. Teilhard views creation as a gradual reduction of the multiple to unity; God's creative act is expressed in the converging evolution of the universe, a universe moving gradually through higher states of unity to the fullness of the Pleroma when all things will be united in Christ. If creation is seen as a long process of unification beginning with an infinite multiplicity and proceeding through the ages along an axis of increasing organization toward a final synthesis in Christ, then, according to Teilhard, the problem of evil is no longer a real problem.[6] In the ancient cosmos that was thought to have come ready-fashioned from the hands of the Creator, it is natural that the reconciliation between a partially bad world and the existence of a God who is both good and all-powerful should appear difficult. But in a cosmos in a state of evolution, of becoming, the problem disappears. It is not because He lacks omnipotence, but by the very structure of the void itself—considered as an infinite multiplicity—that God, in creating, can proceed in only one manner: by a progressive unification. Through a gradual process of attracting elements to Himself, by arranging and unifying little by little through a utilization of the random combinations that occur in quantities of large number, God draws things toward greater unity and toward Himself. At first these elements are almost

---

Teilhard describes evil even more concisely as "the statistical necessity of disorder at the interior of a multitude undergoing organization."

[6] "Comment je vois," 1948, 19.

infinitely numerous, very simple, and with negligible consciousness. Gradually units appear that, although less numerous, are more organized. Finally, man appears, highly complex and gifted with human consciousness. In a process of this kind, it is inevitable that every success be paid for by a certain amount of failure or waste. In pre-life, this waste takes the form of disharmony or decomposition. Among living things, it takes the form of suffering and death. And in the moral order, in the realm of human freedom, this waste and failure appears as sin. There is no order in the process of formation that does not imply disorder at every stage of the process. There is nothing in Teilhard's idea of the inevitability of waste, failure, disorder, that would imply a less than omnipotent Creator. The fact is simply this: because unorganized multiplicity is subject to the play of chance in the arrangements that lead to greater unification, it is absolutely impossible that its progress toward unity be unaccompanied by failure and disorder. Evil occurs by statistical necessity.[7]

The above is an explanation of evil *in general*; it includes both physical evil—that is, every kind of disorder and failure and suffering and death—and the moral evil of sin. Evil appears necessarily in the course of the unification of the multiple, for evil is the very expression of a state of plurality that is not yet completely organized. Evil is not an unforeseen accident in the universe. "It is an enemy, the shadow that God raises by His very decision to create."[8] At every level of created being, precisely because of the evolutionary structure of created being, evil is "relentlessly im-

---

[7] *Ibid.*, 19–20. For an early and much longer general consideration of evil, see "La lutte contre la multitude," 1917, *Ecrits*, 113–24. See also "Les noms de la matière," *Ecrits*, 419–32; "Christologie et évolution," 1933, 3–8; "Réflexions sur le péché originel," 1947, 4–7; "Le néo-humanisme moderne et ses réactions sur le Christianisme," 1948, 56. For a personalistic but still general consideration of evil, see "Equisse d'un univers personnel," 1936, *OE* 6, 105–10.

[8] "Christologie et évolution," 1933, 7.

posed by the play of large numbers at the interior of a multitude undergoing organization."[9] In our universe, "evil appears necessarily and abundantly . . . not by accident (which would not much matter) but by the very structure of the system"; a universe in evolution is necessarily "a universe which labors, which sins, which suffers."[10]

The existence of evil seems to be the rigorously inevitable concomitant of creation. To think that God could create from nothing a world without pain or risks or breakage or sin is simply a conceptual fantasy. To say that God could obtain a creature united to Himself without entering into combat against evil is, for Teilhard, to say a contradiction. God cannot make a square circle; He cannot perform a bad act; and there are certainly physical equivalents to these inflexible laws.[11]

Evil, then, for Teilhard is basically disorder and failure, and we find it at every level of created being. "Statistically, at every degree of evolution, we find evil always and everywhere, forming and reforming implacably in us and around us."[12] We will consider in brief detail the two kinds of evil to which Teilhard gives the most attention, the "evil of decomposition" which includes suffering and death, and the evil that is sin.

One form of evil is suffering. It is inevitable, "bound to the very structure of the cosmos . . . and part of the very law of becoming."[13] "Everything that is not yet finished being organized must

[9] *PM,* 312.
[10] *Ibid.,* 313.
[11] "Note sur les modes de l'action divine dans l'univers," 1920, 10–1. Teilhard's thought is in an evolutionary framework; in a system of thought that takes evolutionary process into account, evil does seem to be rigorously inevitable. To think of an evolving universe without any evil in that universe does seem contradictory. In the static cosmos of Thomistic philosophy, of course, this is not true. It seems quite possible within Thomistic categories to imagine the creation of a universe that would have no evil in it.
[12] *PM,* 312.
[13] "La foi qui opère," 1918, *Ecrits,* 324.

inevitably suffer in its residual lack of organization and in its possible disorganization";[14] this is the human condition, and more—it is the condition of the universe.

In a bouquet, we could be surprised to see imperfect or "suffering" flowers, because the flowers were picked one by one and artificially arranged together. On the other hand, on a tree which has had to fight against the interior accidents of its development and the exterior accidents of weather, broken branches, torn leaves, blossoms that are dried up or drooping or pale—all these are "in their place." They are the manifestations of the more or less difficult conditions of growth met by the tree itself.

The tree is Teilhard's metaphor for the evolving world. Changing metaphor, he goes on to speak of the world's progress as a battle,

a work of conquest that is going on right now; . . . by our birth, we are thrown into full battle. For the success of the universal effort in which we are both the collaborators and the disputed field of battle, it is inevitable that there be suffering. The world, seen experientially from our point of view, is an immense groping, an immense enterprise, an immense attack; its progress is made at the price of much failure and of many wounds. The sufferers, no matter to what species they belong, are the expression of this austere but noble condition. They do not represent useless and lesser elements. They pay for the forward progress and the victory of all. They are fallen on the field of honor.[15]

The "evil" of decomposition that is manifest in suffering has its most serious and aggravated form in death. Taken simply in itself

---

[14] "Esquisse d'un univers personnel," 1936, *OE* 6, 106.

[15] "La signification et la valeur constructrice de la souffrance," 1933, *OE* 6, 63. There is an English translation: "The Meaning and Constructive Value of Suffering," *Teilhard de Chardin, Pilgrim of the Future*, ed. N. Braybrooke, 23–6.

and from a purely natural viewpoint, death is a scandal and a failure, "the worst weakness and the worst enemy."[16] It is the sum and consummation of all the evils of the universe; "it is *evil* itself."[17] All the evils of our life have "a common envelope: the fundamental obligation to be born and to live whether we should have wanted to or not, and they all converge to the same inevitable center: death." As seen by the living, "death is the summing up and the common basis of all that frightens us . . . , the inevitable destiny that is implied in our birth and that circumscribes our life."[18] In an evolutionary universe, death is the law, "the regular indispensable condition of the replacement of one individual by another along a phyletic stem."[19]

As an explanation of most evils, including death and suffering, Teilhard's ideas seem to be not only original but satisfactory. But his general explanation of evil as a statistical necessity in an evolving world applies also to moral evil, to sin. How can he consider sin in more or less the same terms as he considers other forms of evil? And does not his idea of sin as statistical *necessity* tend to deny human freedom?

Sin

Nowhere in Teilhard's writings is there a full theology of sin, or even a single very full treatment of any one aspect of the theology of sin. The theological questions that interested him were those that touched on the question of the evolution of the universe toward Christ-Omega. It is natural, then, that his consideration of sin should be in the context of cosmic and Christ-oriented evolution, and that he should consider the theology of sin only insofar

---

[16] "Mon univers," 1924, *OE* 9, 91.
[17] *DM*, 82.
[18] "La foi qui opère," 1918, *Ecrits*, 312-3.
[19] *PM*, 312.

as it is in that context. We should not look in the writings of Teilhard for considerations of sin as a subjective psychological phenomenon, or of sin as a subjective existential act, or of sin as a personal and subjective rejection of God's love. These notions are outside the scope of his chosen interest: the evolution of the cosmos and what that evolution means for man and for Christianity. His view of sin is in no way impersonal or "cold," but in the context of the evolution of the universe it is fitting that sin be considered not insofar as it is a properly individual and subjective rejection of divine love but as the evil that is proper to that part of evolution which has become reflexively conscious. Teilhard's reflections on sin are almost always in the context of evil in general as the inevitable concomitant of the creative process.

In Teilhard's cosmic perspective, the evil of sin is the form of disorder corresponding to the conscious state of the multiple. In a universe moving toward always greater unity, sin is a return to the multiple, a descent to a less unified state.[20] The unity and the multiplicity in question here are spiritual, although, of course, sin has repercussions, leaves traces, in the material order. Sin is the deliberate movement of the will away from unity; it is evil at the level of moral consciousness. "There is *only one evil*: disunion. We call it moral evil when it affects the free zones of the soul."[21] Objective moral evil is disunion, disorder, and this is why Teilhard can say that sin is inevitable, that it is statistically necessary in a universe in

[20] See the somewhat abstract analysis of sin in "La lutte contre la multitude," 1917, *Ecrits*, 120–2. See also *Cuénot*, 257–8, for a report of a discussion between Teilhard and Father A. M. Dubarle, O.P., on the nature of evil. Teilhard often describes sin as a return to multiplicity, as a movement away from unity and organization. He obviously does not mean that sin is something quantitative; he is using an analogy taken from the scientific concept of entropy, the gradual movement of a more or less organized system to a lower state of organization and energy. His idea of sin as a kind of moral entropy seems to be the chief cause of criticisms that his theology of sin is too "impersonal."

[21] "Mon univers," 1924, *OE* 9, 109, footnote 2.

the process of unification. "Physical disharmony or decomposition among the pre-living, suffering among the living, sin in the domain of freedom: there is no order in the process of being formed that does not at every stage imply disorder."[22]

There is no real difficulty in saying that sin is freely committed and that sin is, at the same time, a statistical inevitability "relentlessly imposed at the interior of a multitude undergoing organization."[23] The inevitability of sin applies to the "multitude" of men, not to any one individual at any particular time. In the multitude of human beings, *because* they are free to choose good or evil, at least some will—in a given period of time—choose evil instead of good; some will sin. This situation could be compared to a national presidential election; there is a statistical inevitability that at least some voters will vote for candidate A instead of candidate B; yet each voter chooses *freely* for whom to vote. A large part of the statistical methods of modern sociology is based on a certain statistical necessity that holds for large populations even in matters of free choice. Sin, for Teilhard, is the free choice of disunion, of disorder; it is free in each case, but it is a statistical necessity for the entire human population moving gradually and even somewhat gropingly toward higher organization and unity. The statistical necessity of sin does not imply obligation, nor does it minimize man's freedom.

Teilhard's opinion is that "Christianity has developed in itself to a probably exaggerated degree—exaggerated because not balanced by compensating factors—and to the point of hypertrophy the ideas of guilt and damnation."[24] He reacted to what he considered an excessive stress on the negative aspects of Christian doctrine, especially man's guilt and the everlasting punishments of hell. Nevertheless, in Teilhard's writings the existence and the impor-

[22] "Comment je vois," 1948, 20.
[23] *PM*, 312.
[24] "L'évolution de la chasteté," 1934, 2.

tance of human freedom to choose good or evil and of human responsibility in choosing are strongly underlined. And in a world in evolution, where evil is the inevitable corollary of creative union, "hell is the natural corollary of heaven,"[25] and the mystery of eternal damnation takes on a cosmic awfulness. It seems well to look briefly at Teilhard's ideas of human freedom and of hell to the extent that these ideas help to understand his conception of sin.

The progress of evolution, far from diminishing freedom in the cosmos, increases it. "Spirit is the term pursued by Nature in its long travail. All that lives—that is, perhaps, all that acts—tends from the beginning toward a little more freedom, power, truth."[26] Man is evolution become conscious of itself, and in man the evolutionary process continues toward an always fuller freedom. The real evolution of the world takes place in human consciousness and in the conscious union of men. Its most important forces are not blindly biological but psychological and moral.[27]

Evolution, continued in man, follows an axis of increasing complexity and consciousness, and the increase of human reflexive consciousness necessarily implies the increase of human freedom to choose good or evil. Human freedom "appears everywhere, and is everywhere increased" by the progress of the evolution of mankind toward greater unity.[28]

For this evolution is in the direction of greater spiritualization, and so in the direction of greater freedom. Socialization increases freedom because "union differentiates"; man becomes more human and so more free by associating with other men. Just as man's freedom grows in the evolutive history of mankind, so does human responsibility; as mankind becomes more tightly organized

[25] "La vie cosmique," 1916, *Ecrits*, 58.
[26] "Le milieu mystique," 1917, *Ecrits*, 156–7.
[27] "Mon univers," 1924, *OE* 9, 76–7.
[28] "The Formation of the Noosphere," 1947, *FM*, 182–3.

in a more and more complex society—that is, as human evolution continues to converge—human responsibility grows along with human freedom. This responsibility or moral obligation is not simply juridical, but based on the organic nature of evolving human society. Finally, with the progressive growth in society of consciousness and freedom and responsibility, evil inevitably increases—if not in quantity, at least in intensity.[29] For evil—and, in the domain of human freedom, sin—is the inevitable counterpart of progress in unity. There is no order in the process of formation that does not imply disorder, and the gradual forging of unity in the realm of the specifically human inevitably means the moral disorder that is sin. It is in the context of the progress of humanity toward greater unification that Teilhard speaks of a growing temptation to revolt. In face of the choice between fidelity and infidelity to the movement of life toward Omega, in the choice between good and evil, man is more and more tempted to choose evil, to sin.

This crisis of human activity is, by its nature, as old as man. It is abundantly clear that we must not confine it to a few brief instants or only to the origins of our race. Born with the intellect, the temptation to revolt must constantly change and *grow* with it. And this is why it has never appeared more acute and more universal than today.[30]

Teilhard's consideration of the mystery of hell and eternal damnation throws more light on his idea of sin as disunion in the domain of human freedom.

The existence of hell is, with the mystery of the Cross, one of the most criticized and disconcerting elements of the Christian creed. And yet, reduced to its essence, nothing could be more in conformity with the perspectives of a universe in evolution than this

[29] "L'évolution de la responsabilité," 1950, *OE* 7, 211–21.
[30] "Hominization," 1925, *VP*, 75.

dogma. All evolution within the limits of our experience entails selection and waste. And so it is impossible for us to imagine, in the totality of its process, the unification of the world in God without making a place for that which might eventually escape this process.

Catholic dogma, Teilhard goes on, does not state that all men will be saved. The dogma of hell tells us that some men may be lost forever, thrown out "to the antipodes of God." Hell is the inverse of heaven, like an "opposite pole" from God.[31]

The history of the kingdom of God is, directly, one of a reunion. The total divine milieu is formed by the incorporation of every elected spirit in Jesus Christ. But to say 'elect' is to imply a choice, a selection. We should not be looking at the universal action of Jesus from a fully Christian point of view if we were to see it merely as a center of attraction and beatification. It is precisely because He is the one who unites that He is also the one who separates and judges. The Gospel speaks of the good seed, the sheep, the right hand of the Son of Man, the wedding feast and the fire that kindles joy. But there are also the tares, the goats, the left hand of the Judge, the closed door, the outer darkness; and, at the antipodes of the fire that unites in love, there is the fire that destroys in isolation. The whole process out of which the New Earth is gradually born is an *aggregation* underlaid by a *segregation*. [32]

The final choice is "revolt or adoration," and those whose final option is revolt will be forever torn away from the ultimate Center of all real organization and unification.[33] Those men who finally resist union with Christ-Omega will be rejected into a conscious and unending decomposition and descent into multiplicity.[34] Hell,

[31] "Introduction à la vie chrétienne," 1944, 8.
[32] *DM*, 146–7.
[33] "A Note on Progress," 1920, *FM*, 19; "Panthéisme et Christianisme," 1923, 12.
[34] "Mon univers," 1924, *OE* 9, 113.

for Teilhard, terrible though it is, is "a structural element in the universe," and it "adds an accent, a gravity, a contrast, a depth" to total reality. The knowledge of the existence of hell, "this negative pole of the world," doubles our understanding of the urgency of Christ's call to all men to union with Him. "The peak can only be measured from the abyss which it crowns."[35]

We have not yet considered one of the most important aspects of Teilhard's thought on the existence of evil in the world. It is his theological hypothesis of original sin. He anticipated by several years the contemporary trend among theologians to reformulate the classical theology of original sin. He considered such a reformulation as vitally necessary to a proper and coherent understanding of Christ's redemption of the world.

Original Sin and Christian Perspective

Teilhard's most complete presentation of his views on original sin was written in 1947 explicitly to be read and criticized by qualified theologians.[36] He begins the essay with his reasons for proposing his theory of original sin. He wants to safeguard the Christian understanding of Christ as Lord of the universe, and he

[35] *DM*, 148. Teilhard writes in 1918: "Only sin is excluded (from the Pleroma). And yet, since the damned are not annihilated, who can say what mysterious complementarity is furnished to the Body of Christ by this immortal waste?" ("Le prêtre," 1918, *Ecrits*, 293.) For other texts on hell and its significance, see: "La vie cosmique," 1916, *Ecrits*, 57–8; "La lutte contre la multitude," 1917, *Ecrits*, 131–2; "Forma Christi," 1918, *Ecrits*, 349–50; "Terre promise," 1919, *Ecrits*, 395; "Les noms de la matière," 1919, *Ecrits*, 429.

[36] "Réflexions sur le péché originel," 1947. Among the theologians for whose consideration this short paper was written was almost certainly Father Pierre Charles, S.J., of the University of Louvain, a thoroughly Thomistic and imaginative theologian and lifelong friend of Teilhard; see *Cuénot*, 6, 13.

wants to be sure that man's place in the forward movement of the universe is not minimized.

In the first place, Christ's power as Lord is a specifically redemptive power.

Christ must continue to be understood as the Head of all creation. . . . The radius of Christ's Lordship and power is "by definition" the radius of the Redemption. No one questions this. Now what would happen from the point of view of Christology if, in our modern perspectives of historical cosmogenesis, original sin were to continue to be thought of on the same small scale—that is, as an accident that happened toward the end of the Tertiary Period in a corner of the planet Earth? Obviously this: Christ's power would not *directly*, *organically*, and *formally* go beyond . . . a short and narrow spindle of the universe around us. In name and juridically, of course, Christ could still be declared Master of the remaining sectors of the cosmos by virtue of His divine dignity. But in a full and real sense, in the sense of St. Paul, He would cease to be "Him in whom all things hold together." And so . . . we are obliged to reflect on the phenomenon of the Fall so that we might conceive and imagine it not as an isolated fact, but as a general condition affecting the whole of history.[37]

Teilhard says the same thing in earlier essays. "The *spirit* of the Bible and the Church is clear: the *entire* world has been corrupted by the Fall, and it is the *entire* world that is the subject of Redemption."[38] To safeguard the Christian view of Christ as Redeemer, it is necessary that we keep original sin as large as the world. Otherwise Christ will be understood as having saved only part of the world, and not understood as the Center of everything.[39]

Further, Teilhard feels that the common understanding of the

[37] "Réflexions sur le péché originel," 1947, 3.
[38] "Chute, rédemption, et géocentricité," 1920, 2.
[39] "Note sur quelques représentations historiques du péché originel," 1924, 8.

dogma of original sin tends strongly to devaluate the place of Christian endeavor in the world, that it tends to devaluate the temporal realities around us and so to devaluate Christian responsibility in promoting human progress. To begin with, it is not clear how the dogma of original sin is consonant with the general contemporary view of the universe. Dogma, of course, is not intrinsically affected by any world view; nevertheless, so that the interior unity of the contemporary Christian's view of reality be preserved it seems necessary that theology show how the doctrine of original sin and man's knowledge of the universe fit together. The doctrine of original sin as it is still formulated today is one of the principal obstacles right now to the progress of Christian thought. "The story of the Fall paralyzes the necessary establishment of a Christian world-view that is fully human and humanizing."[40]

Teilhard's real purpose is not to reconcile science and religion but to integrate the doctrine of original sin into an overall Christian vision of reality, a vision that will not minimize the importance of the world and of Christian responsibility in the world. As long as the dogma of original sin is not somehow seen in the perspective of a unified Christian outlook, it tends to distort Christian ascetical principles. In his first mention of original sin, in 1916, he points out the necessity of providing the theological basis for a healthy Christian outlook on suffering by a further reflection on what "original sin" means. "According to 'classical' views, suffering is *above all a punishment, an expiation*; its force is the force of a sacrifice: born of a sin, suffering makes reparation for it. It is good to suffer so as to check oneself, conquer oneself, liberate oneself." But for Teilhard, "suffering is above all the consequence and the price of a *project of development*. Its force is the force of *effort*. . . . The Cross is the symbol of the difficult work of evolution rather than the symbol of expiation."

[40] "Réflexions sur le péché originel," 1947, 1.

How can these two different points of view be made to coincide? By a rethinking of the theology of original sin so that the original Fall is seen as placing "man in his connatural framework of progression and work 'by the sweat of his brow.' "[41] The negative emphasis on expiation and reparation should be balanced by a positive emphasis on the value of effort and labor. Again in 1933 Teilhard deplores the negative outlook imposed by the current understanding of original sin, an outlook that "opposes at every point the normal expansion of our religion." Original sin as it is usually pictured "suffocates our thought and our heart," it "binds us and weakens us."[42] In 1954 he writes in a letter that

Christianity is not going to recover its power of contagion until it rejects the last traces of Manichaeanism and Platonism and begins to think of original sin no longer in terms of a Fall but in terms of progress. This means that Christians must cease looking upon cosmogenesis as something tainted, outside of God's plan, and representing in its totality a haphazard pasting together with which they need not concern themselves.[43]

Teilhard on Original Sin

What then, is the theological hypothesis of original sin that Teilhard proposes, and how does it differ from the traditional presentation? The dogma of original sin is customarily interpreted as though the state of original sin depended on an event interior to history, an historical event with a "before" and an "after." But, he asks, for important theological reasons should not original sin be considered to be a reality of a transhistoric order, affecting the totality of the world as we know it? The specific effect of original

[41] "La vie cosmique," 1916, *Ecrits*, 60–1.
[42] "Christologie et évolution," 1933, 3–4.
[43] Letter of June 19, 1953, to Mme. Jean Carlhian, quoted by C. Mooney, S.J., *Teilhard de Chardin and the Mystery of Christ*, 79–80.

sin is death, but death is present everywhere in the experimental world. In the form of decomposition death shows itself even at the level of the atom. If there is original sin in the world, then it must be everywhere and from the very beginning. Furthermore, this universal existence of original sin is confirmed "by the most orthodox exigencies of Christology."[44]

How does Teilhard visualize this universality of original sin? He takes as a postulate that the void, the utter nothingness out of which God began His creation, be thought of as an infinite multiplicity and that God's creative act be understood as a gradual process of arrangement and unification. The history of the world, then, can be imagined as a cone with an infinite multiplicity as its base and with the future synthesis of all things in Christ as the apex. In such a universe in a state of converging evolution, evil at every level—moral as well as physical—is, as we have seen, a statistical necessity. And this is original sin: the inevitable existence of evil in the world, a universal condition. Thus, original sin for Teilhard is a negative and inevitable structural element in an evolving universe, a universal condition of existence in a progressively converging world.

It is true that, in Teilhard's explanation, original sin is not an isolated act. It is a state of mankind and of the whole world. For Teilhard, this change of perspective does not at all diminish the

[44] "Réflexions sur le péché originel," 1947, 2–3. See also the very similar explanations of original sin in the following works of Teilhard: "Chute, rédemption, et géocentricité," 1920; "Note sur le Christ universel," 1920, *OE* 9, 41; "Note sur quelques représentations historiques," 1922; "Christologie et évolution," 1933, 3–8; "Quelques vues générales sur l'essence du Christianisme," 1939, 2; "Le Christ Evoluteur," 1942, appendix; "Introduction à la vie chrétienne," 1944, 8; "Two Unpublished Letters of Teilhard," an article by T. Fleming, S.J., *The Heythrop Journal* 6 (1965) 36–45. See Teilhard's brief remarks on original sin in: *HU*, 311; "La vie cosmique," 1916, *Ecrits*, 60–1; "La lutte contre la multitude," 1917, *Ecrits*, 122–3; "L'âme du monde," 1918, *Ecrits*, 231; "Mon univers," 1924, *OE* 9, 108–9.

dogmatic characteristics of the doctrine of original sin; on the contrary, it intensifies them. For one thing, the redemption is seen as truly universal since it is a remedy for a universal state of things. For another, the meaning of baptism is seen more clearly. Each person that comes into the world is, by his solidarity with mankind, contaminated by the total influence of all the sins inevitably and by statistical necessity committed by mankind. "Something in that soul, then, has to be purified."[45] Teilhard adds that among the most harmful to all mankind are the first sins committed on earth, committed with a minimum human consciousness but with a maximum influence on the newly born human race. For each person, the sins committed in his social group and in his family line are particularly harmful.

In Teilhard's theory original sin cannot be localized in time or in space; it is not an event in a historical chain of events. Rather, it is a global modality of evolution. From this point of view our conception of original sin "considered in its cosmic basis—as opposed to its historical actuation by the first human beings—tends to be absorbed by our conception of the very mechanism of creation." For if creation is thought of as progressive unification, then "original sin represents the action of the negative forces of counterevolution."[46] This does not mean that original sin cannot, in Teilhard's hypothesis, also be considered in a more limited sense, insofar as it affects mankind. There is no difficulty in admitting within the boundaries of Teilhard's hypothesis the idea that the evil inherent in the world by virtue of the world's mode of creation should be regarded as being particularly individualized on earth at the time of the appearance of the first responsible human persons. "This would be, in the strict sense, the original sin of the theologians."[47]

[45] "Réflexions sur le péché originel," 1947, 8.
[46] "Le Christ Evoluteur," 1942, appendix.
[47] "Quelques vues générales sur l'essence du Christianisme," 1939, 2.

Teilhard did not propose his ideas on original sin as a way to avoid the necessity of subscribing to the doctrine of monogenism, the doctrine that all men are descended from one couple. Still, as he points out, the acceptance of his hypothesis would "incidentally free us from the obligation, heavier every day, of paradoxically making the whole human race derive from one couple."[48] In Teilhard's theory, Adam is "universalized." "Strictly speaking, there is no Adam. Under this name is hidden the universal and infrangible law of reversion or perversion." Evil is "the ransom of progress."[49] In Teilhard's view Adam is a symbol that all men are born fallen, that all are marked by original sin the instant they become members of mankind. But men are not born in sin because of some aboriginal sin of a primitive Adam. Men are born in original sin because this is the law of the universe, the cosmic condition of a world in evolution.

It is not the purpose here either to attack or to defend Teil-

---

[48] *Ibid.* See Fleming, *op. cit.* As Teilhard points out, although the problem of the monogenetic or polygenetic origin of man is a theological problem—since science deals not with individuals but with populations —there should be at least no contradiction between theological explanations and scientific findings. ("Monogénisme et monophylétisme," 1950, 1–2.) For an excellent treatment of the problem of monogenism from the dogmatic, scriptural, and metaphysical standpoints, see K. Rahner, S.J., "Theological Reflections on Monogenism," *Theological Investigations*, tr. C. Ernst, O.P., 1. 229–96. It seems at least rash to state apodictically, as does J. Connolly (*The Voices of France*, 127–8), that Teilhard's views on polygenism and evolution bring him into "unavoidable conflict with the ordinary teaching of the Magisterium, the Teaching Authority of the Church as expressed by Pope Pius XII in *Humani Generis*." For a more moderate and balanced position regarding Teilhard's ideas on evolution and polygenism, see Philippe de la Trinité, O.C.D., *Rome et Teilhard de Chardin*, 25–8, footnote 12. Father Philippe de la Trinité, however, finds Teilhard's views on original sin to be in direct opposition to the Council of Trent. In general, his book is an aggressive attack on Teilhard and "teilhardisme."

[49] "Chute, rédemption, et géocentricité, 1920, 3. See *Lettres à Léontine Zanta*, 128: Evil can now be seen to be "not punishment for a sin, but 'sign and effect' of progress."

hard's proposed theological hypothesis of original sin. It is presented here because it seems to be an integral part of his thought on evil and on the Redemption and a very important element in the whole structure of his religious thought.[50] It should be noted, however, that there are trends today in Catholic exegesis and dogmatic theology that make Teilhard's suggested theory of original sin seem much less startling than it surely was when he first proposed it. The emphasis in biblical scholarship has shifted from the idea of the Fall to the equally biblical idea of "the sin of the world," the solidarity in sin of all men. And many modern exegetes see in the story of the Fall not the story of an individual event but a kind of parable that illustrates the universal fact of sin in mankind. In general, the Fall has come to be considered less as a localized and unique event and more and more as the expression of a general condition of sin, a condition that envelops mankind and that is actuated, ratified, and continued by the particular sins of individual men. Father Peter Schoonenberg, for example, doubts that Genesis affirms that sin was committed by the first parents of the human race or that we all descend from one human couple. In Genesis Adam is

first of all man unqualified, "Everyman." And even when Adam, as in Romans, Chapter Five, is pictured as a historical figure, we notice nevertheless that the sins committed after him are taken jointly with his in contrast to Christ's redeeming obedience. There is also the fact that John does not mention the sin of Adam but only "the sin of the world," which is "taken away" by Christ (John 1, 29).

[50] Teilhard's hypothesis of original sin was modestly presented to professional theologians precisely as a hypothesis to be considered and reflected on. Nevertheless, its importance for all his theological thought is immense; his theology of creation and of redemption depend on it intrinsically. His religious thought cannot logically be accepted piecemeal; if an element as important as his theory of original sin is rejected in its essentials, then much more of his original religious thought must be rejected.

Is it perhaps permissible to connect the situation induced by original sin, not with the sin of one single individual, but with the sin of the whole world? In such a case it might perhaps be of no importance exactly when and where sin entered the picture, and as a consequence, we could say that revelation tells us nothing about the degree of self-consciousness and freedom of the first human generation.[51]

Even in the light of the Councils, might it not be possible to avoid attributing a separate proper influence to a first sin committed at a definite time by a first universal couple of parents? "If this is possible, . . . we can then refuse to worry about the precise time of the first sin and we do not have to affirm anything about the way the first human beings experienced their relation to God."[52]

Moreover, original sin is being thought of by theologians today more in the light of the Redemption.

Instead of drawing attention to the central reality of the Redemption, some have tried to synthesize history beginning not with salvation itself, with Christ dead and risen, but with a human paradigm that—paradoxically—is supposed to explain everything negative in the world, . . . and this before bringing to light the positive order that governs the world. But if the history of humanity is in fact, by revela-

---

[51] P. Schoonenberg, S.J., *God's World in the Making*, 82–3. See the balanced account of recent research on original sin presented by A. M. Dubarle, O.P., *The Biblical Doctrine of Original Sin*, tr. E. Stewart, 218–45. On the "sin of the world" see especially L. Ligier, S.J., *Péché d'Adam et péché du monde*; two books by J. de Fraine, S.J., *Adam and the Family of Man*, tr. D. Raible, C.PP.S., and *The Bible and the Origin of Man*. On the Genesis story of the Fall, see Dubarle, *op. cit.*, 45–87; Father Dubarle discusses both the mythical and the historical values of the story. On original sin in St. Paul see especially T. Barrosse, C.S.C., "Death and Sin in Saint Paul's Epistle to the Romans," *The Catholic Biblical Quarterly* 15 (1953) 438–59; S. Lyonnet, S.J., "Le péché originel et l'exégèse de Rom. 5:12–4," *Recherches de science religieuse* 44 (1956) 63–84; Dubarle, *op. cit.*, 142–200.

[52] P. Schoonenberg, S.J., *God's World in the Making*, 83.

tion, a holy history, is it not an error in method to make all axes converge backward toward sin? . . . Is this not to inverse the perspective of revelation such as scripture proposes it?[53]

Contemporary theologians tend to see original sin in the context of mankind in evolution toward the fullness of the Body of Christ; there is less stress on original sin as an accident of the past and more stress on original sin as a general disorientation.[54]

Whatever progress present-day theology makes in its investigations of original sin, it will be a progress in the Church guided by the Holy Spirit. Any theory or investigation must take into account the Church's teachings and her directives. It is impossible to say exactly to what extent future progress of the Church's understanding of original sin will be in the direction of or consonant with Teilhard's theological hypothesis.[55]

[53] C. Dumont, S.J., "La prédication du péché originel," *Nouvelle revue theologique* 83 (1961) 117.

[54] See P. Smulders, S.J., *The Design of Teilhard de Chardin,* tr. A. Gibson, 162–88. Father Smulders gives his own views on original sin as the weight of evil that each man carries by reason of his solidarity with mankind and anterior to his own personal sins, a condition that he freely accepts and ratifies by each personal sin. See especially P. Schoonenberg, S.J., *Man and Sin,* tr. J. Donceel, S.J., 177–91. Father Schoonenberg, although stating that "there is a presumption in favor of the classic doctrine of original sin" (191), advances the hypothesis that original sin is identical with the sin of the world. Schoonenberg seems to equate the sin of the world—and so by hypothesis original sin—with the sinful condition of mankind. This is right in line with Teilhard's hypothesis of original sin except that Teilhard's explanation is much more complete in that it tries to account for the existence of evil throughout the universe and not only in mankind.

[55] Certainly any investigation of original sin must be guided by and cannot be in conflict with Catholic dogma, in particular with the dogmas of the Council of Trent. Can original sin be equated with a general condition of humanity, a condition that is freely ratified and perpetrated by the collectivity of personal sins of individual men? This would be in line with Teilhard's hypothesis. The Council of Trent clearly assumed the existence

The Redemption

Christ's death was much more than a historical accident or a consequence of evil in the world and much more than simply an example for Christians. Christ's death marks "the complete immersion of the Divine Unity in the ultimate depths of multiplicity." The coming of Christ into the world by some oblique or indirect route would be incomprehensible. Christ had first to steep Himself in the matter of the cosmos so that He could raise it up to Himself. "It is because Christ has 'inoculated Himself' in matter that He is inseparable from the growth of spirit and so ingrained in the visible world that He could not be uprooted without shaking the foundations of the universe."[56] Christ could not have become the "way out" for the universe and the point of fulfillment for the universe without first becoming immanent in that universe. And to immerse Himself in the experimental world meant to undergo that world with its inevitable evil. Christ could not be Omega without

---

of an individual Adam and the origin of original sin in a unique act; but it did not define these things. "Infallibility guarantees from all error the proposition of the object of faith, but not exactly the theology around it." The theological reasons adduced for showing the truth of what is defined "receive from such a use a very high authority . . . but they are not necessarily free from error, . . . and can be bound up in a still quite imperfect theology." (M. M. Labourdette, O.P., *Le péché originel et les origines de l'homme*, 200.) It is not *defined* that original sin "proceeds from a sin actually committed by an individual Adam and which through generation is passed on to all . . ." (Encyclical *Humani Generis* of Pope Pius XII, Paulist Press, no. 66.) Nonetheless, that part of the Church's teaching which is not strictly infallible must be followed responsibly and serve as the guideline for further research in the area of the interpretation of the dogma of original sin. Teilhard was well aware of the teaching of the Councils and especially of the teaching of the Council of Trent. His intention was not only to leave this teaching intact but to safeguard the essence of the Council's teaching. ("Christologie et évolution," 1933, 8.)

[56] "Mon univers," 1924, *OE* 9, 89.

being immanent to, immersed in the world, and the price of immanence is suffering and death.[57]

We know that God is supremely free as regards His will to create the universe and to become incarnate and to redeem mankind. But God's plan of creation and salvation is perfect, and all the parts of that plan are integrally and perfectly related. As a result, from our standpoint in the experimental world and in the light of divine revelation, all the elements of God's plan appear to us—because of their perfect interconnection—to have a certain necessity. The Incarnation and the Redemption are so organically a part of God's whole creative plan that in the cosmic perspectives of Teilhard we cannot understand the mysteries of creation and the Incarnation and the Redemption without understanding them as intrinsically interrelated. In spite of the perfect freedom of each of God's salvific acts, we cannot understand "creation without God's immersion in the world through the Incarnation, nor the Incarnation without redemptive compensation."[58]

[57] See "Du cosmos à la cosmogénèse," 1951, *OE* 7, 270–3. See F. X. Durrwell, C.SS.R., *In the Redeeming Christ*, tr. R. Sheed, 5–7: "It is not just a question of cancelling a debt; condemnation is built into my nature, and the redemption must be accomplished in a physical transformation." (5.)

[58] "Comment je vois," 1948, 20–1. On the ontological distinction and fundamental unity of the order of creation and the order of redemption, see K. Rahner, S.J., *The Christian Commitment*, tr. C. Hastings, 38–74. Father Rahner's idea of Christian spirituality, however, is quite different from Teilhard de Chardin's. In making an application of his distinction between the creative and redemptive orders to the life of the Christian, Rahner seems to take the "order of creation" as a category of the Christian's positive approach to the world, the "incarnationalist" component of the Christian life. He seems to consider the "order of redemption" as the category of the "eschatological" component, implying renunciation and flight from the world. For Teilhard, of course, there is only one Christian spirituality, the spirituality of the Cross, and it has both "incarnational" and "eschatological" components. The redemptive order implies both renunciation *and* a constructive approach to the world.

Because we ourselves are part of God's plan and see that plan only "from the inside," the redemptive Incarnation appears to us as necessarily connected with the creative process. Teilhard by no means contests God's freedom; he does contest a conceptual pluralism that would artificially separate Redemption from Incarnation or either from the creative process. His viewpoint is the viewpoint of the Old and New Testaments: the history of salvation begins with creation. And for him as for St. Paul, Christ's redemption is the Redemption not just of man but of the universe.[59] Because of the nature of this evolving universe where evil is statistically inevitable at every level, Christ's work of the unification of all things in Himself appears to us as inevitably involving the pain of the Redemption. Christ's work of the Redemption of the world was a painful work, a work of suffering, because it included reparation for the sins of the world or—in Teilhard's somewhat esoteric expression—"compensation for statistical disorders."[60] Teilhard sees Christ's redemptive work as also including the "creative pain" of a "specific effort of unification that goes against a kind of inclination or inertia of existence in virtue of which participated being tends constantly to fall back toward multiplicity."[61]

Reparation for evil, compensation for disorder in the world, is the negative aspect of Christ's redemptive effort. But it is the positive aspect of the Redemption that is most stressed in Teilhard's perspective: the specific effort of the unification of a disordered world. "Jesus is truly He who bears the sins of the world; moral evil is mysteriously compensated for by suffering. But more fundamentally, Jesus is He who structurally overcomes in Himself,

[59] On the Redemption in St. Paul, see S. Lyonnet, S.J., "The Redemption of the Universe," *Contemporary New Testament Studies*, ed. Sister M. Rosalie Ryan, C.S.J., 423–36; M. Emmanuel McIver, O.S.U., "The Cosmic Dimensions of Salvation in the Thought of St. Paul," *Worship* 40 (1966) 156–64.

[60] "Comment je vois," 1948, 20.

[61] *Ibid.*

and for all of us, the resistance to spiritual ascent, a resistance that is inherent in matter."[62] Although Teilhard's vision of the whole structure of the universe, a vision that is theological as well as phenomenological, did not take on definite lines until after 1930, he considered the Redemption in terms of unification from the time of his early works.[63]

Very early too, Teilhard saw the necessity of understanding Christ's redemptive function as *universal*.[64] The idea that Christ's work of redemption is a *universal* work of unification is not without difficulties, as Teilhard well knew. For one thing, it seems to imply a naive notion of the earth as the center of the entire universe. Is the choice of this one small planet among countless possibly inhabited planets an arbitrary choice on the part of the Redeemer as the scene of His painful work of saving the universe? In the face of these and other difficulties, without being able to resolve them all, Teilhard holds firmly to the principle that there is one Christ in whom all things have their stability. This is the fundamental proposition. "Christ is everything or he is nothing."[65] Christ the Redeemer is, as Redeemer, also Christ the Unifier, so much so that it is not from Adam that mankind derives its real unity and solidarity but from Christ.[66]

It is, then, the creative and unificative aspect of Christ's redemptive function that Teilhard emphasizes. Again, in 1933, he writes that "the complete and ultimate sense of the Redemption is not only expiation but labor and conquest."[67] And in 1944 and 1945:

[62] "Christologie et évolution," 1933, 8.

[63] See "La lutte contre la multitude," 1917, *Ecrits*, 124.

[64] "Note sur le Christ universel," 1920, *OE* 9, 41.

[65] "Chute, rédemption, et géocentricité," 1920, 5. For a discussion of this problem, see C. Davis, *Theology for Today*, 164–70.

[66] "Chute, rédemption, et géocentricité," 1920, 3–4; "Mon univers," 1924, *OE* 9, 109.

[67] "Christologie et évolution," 1933, 8. Cf., however, C. Mooney, S.J., *Teilhard de Chardin and the Mystery of Christ*, 133: "We should expect

"The suffering Christ, without ever ceasing to be He who carries the sins of the world, and precisely *as such*, is being understood more and more by the faithful as He who carries and supports the weight of the world in its process of evolution."[68] Christ is "He who carries with the sins of the world the whole weight of the world in progress."[69] By His Passion and Cross Christ did make reparation for the sins of the world, taking them on Himself, and making atonement for them; this is the "negative" aspect of the Redemption. But there is a positive aspect that is brought into relief when the Redemption is put into the context of a world in process, in evolution; this positive aspect of the Redemption is the redemptive effort of Christ to unite all things to Himself.

Thus, in the context of a world in a state of becoming, in a state of converging evolution, creation and the Incarnation and the Redemption are seen as three complementary facets of one single process: pleromization, the gradual unification of all things in Christ in the fullness of the Pleroma. Creation, considered as "creative union," implies a certain immersion of the Creator in His work. Because the creative process inevitably engenders evil as a secondary statistical effect, a certain redemptive compensation on the part of the Creator is implied. Creation, Incarnation, and Redemption, in the framework of Teilhard's thought, are understood as structural elements of one single great mystery. "Taken in their

---

a very strong affirmation of the negative aspect of Redemption, namely, the reparation made by Christ for the sins of the world. . . . Yet no such affirmation is anywhere to be found." This statement seems exaggerated. Father Mooney makes a good point, however, when immediately after the above statement he criticizes Teilhard for not explicitly stating that Christ's reparation for sin is "a bearing of the weight of man's refusal to love." The notion of sin as a "refusal to love" is implicit in Teilhard's writings but he never brings it out. See also J. LeBlond, S.J., "Consacrer l'effort humain," *Etudes* 296 (1958) 63–8.

[68] "Introduction à la vie chrétienne," 1944, 8.
[69] "Christianisme et évolution," 1945, 6.

full sense, creation, Incarnation, and Redemption are not simply facts localized in time and space; they are truly dimensions of the world."[70]

The Cross: Reality and Symbol

Teilhard's views on the cosmic significance of the historical reality of the suffering and death of Christ are summed up in his understanding of what the Cross stands for. Teilhard's idea of the Redemption and what it means for men is condensed in a short but very rich paragraph from *The Divine Milieu.*

To sum up, Jesus on the Cross is both the symbol and the reality of the immense labor of the centuries which has, little by little, raised up the created spirit and brought it back to the depths of the divine milieu. He represents (and in a true sense, he is) creation, as, upheld by God, it reascends the slopes of being, sometimes clinging to things for support, sometimes tearing itself from them in order to pass beyond them, and always compensating, by physical suffering, for the setbacks caused by its moral downfalls.[71]

Christ's suffering and death on the Cross are not simply the suffering and death of an individual or a simple expiation. The death of Christ was an act of creative power. "Jesus crucified is not a reject; He is not defeated. On the contrary, He carries the weight of the universal course of progress with Him toward God."[72] "The Cross is the symbol and the real act of Christ raising the world with its

---

[70] "Quelques vues générales sur l'essence du Christianisme," 1939, 2. See "Christianisme et évolution," 1945, 8; "Réflexions sur le péché originel," 1947, 6–7; "Comment je vois," 1948, 20–1; "Du cosmos à la cosmogénèse," 1951, *OE* 7, 270–3.

[71] *DM*, 104.

[72] "La signification et la valeur constructrice de la souffrance," 1933, *OE* 6, 65–6.

whole burden of inertia and with all its natural vitality—an act of expiation, but also a hard journey of conquest." In Christ's death on the Cross we see "creation in the category of laborious effort."[73]

The Cross is not "a symbol of sadness, of limitation and repression"; it is the symbol of the difficult and painful effort of creative unification. Christianity does not ask man to live in the shadow of the Cross, but in the fire of its intense zeal.[74] In his life, man remains in what we can call the existential structure of the Cross. It is true that we are already "risen with Christ" by the sacrament of baptism and that our life here is pointed toward our own resurrection just as Christ's passion and death are pointed to and inseparable from His resurrection. But in this life the Christian is in the structure of the Cross; it is the life to come that is to be in the existential framework of Christ's resurrection. The Cross, then, is not only the symbol of Christ's whole redemptive function but also the symbol of the life of the Christian. In Christ crucified "each man must recognize his own true image. . . . The truth about our situation in this world is that we are here on the Cross."[75] By its

[73] "Quelques vues générales sur l'essence du Christianisme," 1939, 2. J. Daniélou, S.J., writes that the earliest sermons about the Cross celebrate its cosmic character, and quotes from a sermon of Gregory of Nyssa (*Catechetical Discourse* 23, 3): "I know thy mystery, O cross, for which thou wast raised up. Indeed, thou wast raised up over the world, to make steady that which was unsteady. One part of thee rises into the heavens, to point to the Word on High; another part stretches to right and left, to put to flight the fearsome power of the adversary and to gather the world together in unity; and one part of thee is planted in the earth, so that thou mayest unite the things that are on the earth and the things in hell with the things that are in heaven." (*Christ and Us*, tr. W. Roberts, 141.)

[74] *DM*, 102; "Christologie et évolution," 1933, 8.

[75] "La vie cosmique," 1916, *Ecrits*, 56. That man in this world is in the structure of the Cross is as true for Teilhard as for St. Augustine, for whom historical humanity, both the heavenly and the earthly "cities," is in the interior of the mystery of the Cross of Christ. See J. McCallin, "Christological Unity of the 'De Civitate Dei,'" *Revue des études augustiniennes* 12 (1966) 85–109.

birth and by its very nature, Christianity is marked by the sign of the Cross, and it can remain what it is only by identifying itself always more intensely with the meaning of the Cross.

What is this meaning of the Cross; what does the Cross mean as a symbol of Christianity and in particular of the life of the Christian? A few years before his death Teilhard wrote to his superiors in Rome setting forth his own ideas of how Christianity should be understood in the light of contemporary events and attitudes and how it should be presented in the contemporary world. In the brief essay intended for his superiors, Teilhard puts his ideas in the form of an answer to the question: how can we best state today the meaning of the Cross?[76]

In the usual and oversimplified form in which the Cross is presented today, not only in pious books and in sermons but even in seminary teaching, the Cross is above all a symbol of reparation and expiation. In this symbolism, the Cross has become the vehicle and the expression of a whole set of unfortunate psychological attitudes. For example, the world tends to be viewed as dominated by evil and death, human nature is considered as fallen and somehow twisted and is held in suspicion, whatever is material is mistrusted in an almost manichean way. Happily, these attitudes are in the context of a strong love for Christ suffering. But this love is almost exclusively "upward" instead of "forward," expressed in acts of painful detachment and mortification rather than in constructive activity. This situation, Teilhard continues, should be changed. "The Cross should be to us not just a sign of *escape*, but of forward movement. The Cross should shine before us not just as purifying, but as motivating."[77] And this change is demanded

[76] The full title of the essay is "Ce que le monde attend en ce moment de l'Eglise de Dieu: une généralisation et un approfondissement du sense de la croix," 1952.

[77] *Ibid.*, 4.

not just by the spirit of our age but by all that is most traditional in Christianity.

In Teilhard's theology of the Redemption, Christ not only bears the sins of the world but also the weight of the world in evolution. For Teilhard, then, the Cross is the symbol not only of reparation and expiation but the symbol of the redemptive unification of the world, of the progress of the world toward Christ-Omega. The Cross is the symbol of the synthesis of the "upward" component of sacrifice and adoring reparation and the "forward" component of progress through laborious effort. This is the Cross that Teilhard venerates; it is the same Cross as the Cross of traditional Christian piety, "but much more true." It is not only the symbol of the victory over sin but "the complete and dynamic symbol of a universe in the state of personalizing evolution."[78]

The notion of the Cross as the symbol of true progress runs through Teilhard's writings. The symbolism applies not only to Christ's redemptive work but also to the sharing in that redemptive work by the Christian. Christ's suffering and death are not only the model for the Christian; it is Christ's redemptive act that gives meaning and efficacy to man's work in building the world toward Christ. The Cross, as well as being the expression of what we have to undergo in the way of expiation is also, and primarily, the expression of "the creative but laborious effort of mankind climbing toward Christ who awaits it."[79] "The Cross is the symbol not only of the dark and regressive aspect of the universe, but also and above all of the luminous and conquering aspect; it is the symbol of progress and of victory . . . through difficult labor."[80]

[78] *Ibid.*, 5. See W. Whitla, "Sin and Redemption in Whitehead and Teilhard de Chardin," *Anglican Theological Review* 47 (1965) 81–93.

[79] "Intégration de l'homme dans l'univers," 1930, 13. See "La vie cosmique," 1916, *Ecrits*, 82; "Le prêtre," 1918, 288–9; "La route de l'ouest," 1932, 15.

[80] "Introduction à la vie chrétienne," 1944, 8.

Towards the peaks, shrouded in mist from our human eyes, whither the Cross beckons us, we rise by a path which is the way of universal progress. The royal road of the Cross is no more nor less than the road of human endeavor supernaturally righted and prolonged. Once we have fully grasped the meaning of the Cross, we are no longer in danger of finding life sad and ugly. We shall simply have become more attentive to its barely comprehensible solemnity.[81]

[81] *DM*, 103–4. See "The New Spirit," 1942, *FM*, 95: the Cross is "the Symbol, the Way, the very Act of progress." In spite of the fact that the Cross occupies such an important position in Teilhard's writings, some theologians continue to criticize him for not giving sufficient place to the Cross. This is hard to understand except as indicating a lack of familiarity with his writings. H. Urs von Balthasar objects that Teilhard's Christology seems to leave no place for the Cross; he has other objections to Teilhard's Christology, but this seems to be the main objection; see his "Die Spiritualität Teilhards de Chardin," *Wort und Wahrheit* 18 (1963) 339–50. See also H. Reidlinger, "The Universal Kingship of Christ," tr. T. Westow, *Who Is Jesus of Nazareth?* 119–27; Reidlinger wonders whether "the absence of a theological treatment of the cross in Teilhard constitutes an irreparable and basic lacuna in his synthesis or whether it can still be inserted as an afterthought." (124.)

6 ⋅ CHRISTIAN ENDEAVOR

IN TEILHARD DE CHARDIN'S view of the redemption of the world, Christ's redeeming act on the Cross has two aspects. It is an act of expiation and reparation for the sins of the world. And it is an act of creative unification; in His passion and death, Christ carries not only the weight of sin but the whole weight of the true progress of the world toward the fullness of the Pleroma, toward the final synthesis of all things in Himself. Teilhard views Christ's redemptive act not only as reparation for sin but also, and primarily, as an act of the laborious effort of the unification of the world.

The Christian shares in Christ's work of the redemption of the world, in the work of reparation for sin and of the unification of the world in Christ. Within the framework of Teilhard's religious world view, Christian spirituality can be considered as composed

173

of two complementary movements that correspond to the two aspects of Christ's redemptive act. These two movements are the renunciation of the world and the conquest of the world. Conquest and renunciation are two forms or modalities of the same basic tendency: to be united with God in and through the world.

Teilhard himself neatly summarizes his views on a total spirituality of Christian endeavor by saying that complete Christian endeavor consists of the following three elements:

1. collaborating passionately in the human effort in the conviction that, not only through our fidelity and obedience, but also through the *work* realised, we are working for the fulfillment of the Pleroma by preparing its more or less near-to-our-hand material;

2. in the course of this hard labor, and in the pursuit of an ever widening ideal, achieving a preliminary form of renunciation and of victory over a narrow and lazy egoism;

3. cherishing the "hollownesses" as well as the "fullnesses" of life— that is to say its passivities and the providential diminishments through which Christ transforms directly and eminently into himself the elements and the personality which we have tried to develop for him.[1]

[1] Letter written shortly before *The Divine Milieu*, quoted in *DM*, 93–4. The present chapter is by no means a complete treatise on the Christian life. It is a short outline of Teilhard's expressed views on the Christian life in the world, and it considers the ideas which Teilhard emphasizes the most in his writings. In no one work, not even *The Divine Milieu*, nor even in all his work taken as a whole, does Teilhard present a complete view of the Christian life or a complete Christian spirituality. G. Vass's criticism of *The Divine Milieu*, that it contains nothing in the way of practical hints to prayer or contemplation, treats the problem of moral evil with overwhelming optimism, and does not give great mention to respect for authority, can be applied to all of Teilhard's writings. [G. Vass, "Teilhard de Chardin and Inward Vision," *The Heythrop Journal* 2 (1961) 247.] The fact is simply that there are several areas of the spiritual life that Teilhard does not explicitly treat at great length; this does not at all indicate that he attached little importance to those areas. For example, on Teilhard's outstanding—even heroic—obedience, see R. d'Oince, S.J., "L'épreuve de l'obéissance dans la vie du Père Teilhard de Chardin," *L'homme devant Dieu*, 2. 331–46; L. Barjon, S.J., "Fidelité

In this chapter, we will follow this general outline of Teilhard's thought on the Christian in the world.

An Ethic of Conquest

Teilhard points out that it is the function of religion to give a form to mankind's searching, to give a form to the free psychic energy of the world. In its present state of development, mankind can accept a religion of only one kind: a religion that takes the dynamic and future-directed form of a movement of building toward some supreme unification of the world. Mankind is looking for a religion of conquest.[2]

In Chapter IV we presented Teilhard's views of human effort and activity as cooperating with God's creative action and contributing to the fullness of Christ. Teilhard sees the world as in the process of being created, and this continuous creation is directed to the Pleroma. Man shares in the creative process, contributes to it by his own activity in building the earth. Human endeavor is an essential factor in the development of this world that has been created and elevated in Christ, for the world's movement and progress "take the form of a vast movement of unification that converges toward Christ."[3] By the very work that he does, by his human activity, man is "building up to the fullness of Christ by preparing the more or less proximate matter of the Pleroma."[4] This is because "every movement of material growth is in the

---

chrétienne et fidelité religieuse du Père Teilhard de Chardin," *Foi vivante* 15 (1963) 70–82. Concerning Teilhard's own spiritual development, see H. de Lubac, S.J., *Teilhard de Chardin, the Man and His Meaning*, tr. R. Hague, 3–130.

[2] "Le Christianisme dans le monde," 1933, *OE* 9, 137. See "L'esprit de la terre," 1931, *OE* 6, 36–9.

[3] "Mon univers," 1918, *Ecrits*, 276.

[4] Letter of December 12, 1919, *Archives*, 140.

direction of spirit, and every movement of spiritual growth is ultimately for Christ."[5] The Christian, therefore, has a place in the
world and in the world's activity and work and progress; the Christian has not only the right but the duty to participate fully in the
"things of earth" and to be in the front line of the world's forward
movement. It is on this view of human endeavor as sacred, as
having—in itself—a religious value that Teilhard builds the outline
structure of what he calls an "ethic of conquest."[6]

His ethic of conquest appears in embryonic form in his early
writings.

I think that man has a fundamental obligation to extract from himself
and from the earth all that it can give; and this obligation is all the
more imperative that we are absolutely ignorant of what limits—they
may still be very distant—God has imposed on our natural understanding and power. To grow and to fulfill oneself to the utmost—
that is the law immanent in being. I do not believe that in allowing
us glimpses of a more divine life God has excused us from pursuing,
even on its natural plane, the work of creation. It would, I think,
be "tempting God" to let the world go its own way without trying to
master it and understand it more fully. We must do all we can to

---

[5] "Mon univers," 1924, *OE* 9, 96.

[6] The French is *morale de conquête*. Teilhard's ethic of conquest should
be clearly distinguished from a "spirituality of conquest" in the sense
of converting and Christianizing the world through Catholic Action. For
a description of this spirituality of conquest—which seeks to explicitly
Christianize all areas of human endeavor—as it has existed in France
and Belgium, see G. Thils, *Christian Attitudes*, 11–48. Thils describes a
spirituality of conquest that rests on a naturalistic optimism, that dispenses
with the notions of renunciation and eschatology, and that is explicitly
apostolic. Teilhard, on the other hand, bases his ethic of conquest on
Christian hope, makes renunciation a major element of his ethic, and
situates the notion of "conquest" precisely in eschatological perspectives.
His "conquest" is not a proselytizing attempt to make the world religious.
For him the world *has* a religious value, and his idea of conquest is that
it is a broad effort to build the world in view of the *eschaton*.

lessen death and suffering. We must develop the significance of revealed dogma through a more searching criticism of truth.[7]

Another brief early statement of the ethic of conquest is found in an essay of 1919. Teilhard writes of a "new category of duties" which should "find its place next to the ancient commandments." Up until recently, Christian morality has been for the most part an individualist morality, a morality of conduct and relations between individual persons. "From now on we must take more explicitly into account the obligation of man toward collective groups and even toward the universe: political duties, social duties, international duties. . . . In the first rank of these obligations are the laws of work and of research."[8]

In 1924 Teilhard formulates the ethic of conquest a little more fully.[9] To be faithful to God, man should take it as a primary duty to develop himself and to conquer the world. Teilhard considers both personal development and conquest of the world as a process of unification. The first impulse moving "the multiple," the disordered and unorganized, toward unity is Christ-Omega, who attracts all things to unity in themselves and among themselves and with Him—who moves "from up ahead" the multiplicity toward unity. This fundamental attraction of Christ-Omega takes form

[7] Letter of September 8, 1916, *MM*, 126. See the letter of January 29, 1917, *MM*, 176. These letters and the other letters that form the collection published in *The Making of a Mind*, tr. R. Hague, referred to in this book as *MM*, were written by Teilhard to his cousin, Marguerite Teilhard-Chambon, during the years 1914–1919. They contain much that gives insight into his early thought and into his skill as a spiritual director, as well as a picture of his personality. On Teilhard as seen in these letters as a spiritual director, see the article of his former superior, R. d'Oince, S.J., "Vivre dans la plénitude du Christ," *Christus* 9 (1962) 239–47.

[8] "Note pour l'évangélisation des temps nouveaux," 1919, *Ecrits*, 378–9. See also "La vie cosmique," 1916, *Ecrits*, 23–5; "La maîtrise du monde et le régne de Dieu," 1916, *Ecrits*, 81–5.

[9] "Mon univers," 1924, *OE* 9, 94–7.

and is expressed in man as the obligation and the will to unify and develop himself and to unify and so conquer the world around him. But man's obligation is far more than simply formal obedience to God's will. A juridical type of mind might understand man's obligation to work and to develop the world as an extrinsic obedience owed to a Master in virtue of a more or less arbitrary divine command. Some Christians seem to think that man should work simply to show his good will, that the material results of his work do not count but are just "the evidence of the obedience we have shown in doing useless things."[10] Teilhard reacts against these poor and discouraging views. What we do *is* important. "If Christ is Omega, nothing is foreign to the physical edification of His universal Body. . . . No matter how humble and hidden the action, provided that it be done in the direction of unification, . . . it is ultimately for Christ."[11] If it is true that what we do contributes to the building up of the world, that the tangible, material results of man's effort are important in moving the world closer to the fullness of the Pleroma, then it follows that the Christian should act with the utmost seriousness so that the world comes always a little closer to the fullness of Christ. More than any non-Christian, the Christian should promote human endeavor in all its forms, and especially that human effort that directly increases the general consciousness of mankind. The Christian should move in the direction of human progress audaciously and with Christian hope. The same point of view on the Christian's duty to develop himself and to build the world is found in *The Divine Milieu,* written a few years later. The Christian should be obedient and docile to God's will, and this fidelity should be manifested.

By his fidelity he must *build*—starting with the most natural territory of his own self—a work, an *opus,* into which something enters

10 *Ibid.,* 96.
11 *Ibid.*

from all the elements of the earth. *He makes his own soul* throughout all his earthly days; and at the same time he collaborates in another work, in another *opus*, which infinitely transcends, while at the same time it narrowly determines, the perspectives of his individual achievement: the completing of the world.[12]

The Christian should advance God's kingdom in every domain of mankind, for his faith imposes on him "the right and the duty to throw himself into the things of the earth."[13] The Christian, not less than other men, but more than other men because the perspectives of his endeavor extend to infinity, should "test every barrier, try every path, plumb every abyss. . . . God wills it, who willed that He should have need of it."[14]

Teilhard's ethic of conquest is a dynamic morality that goes beyond what he refers to as the usual and static "morality of equilibrium." "Ultimately, the world is built by moral powers. Reciprocally, morality has as its function the building up of the world. This is a new estimation of morality and it leads to a renewed moral program."[15] In the past, he goes on, moral standards have existed largely to protect the individual and to protect society. Morality has been understood chiefly as a fixed system of rights and duties, a system aimed at establishing and maintaining a static equilibrium among individuals. This has been accomplished primarily by a limitation of energies, by a restraint of forces. The idea has been that each individual person represents a sort of absolute term whose autonomy it is necessary to protect. But if we consider that man is an element in an evolving universe, an element destined to be fulfilled in a higher collective human consciousness that is even now in the process of formation, then we

[12] *DM*, 60–1.
[13] *Ibid.*, 69.
[14] *Ibid.*, 70.
[15] "Le phénomène spirituel," 1937, *OE* 6, 131. See "Quelques réflexions sur la conversion du monde," 1936, *OE* 9, 161–3.

must look again at our moral code. The real problem now is no longer to protect the individual and to safeguard his rights but to guide him to personal fulfillment so that the "personal quantity" that is still diffuse in mankind can be disengaged as much as possible. From now on, the highest morality is that which assumes the best development of the person, of society, and of the world. No longer to protect, but to develop. Up until now the moralist has been a kind of lawyer; he is becoming now "the technician and engineer of the spiritual energies of the world."[16]

Teilhard states three general principles of a renewed and dynamic morality, and briefly develops each of the three. The first principle is this: "that only is ultimately good which is in the direction of the growth of spirit."[17] In virtue of this rule, a number of things that might have been permitted under a static morality of equilibrium are now seen to be intolerable. In the past, a man had a right to use his life as he saw fit just as long as he infringed on no one else's rights. But now we see that no use of life and personal talents is morally correct except a use that is somehow in the service of mankind. Business ethics has tended to be dominated by the ideas of exchange and justice—so much for so much. In a dynamic morality the possession of wealth is morally good only to the extent that the wealth is working in the direction of spirit. Conjugal morality can no longer be satisfied simply by the proper establishment of a family; its principal object should be to render to conjugal love the spiritual power that it is capable of developing between husband and wife. The morality of the individual person can no longer allow room for neutral and harmless existences; it will oblige each person to develop himself, his freedom and personality and gifts, to the highest degree.

A second principle of a dynamic morality is this: "everything is at least fundamentally or partially good which is in the direction of

16 "Le phénomène spirituel," 1937, *OE* 6, 132.
17 *Ibid.*

the growth of spirit."[18] There is no place in a renewed morality for timidity or for "playing it safe." Whatever is good, whatever possesses some ascensional force and can promote greater human consciousness and spiritual growth, must be recognized and developed.

The third principle: "what is ultimately *best* is what assures the highest development of the spiritual powers of earth."[19] In a dynamic and open morality, the general and highest law is to develop everything in the direction of the greatest consciousness, of the greatest spiritual growth. Teilhard is well aware that "these perspectives will seem crazy to those who do not see that life is, from its origins, groping, adventurous, and dangerous. But these perspectives will grow, like an irresistible idea, on the horizon of new generations."[20] Finally, a renewed and dynamic morality is a religious and theistic morality. A morality of equilibrium is closed on itself; logically, it can be agnostic and absorbed in the present. "A dynamic morality," in contrast, "is necessarily inclined to the future in the pursuit of God."[21] In the last analysis Teilhard's renewed and dynamic morality, his ethic of conquest, opens up into a spirituality, a program of Christian holiness and a mystique of union with God in and through the world.

Purity and Personal Unity

Teilhard often states and stresses the importance in the life of the Christian of three basic Christian virtues: purity, charity, self-denial. He further stresses the importance of a proper Christian understanding of all three. In an ethic and a spirituality of con-

[18] *Ibid.*
[19] *Ibid.*, 133.
[20] *Ibid.*, 134–5.
[21] *Ibid.*, 135. See A. Devaux, "Teilhard et la construction d'une morale pour notre temps," *Revue Teilhard de Chardin* 6, no. 23 (1965) 31–8.

quest by unification, purity, charity, and self-denial are the three fundamental operative virtues. They are the virtues of unification. The special effect of purity is to concentrate the multiple powers of the soul; it is the unification of the person. Charity is directed to the unification of persons among themselves. Finally, the function of Christian self-denial is the "de-centering" of each person from his own egoism so that he might be centered on Christ; it is the unification of all in One.[22] More exactly, the Christian virtues of purity (chastity) and charity, practiced in a spirit of Christian self-denial, are functionally directed to unification in Christ.[23] "Renunciation and mortification are basic to purity—and even more basic to charity."[24] But purity and charity are by no means static virtues; seen within an ethic and a spirituality of conquest, they are essentially constructive forces. "Purity, charity —we might think that these Christian virtues are *static* virtues. . . . The ethic of Jesus might seem timid and pale to partisans of a vigorous and aggressive conquest of the summits toward which Life rises. But in reality, *no earthly effort* is more constructive, *more progressive*, than the ethic of Jesus."[25] Let us consider more in detail Teilhard's views on purity, on charity, and on detachment and renunciation.

The specific action of the virtue of purity is to unify the powers of the Christian so that, "rising above the multiple and disorganizing attraction of things," he can "steep his unity—that is, bring his

22 "Science et Christ," 1921, *OE* 9, 60. See "L'âme du monde," 1918, *Ecrits*, 229.

23 "L'union créatrice," 1917, *Ecrits*, 194.

24 "La lutte contre la multitude," 1917, *Ecrits*, 130.

25 *Ibid.*, 127. See "The Mass on the World," 1923, *HU*, 36, where Teilhard asks Christ to teach him "the true meaning of purity: not a debilitating separation from all created reality but an impulse carrying one through all forms of created beauty," and to show him "the true nature of charity: not a sterile fear of doing wrong but a vigorous determination that all of us together shall break open the doors of life."

spirituality to maturity—in the fires of divine simplicity."[26] Purity
is not a negative virtue but a positive unification and spiritualization of forces. It is a personalizing virtue. Sins against purity can
now be seen for what they really are: a waste of the energy of
personalization. They introduce into the soul a principle of corrup-
tion and disaggregation; they destroy part of the person's potential
for interior unity.[27]

In a dynamic Christian ethic, chastity is the opposite of waste; it
is a unification and a conservation by sublimation, a progressive
spiritualization of profound human drives. "Purity . . . knits together the fibers of the soul."[28] There is nothing puritanical in
Teilhard's idea of chastity. It is not a virtue of flight or withdrawal
from sex but the virtue of "conquest by sublimation of the profound spiritual powers still dormant under the mutual attraction of
the sexes."[29] "To be pure has heretofore meant principally to
abstain, to guard oneself undefiled. The chastity of tomorrow will
be understood above all as the sublimation of the powers of the
flesh and of every passion."[30] In spite of outward appearances,
purity is not a passive virtue but "essentially an active one, because it concentrates God in us and in those who are subject to our
influence."[31] Neither the chastity proper to the married state nor
the chastity of celibacy is "a refusal to love." Chastity is, rather,

[26] "La lutte contre la multitude," 1917, *Ecrits*, 126.
[27] "Esquisse d'un univers personnel," 1936, *OE* 6, 93; "Les noms de la
matière," 1919, *Ecrits*, 426.
[28] "Mon univers," 1924, *OE* 9, 99.
[29] "Le coeur de la matière," 1950, 34. "L'évolution de la chasteté," 1934,
is a dense and carefully written consideration of the Christian virtue of
chastity in the perspectives of an ethic of unification and conquest. See
also "L'éternel féminin," 1918, *Ecrits*, 253–62, written in a kind of prose-
poem style in the manner of the wisdom literature of the Old Testament;
"Esquisse d'un univers personnel," 1936, *OE* 6, containing a section on
sexuality (91–6) that ends in a consideration of chastity.
[30] "Christologie et évolution," 1933, 13.
[31] Letter of December 5, 1916, *MM*, 149.

an increasing refinement of the power to love. It is not weakness but strength, not flight but conquest, not waste or dissolution but a growing interior unity, not a curtailment of the power to love but a concentration and spiritualization of that power.

In *The Divine Milieu* Teilhard expands his consideration of chastity to include purity in the broad sense, purity of heart. It is well worth quoting him at some length.

Purity, in the wide sense of the word, is not merely abstaining from wrong (that is only a negative aspect of purity), nor even chastity (which is only a remarkable special instance of it). It is the rectitude and the impulse introduced into our lives by the love of God sought in and above everything.

He is spiritually impure who, lingering in pleasure or shut up in selfishness, introduces, within himself and around himself, a principle of slowing-down and division in the unification of the universe in God.

He is pure, on the other hand, who, in accord with his place in the world, seeks to give Christ's desire to consummate all things precedence over his own immediate and momentary advantage.

Still purer and more pure is he who, attracted by God, succeeds in giving that movement and impulse of Christ's an ever greater continuity, intensity and reality—whether his vocation calls him to move always in the material zones of the world (though more and more spiritually), or whether, as is more often the case, he has access to regions where the divine gradually replaces for him all other earthly nourishment.

Thus understood, the purity of beings is measured by the degree of the attraction that draws them towards the divine center, or, what comes to the same thing, by their proximity to the center. Christian experience teaches us that it is preserved by recollection, mental prayer, purity of conscience, purity of intention, and the sacraments. Let us be satisfied, here, with extolling its wonderful power of condensing the divine in all around us.[32]

[32] *DM*, 132–3.

Love as the Basic Energy of Evolution

In Teilhard de Chardin's continuing reflection on supernatural revelation and its meaning in terms of the experimental world, nowhere is there a more marked development than in his thought on love and Christian charity. In 1916 he writes that he "would be hard put to it to defend rationally, or at any rate scientifically (in the wide sense of the word) the precept of charity." He has not yet even begun to develop a theory, much less a theology of charity. "It's a good thing," he adds, "that facts are more important than theory and that we know for certain, from Our Lord's own words, that we must love our neighbor as ourselves. Explanations don't matter."[33] In 1917 he still considers charity to be a unifying but *static* virtue.[34] In his early essays Teilhard considers charity as unifying persons among themselves, "a role particularly divine and providential in a world where the appearance of intelligence began a crisis of autonomy and individualism."[35] Two years later he decries the fact that there is no adequate theology of human love and of its transformation into the love of God.[36] His views on charity begin to take some form finally in *The Divine Milieu*.

Christian charity, which is preached so fervently by the Gospels, is nothing else than the more or less conscious cohesion of souls engendered by their communal convergence *in Christo Jesu*. It is impossible to love Christ without loving others (in proportion as these others are moving towards Christ). And it is impossible to love others

[33] Letter of August 4, 1916, *MM*, 117. In later letters to his cousin, Teilhard comments on the remarks about Christian charity in her letters to him. See *MM*, 133, 137, 146, 180–1.

[34] Letter of February 5, 1917, *MM*, 181.

[35] "L'union créatrice," 1917, *Ecrits*, 194. See "L'âme du monde," 1918, *Ecrits*, 229; "L'éternel féminin," 1918, *Ecrits*, 253–62. See "Panthéisme et Christianisme," 1923, 11; "Mon univers," 1924, *OE 9*, 99.

[36] "Note pour l'évangélisation des temps nouveaux," 1919, *Ecrits*, 378.

(in a spirit of broad human communion) without moving nearer to Christ. Hence automatically, by a sort of living determinism, the individual divine *milieux*, in proportion as they establish themselves, tend to fuse one with another; and in this association they find a boundless increase of their ardour. This inevitable conjunction of forces has always been manifested, in the interior lives of the saints, by an overflowing love for everything which, in creatures, carries in itself a germ of eternal life.[37]

In the early 1930's Teilhard indicates that he is beginning to see Christian charity as a dynamic force. "Until now, to love my neighbor has meant to do him no harm and to bandage his wounds. From now on, charity—without ceasing to be compassionate—will find its consummation in a life given for the advancement of all."[38] But this is still a somewhat vague position; Teilhard will not begin to develop a full theory of Christian charity until after 1940. It will be necessary first to elaborate in evolutionary perspectives a general theory of love.

Beginning in 1931 Teilhard is occupied for a decade in working out a general scientific phenomenology of love as the energy of evolution. Love is described as the strongest, most universal, and most mysterious of cosmic energies. The cosmic energy of love is, in essence, the attraction of each element of the universe by the term of universal evolution, Omega; it is the primitive and universal psychic energy.[39] In this cosmic view, love exists at all levels of the universe. In its most primitive forms it is hardly distinguishable from molecular forces. Later in the evolutionary process it tends to be almost identifiable with reproductive drives.

[37] *DM*, 144.

[38] "Christologie et évolution," 1933, 13. There is a similar statement in "Essai de l'intégration de l'homme dans l'univers," 1930, fourth lecture, 13–4.

[39] "L'esprit de la terre," 1931, *OE* 6, 41.

With the appearance of man, love enters the realm of reflexive consciousness, of the spiritual. Love is a sacred reserve of energy; it is the lifeblood of spiritual evolution.[40]

Five years later Teilhard develops this point of view in a tightly reasoned three-part analysis of human love.[41] Beginning with sexual love, the analysis moves to a love that he calls the "human sense." It differs from sexual love in that it is not exclusive but outgoing to all men. In its simplest form the "human sense" is manifested in the love of friendship; in higher forms it is shown in the larger friendships engendered by devotion to a common cause or project, in patriotism, in a sense of world unity. In the third stage of his analysis, he considers the "cosmic sense," "the more or less undetermined affinity that binds us psychologically to the whole of the universe that envelops us."[42] Ultimately and fundamentally, the cosmic sense is the love of Omega, the Center of centers, toward whom universal evolution is converging.

The cosmic sense is a love; it cannot be anything else. It is a love because it is directed to a unique and complementary object of a personal nature. It must be a love, for its role is to dominate by bringing them to fulfillment the love of man for woman and the love of the human being for all other human beings. In the cosmos as I have described it, the possibility is clear—as unlikely as the expression may seem—of *loving the universe*. And it is only within this act that love can grow and develop with unlimited intensity.[43]

40 *Ibid.*, 42.

41 "Esquisse d'un univers personnel," 1936, *OE* 6, 89–105.

42 *Ibid.*, 101. For a later and fuller analysis of the "human sense," see "La montée de l'autre," 1942, *OE* 7, 77–81. *Le sens humain*, translated in this chapter as "human sense," is translated in Chapter I as "human point of view." The expression *le sens humain* is a somewhat flexible one for Teilhard; I have translated it according to the context in which he uses it.

43 "Esquisse d'un univers personnel," 1936, *OE* 6, 104.

At each stage of his three-stage analysis Teilhard shows that love
—sexual love and the human sense and the cosmic sense—is personalizing. More precisely, love leads to and is itself a form of
union. And every true union, far from confusing the elements
united, individualizes them and makes them more themselves.
Union differentiates the members united. Thus love, because it is a
unitive energy, is the energy of personal development and fulfillment, the energy of personalization.

A little later Teilhard writes in a letter that he is discovering
more clearly the great value and function of the love of God in
man's effort to build the world, and that he intends to include this
consideration in his next essay on human energy.[44] In an essay
written soon after, he sums up what he has written about love in
the previous essays, and goes further in marking the importance of
Omega. Through human evolution the universe has reached a
superior level where its physical and spiritual powers progressively
take the form of a fundamental affinity that binds individuals among
themselves and to Omega. The elements of the world tend to
become more and more personalized through accession to a Center
of unification that is itself personal. Further, this Center of ultimate
confluence radiates the basic energy of the world. Teilhard asks
what term we can give to this influence, to this basic universal
energy. "Only one," he answers, "love."[45] Teilhard then goes on
to verify his hypothesis that love is the basic human energy,
human energy in its pure state. He proceeds first by a psychological
analysis to show that love carried to a certain universal degree by
the perception of the Center Omega is the only power capable of
totalizing the possibilities of human action.[46] With very close and

[44] Letter of June, 1937, quoted in L. Swan, "Memories and Letters,"
Teilhard de Chardin: Pilgrim of the Future, ed. N. Braybrooke, 45.

[45] "L'énergie humaine," 1937, *OE* 6, 180–1. See "La centrologie," 1944,
OE 7, 127–9.

[46] L'énergie humaine," 1937, *OE* 6, 181.

sometimes difficult reasoning, he tries to show that only love can unify in a coherent synthesis the actions of the person, the person himself, and—finally—all persons in one unified mankind.[47]

But, as Teilhard admits at the end of the psychological analysis, he could not have made it without a model. The model is Christianity, and Teilhard now does an analysis of Christianity considered simply as historical phenomenon. He finds that Christ "considered in the full realism of His Incarnation" is perfectly comparable to the Omega of his previous analysis, and that Christ tends to produce exactly the spiritual totalization that is anticipated.[48] Christ presents Himself as a personal Term of union in His Church. Christianity, then, is precisely a phylum of love, the axis of love along which the evolution of the universe is progressing toward a final synthesis of love and unity and personalization in Christ. Teilhard is still in a generalized scientific phenomenology of love, even in his consideration of Christianity. It is not until later that he reflects theologically on his general theory or hypothesis of love as the basic energy of evolution, the basic energy of human unification, and an energy that, phenomenologically, finds its clearest expression and most elevated action in "the Christian phenomenon."

In a final period of the development of his scientific phenomenology of love, Teilhard concentrates on the place of love in the evolutionary process of social totalization. Human evolution is going on, even now, and progressing along an axis of increasing complexity and of correlatively increasing consciousness. Mankind is moving—converging—toward a maximum point of organization or complexity and of mass consciousness; this point is the final

[47] *Ibid.*, 182–91. See "L'apport spirituel de l'extrême orient," 1947, *Monumenta Nipponica* 12 (1956) 9.

[48] "L'énergie humaine," 1937, *OE* 6, 192. Teilhard presents a brief synthesis of his theory of love in *PM*, 264–9, 295–6. It includes the main elements of the essays written between 1931 and 1937.

synthesis with Omega. The basic process of mankind's evolution toward Omega is one of social totalization. But, Teilhard asks, "does it not appear . . . that social totalization leads directly to spiritual retrogression and greater materialism?"[49] Is this not the experience of all totalitarian states? If social totalization sometimes leads to the subhuman conditions of totalitarian society, Teilhard answers, it is not the principle of social totalization that is wrong but that the principle has been misunderstood and wrongly applied. If mankind is to achieve spiritual growth through collectivization,

the first essential is that the human units involved in the process shall draw closer together, not merely under the pressure of *external* forces, or solely by the performance of material acts, but directly, center to center, through *internal* attraction. Not through coercion or enslavement to a common task, but through *unanimity* in a common spirit.[50]

True union, union of heart and spirit, does not enslave or in any way diminish the persons it unites. It *personalizes* them. "In a world where the formula is 'toward personalization through union,' it is obvious that the forces of love have a dominating place—for love is precisely the bond that draws together and unites persons among themselves."[51] True union is union of love, and this is the fundamental and necessary place of love in the evolution of mankind.

Only union *through* love and *in* love (using the word "love" in its widest and most real sense of "mutual internal affinity"), because it brings individuals together not superficially and tangentially but center to center, can physically possess the property of not merely differenti-

[49] "Life and the Planets," 1945, *FM*, 118–9.
[50] *Ibid.*, 119.
[51] "La centrologie," 1944, *OE* 7, 125.

ating but also personalizing the elements which comprise it. Even under the irresistible compulsion of the pressures causing it to unite, mankind will only find and shape itself if men can learn to love one another in the very act of drawing closer.[52]

In three essays written between 1950 and 1954, Teilhard completes his analysis of love. He fills out his general hypothesis of love as the psychic energy of evolution by pointing out the necessity of some existing autonomous center that would be structurally and functionally capable of inspiring and releasing within mankind the necessary forces of love and unanimity. He reasons that "only a veritable *super-love,* the attractive power of a veritable 'super-being,' can of psychological necessity dominate, possess, and synthesize the host of earthly loves."[53] If there is no really existing and personal center of universal coherence, there can be no true union among totalized mankind. Man's urge toward something ahead of him "cannot achieve its full fruition except by combining with another and still more fundamental aspiration—one from above, urging him toward Someone."[54]

Teilhard suggests that the increasing contemporary interest in scientific and social progress and in the research that makes that progress possible is evidence of a new attitude of man toward the universe, of a growing mystical current that has as its basis the conviction that "the universe, viewed in its complete workings, is *ultimately lovable and loving.*" At the same time, the charity of the Gospels is beginning to appear basically as a love of a universal evolution that is "christified to its roots." Teilhard suggests that

[52] "The Directions and Conditions of the Future," 1948, *FM,* 235. See "La centrologie," 1944, *OE* 7, 126.

[53] "How May We Conceive and Hope that Human Unanimization Will Be Realized on Earth?" 1950, *FM,* 286–7. See "On the Probable Coming of an 'Ultra-Humanity,'" 1950, *FM,* 277–80.

[54] "How May We Conceive and Hope that Human Unanimization Will Be Realized on Earth?" 1950, *FM,* 288.

this is more than a coincidence. Is Christianity justified, he asks, in its claim to bind objectively the rapidly convergent portions of the human wave to the real and existing Center of their evolutionary convergence? "If I were not convinced from birth that this is so, I think I should ask myself the question."[55] In its final stages, Teilhard's theory of love has become a sign that points to Christianity, an *apologia* in the classic sense of the word. The scientific phenomenology of love is open to and even demands a complementary theological consideration of Christian charity.

Christian Charity

In 1940 Teilhard de Chardin picks up his theological reflection on charity where he left it about a decade earlier. But now he has already developed the main outline of his phenomenology of love, and it is within this new framework of love as the driving force and unitive factor of evolution that he restudies Christian charity. For the next decade he will work along two converging lines, extending his phenomenological hypothesis of love and constructing a theological theory of Christian charity. The two lines are converging, but they are distinct. In his theory of love, while admitting the extrinsic influence of Christianity as a partial model of his theory, he uses only the "observable phenomena" as a source. His reflection on Christian charity, on the other hand, draws from two sources: his broadly scientific theory of love and the data of Christian revelation; it is a properly theological reflection. The two distinct but converging lines of thought, the theory of love and the theological reflection on charity, do influence one another; the distinction between them, however, remains clearly marked.

An insight into the direction that his thought on charity will take can be gained from a note written during his annual retreat in 1940. "Into the famous text of Romans 8:38, . . . 'who will

[55] "The Singularities of the Human Species," 1954, *AM*, 273.

separate us from the love of Christ,' I introduce a shade of meaning that differs from St. Paul's (even though it follows his line).
For St. Paul, charity is the force greater than all forces; for me, it
is the *dynamic* milieu that embraces and superanimates them
all."[56]

About the same time, Teilhard writes of the need to incorporate
into our charity the love of mankind and the love of the entire
universe, to make our own in Christian charity "the anxieties, the
hopes, the growth" of mankind and "to make the progress of the
world part of our perspective on the Kingdom of God."[57] Charity
is not just a sentiment. We are destined in the evolution of the
cosmos to be *one,* and "the fundamental law and operative guideline of all our activity is to work toward this synthesis." The
precept of charity, then, is not in the domain of pure sentiment but
at the center of "the system of universal energies and necessary
laws."[58] Charity is, and must be, not static but dynamic.

What the modern mind finds disconcerting in Christian charity is
its negative or at least static aspect, and also the "detached" quality
of this great virtue. "Love one another . . ." Hitherto the evangelical
precept has seemed simply to mean, "Do not harm one another," or,
"Seek with all possible care and devotion to diminish injustice, heal
wounds and soften enmities in the world around you." Hitherto, also,
the "supernatural" gift of ourselves which we were required to make
to God and to our neighbour appeared to be something opposed to
and destructive of the bonds of feeling attaching us to the things of
this world.

But if charity is transplanted into the cone of time nothing remains
of these apparent limitations and restrictions. Within a universe of

[56] Quoted in H. de Lubac, S.J., *Teilhard de Chardin, the Man and His
Meaning,* tr. R. Hague, 37, footnote 28.
[57] "La parole attendue," 1940, *Cahiers Pierre Teilhard de Chardin,* 4,
La parole attendue, 26.
[58] "L'atomisme de l'esprit," 1941, *OE* 7, 59.

convergent structure the only possible way in which an element can draw closer to its neighbouring elements is by *tightening the cone—* that is to say, by causing the whole layer of the world of which it is a part to move towards the apex. In such an order of things no man can love his neighbour without drawing nearer to God—and, of course, reciprocally (but this we knew already). But it is also impossible (this is newer to us) to love either God or our neighbour without assisting the progress, in its physical entirety, of the terrestrial synthesis of the spirit: since it is precisely the progress of this synthesis which enables us to draw closer together among ourselves, while at the same time it raises us towards God. Because we love, and in order that we may love even more, we find ourselves happily and especially compelled to participate in all the endeavours, all the anxieties, all the aspirations and also all the affections of the earth—*in so far as these embody a principle of ascension and synthesis.*[59]

When placed in the context of a universe converging on Christ-Omega, charity becomes *universal, dynamic,* and *synthesizing.* Since everything in the universe is moving toward Christ-Omega, since the evolution of the world is in reality a Christogenesis, the whole universe and all in it is charged with the presence of Christ and is the object of Christian charity. And because the forward movement of the world is a Christogenesis, because Christ is fully attainable only at the term and the summit of cosmic evolution, we cannot enter into the progress of the world except in the effort to complete and synthesize everything in Him. The most active and the most complete agent of evolution is charity; it is impossible to adhere to Christ without involving oneself in the forward movement of the world. Charity is the force by which mankind is built toward its final fulfillment. It is, then, the entire human effort that "enters, organically and with full right, into the preoccupations

[59] "The New Spirit," 1942, *FM*, 95. See "Introduction à la vie chrétienne," 1944, 1.

and the ambitions of charity."[60] To love Christ, we must help advance mankind and the whole universe toward Him. Furthermore, charity synthesizes all our aims and activities. On the scale of ordinary daily life, most of our activities fall outside the scope of charity. To love is always to love a person, to come closer to a person "center to center"; but most of our daily activities involve things, impersonal matters, the mundane business of living. Yet if all things are directed toward Christ-Omega in a world of convergent evolution, then we can love Christ in every aim and activity, provided only that it is somehow in the direction of the world's forward movement toward Him. Our every aim and activity can be a "center to center" relation to Christ, an act of Christian love. Charity is the superior form of spiritual energy in which all the other energies of the soul are transformed insofar as they come into the field of force of Omega. The Christian can love not only while he acts, but in *acting*; he can unite himself directly to the Divine Center by his very action no matter what the form of that action.[61]

In the last five years of his life Teilhard sees Christian charity more clearly than ever as the plenitude and the fulfillment of human love in all its forms. Charity is natural love elevated into "the Christocentric zone of the universe . . . where it manifests its astonishing power to transform everything."[62] During this period he gives special emphasis to the idea that Christian charity can and should be not only love of God and love of neighbor but also a love of all creation. Love is the psychic energy of evolution, and

[60] "Super-humanité, super-Christ, super-charité," 1943, *OE* 9, 214.

[61] "Super-humanité, super-Christ, super-charité," 1943, *OE* 9, 215–6. See also "Christianisme et évolution," 1945, 9.

[62] "Le coeur de la matière," 1950, 28. In more traditional terms we could say that grace elevates and perfects nature, that supernatural charity is natural love elevated to the level of the supernatural, into "the Christocentric zone."

evolution itself is a universal forward movement converging on Christ, a Christogenesis. Christian charity, then, can and should include a love of the universe and of universal evolution. Love in all its forms can and should be "christified" into Christian charity.[63] Teilhard has fully integrated his scientific phenomenology of love and his theological reflection on charity.

Human Endeavor and Christian Detachment

It would be a serious mistake to see Teilhard as a proponent of a spirituality that is only "creative," a spirituality that stresses only development and progress and that neglects Christian mortification and renunciation.[64] His spiritual doctrine is the doctrine of the Cross. A constantly recurring theme in his writings is the necessary connection between detachment and true development or progress. A spirituality of conquest is necessarily a spirituality of detachment and renunciation; "the world, being subject to the world, the duty to serve the world, these are as heavy to carry as a Cross," and in Christ on the Cross "each man must recognize his own true image."[65] For in this world we are on the Cross, and nowhere more than in our efforts to help advance the world along its path to Christ-Omega. As a matter of fact, the sincere Christian promoter of progress is a person of continuous mortification. "He works; he forgets himself; he even becomes detached, for he loves the causes he is working for more than himself and he looks for the success of life more than for egotistical satisfaction of his own personal success."[66]

---

[63] See "Du cosmos à la cosmogénèse," 1951, *OE* 7, 273–5; "Le Christique," 1955, 12–3.

[64] See Louis Bouyer, *Introduction to Christian Spirituality*, tr. Mary Perkins Ryan, 163–4.

[65] "La vie cosmique," 1916, *Ecrits*, 56.

[66] "La maîtrise du monde et le régne de Dieu," 1916, *Ecrits*, 82.

Even though his suffering does not immediately appear to be an expiation or a sign of rupture with the world—but, rather, as the ransom of progress—he can certainly consider himself an authentic servant of the Cross. He does not hate the world in any puritanical sense, but he does hate the world in the sense of the Gospels. He hates the world cultivated just for its own sake or only for pleasure, the world that is closed and turned in on itself, the world that regresses from Omega and adores itself. But the world that moves toward Christ he loves, and he gives himself to it. In so giving himself, he "loses himself"; he practices Christian renunciation and detachment. He adheres to Christ in Christian purity and charity and in detachment, the base and inevitable concomitant of purity and charity.[67]

Attachment to the world and its progress toward Christ necessarily implies a high degree of detachment. Attachment and detachment go together in an effort that is devoid of self-interest; when a person works so as to bring himself and the world closer to God, he simultaneously—in the same act—personalizes himself and loses himself in Christ. "Christian action, by its nature, both detaches one and unites one to Our Lord."[68] Christian action detaches the Christian because true attachment to the world's forward movement is identical with an austere detachment from self-seeking.[69] In other words, Christian detachment *proceeds* from Christian action. The Christian option, then, is not a choice between detachment from the world's progress and attachment to that progress; it is not a choice between heaven and earth. It is a choice "between two kinds of effort to build the earth: in Christ or outside Him."[70]

[67] See "La lutte contre la multitude," 1917, *Ecrits*, 130; "L'union créatrice," 1917, *Ecrits*, 194; "L'âme du monde," 1918, *Ecrits*, 229.

[68] Letter of July 4, 1915, *MM*, 58.

[69] See "Le prêtre," 1918, *Ecrits*, 292; "Forma Christi," 1918, *Ecrits*, 346–7.

[70] "Note pour l'évangélisation des temps nouveaux," 1919, *Ecrits*, 379.

Teilhard's point of view on detachment through action is found scattered among his essays of 1916–1919. In late 1919, this point of view is presented in a more developed form in an exchange of letters between Teilhard, then studying for a doctorate in geology at Paris, and Maurice Blondel, older and well established as a Catholic philosopher.[71] A mutual friend, Father Auguste Valensin, S.J., sent two or three of Teilhard's essays to Blondel; Blondel returned the essays with his comments.[72] In his reply to Blondel's first criticism, Teilhard remarks on their fundamental agreement but adds that there seems to be a divergence of views that it would be profitable to state as accurately as possible. Since the difference in views concerns the question of Christian detachment and renunciation, Teilhard tries to present as clearly as possible his idea of detachment through action.

The first form of Christian renunciation that comes to mind, Teilhard writes to Blondel, is renunciation through a rupture with the world. According to this form of renunciation, the Christian should close all doors to the outside world, cut out its light and not listen to its voice. There are two lights and two voices, that of God and that of the world. It is by shutting out the world that we will hear God's voice and enter into His light. Teilhard has no personal objection to this idea of detachment. But he finds it impracticable, unworkable as a way of life for the vast majority of Christians. It is not, therefore, a general solution to the problem of what our attitude should be in face of the supernatural; it does not promise for the majority of men the possibility of a maximum union with Christ.[73] There must be another and more general view of Chris-

---

[71] The letters are presented and commented on by H. de Lubac, S.J., in *Archives*.

[72] Father de Lubac thinks that these essays probably included some of the following, all now published in *Ecrits*: "La vie cosmique," 1916; "Le Christ dans la matière," 1916; "La lutte contre la multitude," 1917; "La puissance spirituelle de la matière," 1919. See *Archives*, 125.

[73] *Archives*, 135–7.

tian renunciation. Teilhard goes on to present his own idea of what this view should be.

An immense and necessary part of the life of each of us is given over to positive work, to the natural human and social effort. This effort is imposed on us by circumstances outside our control, and it is a penance. But it also possesses a spiritualizing value of the first order, not only by the moral training it gives us *but also* by the positive results of the *work itself.* . . . Can we really affirm that charity, cut off from the life-blood and the battle of daily human life, would not perish in a world transformed into a monastery?

In the routine of each life and in the history of the human race as a whole there is an enormous potential for positive achievement, and it must not be allowed to miscarry. It is absolutely necessary that Christ be as large as my life, my *whole* life, so that I can be conscious of growing in Him not only by ascetical restrictions and the supremely unifying pains of suffering but also by the whole positive effort of my human tasks. This is necessary. Otherwise, Christianity would be robbing me of the courage to act.[74]

The formation of the Pleroma, then, must operate not according to a process of rupture with the natural world but by a law of *transformation* of the natural world. "The supernatural plenitude of Christ rests on the natural plenitude of the world."[75] Teilhard is simply applying the principle that grace builds on and transforms nature. His originality lies in the fact that he sees clearly the implications of this law of transformation for a practical Christian attitude of renunciation.

In general, Christ gives Himself to us in and through the world, a world to be fulfilled in Him. We cannot simply and naively throw aside all created things for the "pearl of great price"; that attitude is just not applicable to real life. To abandon the world in

74 *Ibid.,* 138.
75 *Ibid.,* 139.

order to search for union with God can even be an illusion, a
temptation to avoid reality and the hard effort it demands. The
ordinary way to Christian detachment is through an enthusiastic
collaboration with the whole human effort in the consciousness
that "by the results of our work we are . . . preparing the more or
less proximate matter of the Pleroma."[76] In this difficult labor in
pursuit of an ideal, we will find a call to renunciation and to
victory over selfishness and egotistical laziness. "In spite of our
attachment to things, we will detach ourselves from them."[77] Our
very attachment, in a sense, detaches us, because in nature—seen
properly—there is a logic and a power of renunciation, of "creative death," that is precisely the beginning of the renunciation
imposed by Christ on the members of His Body. Detachment and
human effort, seen in this perspective, are harmonized.

There is, of course, an infinite variety of combinations of effort
and renunciation. There is an infinity of vocations, and in each
vocation there is an infinity of phases. Saint Thomas Aquinas and
Saint Vincent de Paul and Saint John of the Cross are side by side
in the Church. And in the life of each Christian, there is a time for
growth and a time for diminishment. In any case, Christian renunciation is a renunciation that implies not rupture with the natural
order but the transformation of the Christian and of the world in
Christ.[78]

Teilhard expresses this same idea of "detachment through action" in *The Divine Milieu*. The idea is the same as in his corre-
spondence with Blondel, but more clearly and concisely expressed.

Anyone who devotes himself to human duty according to the Christian
formula, though outwardly he may seem to be immersed in the

[76] *Ibid.*, 140.
[77] *Ibid.*, 141.
[78] For an outline and discussion of the views of Teilhard and Blondel
in this exchange of letters, see C. Mooney, S.J., "Blondel and Teilhard de
Chardin," *Thought* 37 (1962) 543–62.

concerns of the earth, is in fact, down to the depths of his being, a man of great detachment.

Of its very nature work is a manifold instrument of detachment, provided a man gives himself to it faithfully and without rebellion. In the first place it implies effort and a victory over inertia. And then, however interesting and intellectual it may be (and the more intellectual it is, the truer this becomes), work is always accompanied by the painful pangs of birth. . . . The Christian knows that his function is to divinise the world in Jesus Christ. In him, therefore, the natural process which drives human action from ideal to ideal and towards objects ever more internally coherent and comprehensive in their embrace, reaches—thanks to the support of Revelation— its fullest expansion. And in him, consequently, detachment through action should produce its maximum effectiveness.

And this is perfectly true. The Christian as we have described him in these pages, is at once the most attached and the most detached of men. Convinced in a way in which the "worldly" cannot be of the unfathomable importance and value concealed beneath the humblest worldly successes, the Christian is at the same time as convinced as the hermit of the worthlessness of any success which is envisaged only as a benefit to himself (or even a general one) without reference to God. It is God and God alone whom he pursues through the reality of created things.[79]

The doctrine of detachment through action, of Christian renunciation in the interests of a higher cause, is referred to in different contexts in several of Teilhard's works written during the 1930's and early 1940's. Christian detachment is spiritual detachment, the detachment of the interior man; for Teilhard, it takes the form not of a rejection or a withdrawal but of a conquest. Detachment is the inner attitude of the Christian who immerses himself in the world in order to participate in the things of the world so as to lead them

---

[79] *DM*, 71–3. See also "Mon univers," 1924, *OE* 9, 97–9, where Teilhard describes interior detachment in terms of spiritual progress.

to God. This idea of detachment is patterned on and is in perfect harmony with the fact and the purpose of the Incarnation, immersion in the world so as to lead the world to God. Christian detachment "permits us to love things without resting in them, . . . to go beyond them while leading them on with us . . . to go beyond every truth and every beauty precisely by the force of our love for them."[80] The Christian ideal of "perfection" is seen by Teilhard "less as a matter of purifying this soiled world than as an effort to divinize creation."[81]

Diminishment and Christian Detachment

There is a detachment through action and there is also, more importantly, a detachment through the passive undergoing of unavoidable evil. Teilhard calls the inevitable and unavoidable evils that we are obliged to suffer through, to undergo, the "forces of diminishment." There are forces of diminishment whose origin lies outside us: deaths of those close to us, accidents of all kinds, sickness, lack of opportunity for advancement, obstacles and barriers and bad circumstances. But more frightening are the *internal* passivities of diminishment; they "form the darkest element and the most despairingly useless years of our life . . . natural failings, physical defects, intellectual or moral weaknesses." Add to these the conflicts and confusion within our own personality, anxieties, old age. Finally, waiting for each of us at the end of our life is "the sum and consummation of all our diminishments," death.[82]

In the passive experience of undergoing these forces of dimin-

[80] "Essai de l'intégration de l'homme dans l'univers," 1930, 13; "Christologie et évolution," 1933, 13. See "The New Spirit," 1942, *FM*, 96: Teilhard says of Christian detachment that "instead of leaving behind, it leads on; instead of cutting off, it raises. It is no longer a break-away but a way through; no longer a withdrawal but an act of emerging."

[81] "L'évolution de la chasteté," 1934, 7.

[82] *DM*, 81–2.

ishment, what is the Christian attitude? How can this passive experience lead to greater union with God? "It is easy enough to understand that God can be grasped in and through every life. But can God also be found in and through every death?"[83] We have a Christian duty to resist evil in all its forms, and in this fight against evil we are united with Christ and become more closely united with Him. But what about our failures? There are evils, forces of diminishment, that we lose out to; even at best, all of us will die. Teilhard finds the Christian answer to the problem of passive suffering and death at two levels: in a Christian understanding of Divine Providence, and in an analysis of the process by which God uses our passivities to unite us more closely with Himself.

In the first place, God—in virtue of His perfections—cannot ordain that the elements of a world in process of growth should avoid shocks and diminishments. "A world assumed to be progressing toward perfection, or 'rising upward,' is of its nature precisely still partially disorganized. A world without a trace or a threat of evil would be a world already consummated."[84] God's perfections cannot run counter to the nature of things. But God integrates evil into His total plan; he uses the forces of diminishment to serve a higher purpose.

But God will make it good—he will take his revenge, if one may use the expression—by making evil itself serve a higher good of his faithful, the very evil which the present state of creation does not allow him to suppress immediately. Like an artist who is able to make use of a fault or an impurity in the stone he is sculpting or the bronze he is casting so as to produce more exquisite lines or a more beautiful tone, God, without sparing us the partial deaths, nor the final death, which form an essential part of our lives, transfigures them by integrating them in a better plan—*provided we lov-*

83 *Ibid.*, 80.
84 *Ibid.*, 86, footnote 3.

ingly trust in him. Not only our unavoidable ills but our faults, even our most deliberate ones, can be embraced in that transformation, provided always we repent of them. Not everything is immediately good to those who seek God; but everything is capable of becoming good.[85]

Within this general understanding of Divine Providence Teilhard tries to analyze the overall process by which we are led to closer union with God through our passive experience of the forces of evil, through our undergoing of the innumerable daily deaths in our life and the final complete physical death at the end of our life.

Teilhard's basic idea is that every union necessarily implies a going out of oneself to the other; every union is a kind of migration and a partial death. Union for him means a union of love, and love is fundamentally the giving of self to the one loved. "But if, as we are sure, this being reduced to nothing in the other must be all the more complete the more we give our attachment to one who is greater than ourselves, then we can set no limits to the tearing up of roots that is involved on our journey into God."[86] This initial attachment to God, although it demands "detachment through action" and does require a certain dying to self, has as its effect the development to its furthest limits of the center of our personality.

But Christian detachment goes further than this. Ultimately, the whole purpose of detachment is to center us less on ourselves and to center us more on God. Death to self, then, is an excentration, a decentering of ourself so as to be more centered on God. It is in particular the passivities of diminishment that serve to excentrate us, to take us out of ourselves and to center us on God. The forces of diminishment are forces of disaggregation, even of disintegration; they break up the provisory unity of self. This breaking-up of

[85] *Ibid.,* 86.
[86] *Ibid.,* 88.

self, this disintegration and partial death, is a necessary step to a further integration—at a higher level—in God. "By being diminished in Christ Jesus, those who are mortified, who suffer, and who grow old in patience go beyond the critical point where death turns into life. In forgetting themselves they find themselves again."[87] "The more we progress in life, the more we change. And the more we change, the more we die. It is the law of becoming."[88] In the devotional prose-poem, *The Mass on the World*, Teilhard, at the moment of Communion, prays:

The world can never be definitely united with You, Lord, save by a sort of reversal, a turning about, an *excentration*, which must involve the temporary collapse not merely of individual achievements but even of everything that looks like an advancement for humanity. If my being is ever to be decisively attached to Yours, there must first die in me not only . . . the ego but also the world; in other words I must first pass through an agonizing phase of diminution for which no tangible compensation will be given me. That is why, pouring into my chalice the bitterness of all separation, of all limitations, and of all sterile fallings away, You then hold it out to me. "Drink ye all of this."[89]

The evil in the world, the forces of diminishment that make us suffer—these are not divine or positively willed by God. They represent the unfinished part, the disorder, of a universe that is not yet perfectly unified. Nevertheless, Christ is victorious over evil, and if in this life we will not see the final unification of all things in Christ, Christ is not for that reason defeated. Christ dominates the limitations and the diminishments of the universe by transforming

[87] "Le prêtre," 1918, *Ecrits*, 293. See also "La lutte contre la multitude," 1917, *Ecrits*, 129–30; "L'union créatrice," 1917, *Ecrits*, 195; "Forma Christi," 1918, *Ecrits*, 344–9.
[88] "La foi qui opère," 1918, *Ecrits*, 324.
[89] "The Mass on the World," 1923, *HU*, 31.

them, by integrating them—without really changing them—into the process of our growth in union with Him. Christ operates in us not only by the vitality of life, but by the terrible disorders of defeat and of death. What is apparently the darkest sector of the world is, ultimately, the most luminous.[90]

The final evil and the final excentration and the final passage to union with Christ is death. Nothing in this world can grow indefinitely without at last eventually reaching a point of "change of state," a critical point where it can no longer grow without a complete metamorphosis. In the growth of the person, "there comes a time when a complete rearrangement of elements becomes necessary so that the person can enter into a new domain of advancement."[91] There comes a point where a complete transformation is necessary; the agent of this definitive transformation is death. Death is the final "critical point of our excentration, of our reversion to God."[92] Christ's greatest victory is the victory over death. In itself, death is a scandal and a failure, the worst enemy of man, the blind revenge of the insufficiently dominated elements of this world. But in His own death on the Cross, Christ has transformed death itself, giving it the value of the final and most important force of excentration and so of transformation and union with God. "He has conquered death. He has given it the ontological value of a metamorphosis. And with Him, through death, the world has penetrated into God."[93]

[90] "Mon univers," 1924, *OE* 9, 101.

[91] "Esquisse d'un univers personnel," 1936, *OE* 6, 108. See "Le milieu mystique," 1917, *Ecrits*, 151; "L'union créatrice," 1917, *Ecrits*, 195.

[92] *DM*, 88. In a letter of November 13, 1916, Teilhard writes: "Death surrenders us totally to God; it makes us enter into Him; we must, in return, surrender ourselves to death with absolute love and self abandonment,—since, when death comes, all we can do is surrender ourselves completely to the domination and guidance of God." (*MM*, 145.)

[93] "Mon univers," 1924, *OE* 9, 92. See "La centrologie," 1944, *OE* 7, 128–9. On Holy Thursday, 1955, three days before his sudden death, Teilhard wrote in the final page of his personal journal: "The last enemy to

Christian Holiness

In Teilhard de Chardin's analysis of growth in union with God there are, as we said at the beginning of this chapter, three levels or phases, overlapping but distinguishable. The first phase is one of enthusiastic attachment to the world, of whole-hearted collaboration in the human effort in the realization that we are helping to build the world toward the Pleroma, the fulfillment of all things in Christ. Secondly, in the course of this endeavor we achieve a first stage of Christian detachment, of detachment from selfish interests and from a narrow egoism. Finally, we accept and even cherish the passivities and diminishments that serve, in a transforming process of excentration, to center us not on ourselves but on God. In Teilhard's view, growth in Christian holiness, in union with God, is a progressive movement that contains a double polarity: action and attachment to progress, and resignation and detachment.

"Thus, in the general rhythm of Christian life, development and renunciation, attachment and detachment, are not mutually exclusive. . . . They are . . . two components by which the Christian life uses things as a springboard from which to mount beyond them."[94] If it is true that there is in the life of the Christian a certain primacy given to development and attachment, it is just as true that there is a continual and final ascendancy of that side of the Christian life that is detachment and renunciation. With spiritual growth and progress,

the perspectives of renunciation implied in the exercise of life itself are gradually expanded. Ultimately we find ourselves thoroughly uprooted, as the Gospel desires, from everything perceptible on earth.

---

be destroyed is death, for Christ has put everything under His feet." (Quoted in H. de Lubac, S.J., *La pensée religieuse du Père Teilhard de Chardin*, 73.)
  [94] *DM*, 99.

But the process of uprooting ourselves has happened little by little and according to a rhythm which has neither alarmed nor wounded the respect we owe to the admirable beauties of the human effort.[95]

Teilhard's approach to growth in holiness is a balanced approach. It avoids the excesses of paying too much attention to development and attachment, of falling into "the error of seeking divine love and the divine kingdom *on the same level* as human affections and human progress." It further avoids excessive emphasis on renunciation as if sanctity were "built on the destruction of nature."[96] Teilhard stresses neither the purely "natural" aspects of the Christian life nor the idea of rupture with "nature." His basic idea is that of the gradual *transformation* and sublimation of the natural by the supernatural, the gradual transformation of the Christian in his growth and progress in union with God.[97] It is a transformation in and through the universe seen with the eyes of faith.

My whole interior life is more and more oriented toward and strengthened in the union with God that is found in all the interior and exterior forces of this world. But in order for this attitude to have results, I can't exclude any of these forces, neither death nor "persecution" because of my ideas. Everything is transformable in Our Lord if we believe. . . . The general formula for the Christian life is contained for me in this phrase: to be united through fidelity to the world consecrated by faith. I think that this statement is complete and quite sound.[98]

---

[95] *Ibid.*, 103.
[96] *Ibid.*, 110, footnote 1.
[97] See "Note sur la notion de la perfection chrétienne," 1942, *OE* 9, 41.
[98] Undated extract from the book, *Lettres à Léontine Zanta*, published by Desclée de Brouwer, quoted in *Christus* 12 (1965) 509.

7 ⋅ THE SECOND COMING OF CHRIST

THIS SHORT chapter is intended to serve as a partial summary and an epilogue to the entire present study. Teilhard de Chardin's vision of the world, of the place of man and his endeavor in the world, and of God's saving plan, is condensed and brought into focus in his understanding of the end of the world and its transformation in Christ at Christ's second coming. Teilhard, who thought in terms of growth and evolution, considered endings— terminal states of growth—of more importance and interest than beginnings. As a result, his reflection on the terminal point of the evolution of the world has a dominating position in the structure of his thought. It could be said that he sees the whole universe and its evolution from the projected vantage point of "the end of the world."

It is a central part of Teilhard's general theory that mankind is evolving, progressing along an axis of greater organization and higher collective consciousness toward an ultimate and maximum point of complete maturity. Mankind's progress is convergent in the sense that the growth and maturation of the human race are approaching a point in the future, a point of maximum organization and of maximum consciousness. It is as though human progress were taking place on the surface of a cone and following a spiraling line that goes from the base to the cone's apex. Will mankind reach its final point of fulfillment? As a Christian, Teilhard is certain that it will, for he considers the "collective consummation of earthly mankind" to be "not a meaningless and still less a hostile event, but a pre-condition of the final 'parousiac' establishment of the Kingdom of God." It is a pre-condition that is "necessary, but not sufficient in itself."[1]

When Teilhard writes strictly within the self-imposed limits of a scientific phenomenology without introducing any elements from Christian revelation, he describes the extrapolated terminal point of mankind's evolution without reference to the Parousia, to the second coming of Christ.[2] A careless reading might give the impression that Teilhard conceives passage through the last critical point of evolution, the ultimate point of mankind's maturation, as a natural process attainable simply by human forces, simply a natural outcome of human evolution. To think this would be to completely misunderstand his thought. In his essays that explicitly consider the Christian revelation of the Parousia, it is clear that there is no ambiguity in Teilhard's thought. The terminal point of human evolution is not simply a natural outcome of evolution; it is an event in which the supernatural predominates. In other words,

---

[1] "The Directions and Conditions of the Future," 1948, *FM*, 237.

[2] See, for example, "Life and the Planets," 1946, *FM*, 120–3; *MPN*, 112–21.

the collective effort of human evolution cannot by itself bring about the Parousia.

That mankind reach a point of maximum maturation is, in Teilhard's evolutionary framework of thought, *not* a sufficient condition for Christ's second coming. It is, however, a necessary condition. According to this viewpoint, the final point of human maturation and the second coming of Christ, although taking place at different depths of existence, "coincide in the concrete unity of a single event."[3] This is because Christ will not come at the end of the world until the world reaches its end, its terminal point of growth. Christ will not come until the world is sufficiently evolved and prepared for His coming. This is, Teilhard remarks, "in perfect analogy with the mystery of the first Christmas which (as everyone agrees) could only have happened between Heaven and an Earth which was prepared, socially, politically, and psychologically to receive Jesus."[4]

Teilhard has no intention whatever of denying the gratuity of God's intervention in the world at the end of time, of denying the gratuity of the Parousia. Christ's second coming could never be brought about merely by the powers of natural evolution and human effort. The Parousia is a supernatural event. What Teilhard does deny is that the Parousia will be an *arbitrary* event, unconnected with human evolutionary progress. It is just as true of

[3] "Trois choses que je vois," 1948, 4. For a similar statement, see "The Heart of the Problem," 1949, *FM*, 267–8. As F. Viallet remarks in commenting on a pencil sketch, reproduced in his book, that Teilhard drew to show schematically how the universe converges on Christ-Omega, Teilhard sees the world's end as having two "faces": the total maturation of mankind and the saving action of Christ. "Thus Teilhard clearly shows the structure of his vision of evolution: he wants to conserve both the value of *human* effort and the idea of a *transcendent* God." (F. Viallet, *Le dépassement*, 215–6).

[4] "The Heart of the Problem," 1949, *FM*, 267, footnote 1. See "A Note on Progress," 1920, *FM*, 22.

Christ's second coming in the Parousia as of His first coming in the Incarnation that only a strictly supernatural intervention of God can bring it about. It is equally true that God does not act arbitrarily; just as the Incarnation took place in "the fullness of time," so will the Parousia take place only in a greater and ultimate fullness of time.[5]

Teilhard envisages the end of mankind in this world not as a mass death and destruction but as a transformation. The end of the "thinking species" will not be "disintegration and death, but a new break-through and a re-birth, this time outside time and space, through the very excess of unification and co-reflexion."[6] The end of the world as we know it will not be through some sidereal disaster, through a natural cataclysm, but through "the wholesale internal introversion upon itself of the noosphere, which has simultaneously reached the uttermost limits of its complexity and its centrality."[7] It will be a psychic reversal rather than a natural catastrophe, perhaps resembling death, but in fact a liberation beyond the conditions of matter and history, "an ecstasy in God."[8] This explanation and way of imagining the manner in which the world will end as "an eruption of interior life, an ecstasy,"

---

[5] O. Rabut, O.P., commenting on Teilhard's idea of the Parousia and final Pleroma in *Dialogue with Teilhard de Chardin*, 167, writes: "The enormous problem that evolution sets us is that it seems to save mankind. But, in Teilhard's thought, salvation in the Christian sense is neither eliminated nor replaced. It is the grace of Christ which saves, and not the forces of evolution; yet grace makes use of evolution. . . . Christian salvation makes use of natural instruments which *dispose* men to accept God's gifts in a more fitting manner, and thus enable these gifts to bear fruit. The one essential is not to confuse the disposition to receive with the gift that has been received."

[6] "The End of the Species," 1952, *FM*, 302. See also: *DM*, 68; *PM*, 287–8; "L'atomisme de l'esprit," 1941, *OE* 7, 51–2; "Comment je vois," 1948, 14; "Du cosmos à la cosmogénèse," 1951, *OE* 7, 270; "L'activation de l'énergie humaine," 1953, *OE* 7, 415.

[7] *PM*, 287.

[8] "L'esprit de la terre," 1931, *OE* 6, 57.

is sufficient. "There is no need for us to rack our brains in trying to understand how the immensity of the material universe might vanish. It is enough that the spirit should be reversed, that it should enter another sphere, for the face of the world to be instantly altered."[9]

The world's end, then, will be a transformation and rebirth, but—at the same time—it will be a kind of death. The world's final transformation in Christ will involve a partial disintegration, a disassembling of its elements, a kind of death. This will be necessary in order that the world be finally and definitively decentered from itself and transformed so as to be wholly centered on Christ. The decentering or excentration of the world is part of the passage into the next life. The final point of human maturation and of the transformation of all things in Christ is also the final critical point and "threshold of reversal and excentration."[10] The end of the world will necessarily entail "the overthrow of equilibrium, detachment of the mind, fulfilled at last, from its material matrix, so that it will henceforth rest with all its weight on God-Omega." The critical point for mankind will be, then, both transformation and excentration, the "critical point simultaneously of emergence and emersion, of maturation and escape."[11]

In an essay written in 1924 Teilhard summarizes his views on the Parousia. The ideas expressed in this text are brought out in diverse ways in his later works, but the thought itself never changes.

Pressed tightly against one another by the increase in their numbers and relationships, forced together by the growth of a common power and the sense of a common travail, the men of the future will in some sort form a single consciousness; and because, their

[9] "Mon univers," 1924, extract translated in *FM*, 307.
[10] "Note sur la notion de perfection chrétienne," 1942, 3.
[11] *PM*, 287.

initiation being completed, they will have measured the power of their associated minds, the immensity of the universe, and the narrowness of their prison, this consciousness will be truly adult, truly major. May we not suppose that when this time comes mankind will for the first time be confronted with the necessity for a truly and wholly human act, a final exercise of choice—the yes or no in face of God, individually affirmed by beings in each of whom will be fully developed the sense of human liberty and responsibility? . . .

As the end of time approaches a terrifying spiritual pressure will be brought to bear on the limits of the Real, born of the effort of souls desperately straining in their desire to escape from the Earth. This pressure will be unanimous. But the Scriptures teach us that at the same time it will be rent by a profound schism between those who wish to break out of themselves that they may become still more masters of the world, and those who, accepting Christ's word, passionately await the death of the world that they may be absorbed with it into God.

And no doubt it is then, in a Creation brought to the paroxysm of its aptitude for union, that the Parousia will occur. The unique process of assimilation and synthesis, pursued from the beginning of time, being at length revealed, the universal Christ will appear like a flash of lightning amid the storm-clouds of a slowly consecrated World. . . .

Then the organic complex will have been constituted of God and the World, the Pleroma. . . .

Like a vast tide the Being will have dominated the trembling of all beings. The extraordinary adventure of the World will have ended in the bosom of a tranquil ocean, of which, however, each drop will still be conscious of being itself.[12]

Twenty-five years later he writes of the Parousia in the context of the "problem of the two faiths." At the source of mankind's contemporary crisis he sees a real but unnecessary conflict, a con-

---

[12] "Mon univers," 1924, extract translated in *FM*, 306–8.

flict between the modern forward impulse of faith in man, in the world, in human progress, and the traditional upward impulse of religious worship. These two impulses or drives, "the Forward" and "the Upward," meet in the heart of contemporary man and they seem to be in irreconcilable conflict. It is of the essence of Teilhard de Chardin's Christian vision that in that vision the Forward and the Upward can and should be brought into harmony and mutually complement and support one another in a synthesis.

To show how faith in human progress and faith in Christ are the two elements of a possible and necessary synthesis, he selects "a single case, one which sums up everything," the second coming of Christ. If it is truly necessary that mankind should have attained the natural completion of its evolutionary growth in order that the Kingdom of God be established in its fullness, that the fullness of the Pleroma be achieved, "then it must mean that the ultra-human perfection which neo-humanism envisages for evolution will coincide in concrete terms with the crowning of the Incarnation awaited by all Christians."[13] That is, the forward human impulse toward progress, toward the development of mankind to its utmost and toward the building of the world, finds its fulfillment in the ultimate maturation of mankind. This final maturation provides the material for the final transformation in Christ.

What is more, mankind's ultimate point of evolutionary progress and the point of its transformation by the transcendent action of God form one single event. Thus man's forward impulse toward progress and his upward impulse of adoration of God find their reconciliation and their synthesis in the light of the second coming of Christ. The two components of modern man's striving, the Forward and the Upward, draw together in synthesis.[14]

[13] "The Heart of the Problem," 1949, *FM*, 267–8.
[14] See the Second Vatican Council's *Constitution on the Church in the Modern World*, Part 1, Chapter 3, no. 39: ". . . the expectation of a new earth must not weaken but rather stimulate our concern for cultivating

The supernaturalising Christian Upward is incorporated (not immersed) in the human Forward! And at the same time Faith in God, in the very degree in which it assimilates and sublimates within its own spirit the spirit of Faith in the World, regains all its power to attract and convert! . . . Let there be revealed to us the possibility of believing *at the same time and wholly* in God *and* the World, the one through the other; let this belief burst forth, as it is ineluctably in process of doing under the pressure of these seemingly opposed forces, and then, we may be sure of it, a great Flame will illumine all things: for a Faith will have been born (or re-born) containing and embracing all others—and inevitably, it is the strongest Faith which sooner or later must possess the Earth.[15]

---

this one. . . . For after we have obeyed the Lord, and in His Spirit nurtured on earth the values of human dignity, brotherhood and freedom, and indeed all the good fruits of our nature and enterprise, we will find them again, but freed of stain, burnished and transfigured . . . when Christ hands over to the Father a kingdom . . . already present in mystery. When the Lord returns, it will be brought into full flower."

[15] "The Heart of the Problem," 1949, *FM*, 268–9.

BIBLIOGRAPHY

I. Works by Pierre Teilhard de Chardin

BOOKS BY TEILHARD DE CHARDIN AND ANTHOLOGIES OF HIS WRITINGS

Oeuvres de Pierre Teilhard de Chardin:
1. *Le phénomène humain,* Paris, 1955. American edition: *The Phenomenon of Man,* tr. B. Wall, revised translation, New York, 1965.
2. *L'apparition de l'homme,* Paris, 1956. American edition: *The Appearance of Man,* tr. J. Cohen, New York, 1965.
3. *La vision du passé,* Paris, 1957. American edition: *The Vision of the Past,* tr. J. Cohen, New York, 1967.
4. *Le milieu divin,* Paris, 1957. American edition: *The Divine Milieu,* tr. B. Wall, A. Dru, N. Lindsay, D. MacKinnon, *et al.,* New York, 1960.

5. *L'avenir de l'homme*, Paris, 1959. American edition: *The Future of Man*, tr. N. Denny, New York, 1964.
6. *L'énergie humaine*, Paris, 1962.
7. *L'activation de l'énergie*, Paris, 1963.
8. *Le groupe zoologique humain*, Paris, 1956; also published later as vol. 8 of the "Oeuvres de Pierre Teilhard de Chardin." American edition: *Man's Place in Nature*, tr. R. Hague, New York, 1966.
9. *Science et Christ*, Paris, 1965.

Ecrits du temps la guerre (1916–1919), Paris, 1965. (This work will be published in English in 1968 by Wm. Collins Sons & Co., London, and Harper & Row, New York.)

Hymne de l'univers, Paris, 1961. American edition: *Hymn of the Universe*, tr. S. Bartholomew, New York, 1965.

OTHER PUBLISHED ESSAYS OF TEILHARD DE CHARDIN

"La parole attendue," *Cahiers Pierre Teilhard de Chardin, 4, La parole attendue*, Paris, 1963, 22–9.

"Le Christ Evoluteur," *Cahiers de la fondation Teilhard de Chardin, 5, Le Christ Evoluteur, Socialisation et Religion*, Paris, 1965, 17–27.

"L'apport spirituel de l'extrême orient. Quelques réflexions personnelles," *Monumenta Nipponica* 12 (1956) 2–11.

"La pensée du Père Teilhard de Chardin," *Les études philosophiques* 10 (1955) 580–1.

"Un sommaire de ma pensée 'phénoménologique' du monde," *Les études philosophiques* 10 (1955) 569–71.

"The Antiquity and World Expansion of Human Culture," *Man's Role in Changing the Face of the Earth*, ed. W. Thomas, Jr., Chicago, 1956, 103–12.

PUBLISHED LETTERS OF TEILHARD DE CHARDIN

The Making of a Mind, tr. R. Hague, New York, 1965.

Letters from a Traveller, tr. B. Wall, R. Hague, V. Hammersley, N. Lindsay, *et al.*, New York, 1962.

Lettres à Léontine Zanta, Paris, 1965.

de Lubac, H., S.J., "Maurice Blondel et le Père Teilhard de Chardin, mémoires échangés en décembre 1919, présentés par H. de Lubac," *Archives de philosophie* 24 (1961) 123–56.

UNPUBLISHED ESSAYS OF TEILHARD DE CHARDIN

"Note sur les modes de l'action divine dans l'univers," 1920.

"Chute, rédemption, et géocentricité," 1920.

"Note sur quelques représentation historiques," 1922.

"Panthéisme et Christianisme," 1923.

"Note sur quelques représentations historiques du péché originel," 1924.

"Le sens humain," 1929.

"Intégration de l'homme dans l'univers," 1930.

"La route de l'ouest," 1932.

"Christologie et évolution," 1933.

"L'évolution de la chasteté," 1934.

"Comment je crois," 1934.

"Quelques vues générales sur l'essence du Christianisme," 1939.

Appendix on original sin at the end of "Le Christ Evoluteur," 1942.

"Note sur la notion de perfection chrétienne," 1942.

"Introduction à la vie chrétienne," 1944.

"Christianisme et évolution," 1945.

"Réflexions sur le péché originel," 1947.

"Le néo-humanisme moderne et ses réactions sur le Christianisme," 1948.

"Trois choses que je vois," 1948.

"Comment je vois," 1948.

"Pré-humain, humain, ultra-humain," 1949.

"Le coeur de la matière," 1950.

"Monogénisme et monophylétisme," 1950.

"Le phénomène chrétien," 1950.

"Quelques remarques 'pour y voir clair' sur l'essence du sentiment mystique," 1951.

"Ce que le monde attend en ce moment de l'Eglise de Dieu: une généralisation et un approfondissement du sens de la croix," 1952.
"Le Dieu de l'évolution," 1953.
"Contingence de l'univers et goût humain de survivre," 1953.
"Le Christique," 1955.

II. Works on the Thought of Teilhard de Chardin

BOOKS

Barthélemy-Madaule, M. *Bergson et Teilhard de Chardin.* Paris, 1963.

Braybrooke, N. (ed.). *Teilhard de Chardin, Pilgrim of the Future.* New York, 1964.

Chauchard, P. *Man and Cosmos,* tr. G. Courtright. New York, 1965.

Corte, N. *Pierre Teilhard de Chardin,* tr. M. Jarrett-Kerr, C.R. London, 1960.

Crespy, G. *La pensée théologique de Teilhard de Chardin.* Paris, 1961.

Cuénot, C. *Teilhard de Chardin.* Paris, 1962.

————. *Teilhard de Chardin,* tr. V. Colimore. Baltimore, 1965.

————(ed.). *Teilhard de Chardin et la pensée catholique.* Paris, 1965.

Francoeur, R. (ed.). *The World of Teilhard,* Baltimore, 1961.

Garaudy, R. *Perspectives de l'homme: existentialisme, pensée catholique, marxisme.* Paris, 1959.

Grenet, P. *Pierre Teilhard de Chardin, ou le philosophe malgré lui.* Paris, 1960.

Lepp, I. *Teilhard et la foi des hommes.* Paris, 1963.

de Lubac, H., S.J. *La pensée religieuse du Père Teilhard de Chardin.* Paris, 1962.

————. *Teilhard de Chardin, the Man and His Meaning,* tr. R. Hague. New York, 1965.

Martin-Deslias, N. *Un aventurier de l'esprit: Teilhard de Chardin.* Paris, 1963.

Mooney, C., S.J. *Teilhard de Chardin and the Mystery of Christ.* New York, 1966.

Murray, M. *The Thought of Teilhard de Chardin.* New York, 1966.

Philippe de la Trinité, O.C.D. *Rome et Teilhard de Chardin.* Paris, 1964.

──────. *Teilhard et teilhardisme.* Rome, 1962.

Rabut, O., O.P. *Dialogue with Teilhard de Chardin.* New York, 1961.

Rideau, E., S.J. *La pensée du Père Teilhard de Chardin.* Paris, 1965.

Smulders, P., S.J. *The Design of Teilhard de Chardin,* tr. A. Gibson. Westminster, 1967.

Tresmontant, C. *Pierre Teilhard de Chardin,* tr. S. Attanasio. Baltimore, 1959.

Viallet, F. *Le dépassement.* Paris, 1961.

Wildier, N. *Teilhard de Chardin.* Paris, 1960.

ARTICLES

d'Armagnac, C., S.J. "Philosophie de la nature et méthode chez le Père Teilhard de Chardin," *Archives de philosophie* 20 (1957) 5–41.

Barjon, L., S.J. "Fidelité chrétienne et fidelité religieuse du Père Teilhard de Chardin," *Foi vivante* 15 (1963) 70–82.

Barthélemy-Madaule, M. "La perspective teilhardienne et l'action," *Europe* 43, no. 431–2 (1965) 70–88.

──────. "Teilhard de Chardin, Marxism, Existentialism," *International Philosophical Quarterly* 1 (1961) 648–67.

Brunner, A., S.J. "Pierre Teilhard de Chardin," *Stimmen der Zeit* 165 (1959) 210–22.

Chauchard, P. "Teilhard de Chardin et Saint Thomas d'Aquin," *Revue Teilhard de Chardin* 1, no. 1–2 (1960) 11–2.

Cuénot, C. "Teilhard et le marxisme," *Europe* 43, no. 431–2 (1965) 164–85.

Dallaire, J., S.J. "Teilhard et l'évolution," *Revue Teilhard de Chardin* 5, no. 19 (1964) 25–31.

Devaux, A. "Teilhard et la construction d'une morale pour notre temps," *Revue Teilhard de Chardin* 6, no. 23 (1965) 31–8.

Donceel, J. "Teilhard de Chardin: Scientist or Philosopher?" *International Philosophical Quarterly* 5 (1965) 248–66.

Fleming, T., S.J. "Two Unpublished Letters of Teilhard," *The Heythrop Journal* 6 (1965) 36–45.

Frank, R. "Social Evolution and the Human Species," *American Catholic Sociological Review* 33 (1962) 291–337.

Garaudy, R. "Le Père Teilhard, le Concile et les marxists," *Europe* 43, no. 431–2 (1965) 185–208.

Guérard des Lauriers, M., O.P. "La démarche du P. Teilhard de Chardin, réflexions d'ordre épistemologique," *Divinitas* 3 (1959) 221–68.

Jeannière, A., S.J. "Sur le mal, l'union et le point Oméga," *Esprit* 32 (1964) 361–6.

Journet, C. "La vision teilhardienne du monde," *Divinitas* 3 (1959) 330–44.

————. "L'effort théologique du P. Teilhard de Chardin," *Nova et vetera* 39 (1964) 305–10.

Labourdette, M., O.P. "L'oeuvre du Père Teilhard de Chardin," *Revue thomiste* 64 (1964) 403–36.

LeBlond, J., S.J. "Consacrer l'effort humain," *Etudes* 296 (1958) 58–68.

de Lubac, H., S.J. "Maurice Blondel et le Père Teilhard de Chardin, mémoires échangés en décembre 1919, présentés par H. de Lubac," *Archives de philosophie* 24 (1961) 123–56.

Luyten, N., O.P. "La méthode du Père Teilhard," *Teilhard de Chardin et la pensée catholique,* ed. C. Cuénot. Paris, 1965, 19–63.

Malevez, L., S.J. "La méthode du P. Teilhard de Chardin," *Nouvelle revue théologique* 29 (1957) 579–99.

Monestier, A. "Teilhard et Aurobindo," *Revue Teilhard de Chardin* 4, no. 14 (1963) 11–3.

Mooney, C., S.J. "Blondel and Teilhard de Chardin," *Thought* 37 (1962) 543–62.

Morel, G., S.J. "Karl Marx et le P. Teilhard de Chardin," *Etudes* 304 (1960) 80–7.

North, R., S.J. "Teilhard de Chardin and the Problem of Creation," *Theological Studies* 24 (1963) 557–601.

d'Oince, R., S.J., "L'épreuve de l'obéissance dans la vie du Père Teilhard de Chardin," *L'homme devant Dieu* (3 vols.; Paris, 1964) 3. 331–46.

————. "Vivre dans la plénitude du Christ," *Christus* 9 (1962) 239–47.

Reidlinger, H. "The Universal Kingship of Christ," tr. T. Westow, *Who is Jesus of Nazareth?* "Concilium," vol. 11, ed. E. Schillebeeckx, O.P. New York, 1966, 107–27.

Russell, J., S.J. "The Principle of Finality in the Philosophy of Aristotle and Teilhard de Chardin," *The Heythrop Journal* 3 (1962) 347–57; 4 (1963) 32–41.

Russo, F., S.J. "La méthode du Père Teilhard de Chardin," *Recherches et débats* 40 (1962) 13–23.

————. "La socialisation," *Teilhard de Chardin et la pensée catholique,* ed C. Cuénot, 171–87.

Sorokin, P. "Discussion," *American Catholic Sociological Review* 33 (1962) 330–5.

Swan, L. "Memories and Letters," *Teilhard de Chardin, Pilgrim of the Future,* ed. N. Braybrooke. New York, 1964, 40–9.

Varga, I. "Teilhard, Marx et progrès social," *Europe* 3, no. 431–2 (1965) 152–8.

Vass, G. "Teilhard de Chardin and Inward Vision," *The Heythrop Journal* 2 (1961) 237–49.

von Balthasar, H. Urs. "Die Spiritualität Teilhard de Chardin," *Wort und Wahrheit* 18 (1963) 339–50.

Wallace, W., O.P. "The Cosmogony of Teilhard de Chardin," *The New Scholasticism* 36 (1962) 353–67.

Whitla, W. "Sin and Redemption in Whitehead and Teilhard de Chardin," *Anglican Theological Review* 47 (1965) 81–93.

III. OTHER WORKS CITED

BOOKS

Bertoni, A. *Jean Duns Scot*. Levanto, 1917.

Bonsirven, J., S.J. *The Theology of the New Testament*, tr. S. Tye. Westminster, Md., 1963.

Bouyer, L. *Introduction to Christian Spirituality*, tr. Mary Perkins Ryan. Collegeville, 1961.

—————. *Liturgical Piety*. Notre Dame, 1955.

—————. *The Meaning of the Monastic Life*, tr. K. Pond. New York, 1955.

The Christian and the World, ed. at Canisianum, Innsbruck. New York, 1965.

Connolly, J. *The Voices of France*. New York, 1961.

Constitution on the Church in the Modern World. Second Vatican Council, 1965.

Danielou, J., S.J. *Christ and Us*, tr. W. Roberts. New York, 1961.

Davis, C. *Theology for Today*. New York, 1962.

Devlin, C., S.J. (ed.). *The Sermons and Devotional Writings of Gerard Manley Hopkins*. London, 1959.

Dubarle, A.M., O.P. *The Biblical Doctrine of Original Sin*, tr. E. Steward. New York, 1964.

Durrwell, F. X., C.SS.R. *In the Redeeming Christ*, tr. R. Sheed. New York, 1963.

de Fraine, J., S.J. *Adam and the Family of Man*, tr. D. Raible, C.PP.S. New York, 1965.

—————. *The Bible and the Origin of Man*. New York, 1962.

Frankl, V. *Man's Search for Meaning*, tr. I. Lasch. New York, 1963.

Labourdette, M.M., O.P. *Le péché originel et les origines de l'homme*. Paris, 1953.

L'homme devant Dieu, 3 vols. Paris, 1964.

Ligier, L., S.J. *Péché d'Adam et péché du monde*, 2 vols. Paris, 1961.

Merton, T. *Life and Holiness*. New York, 1963.

Nogar, R., O.P. *Evolutionism, Its Power and Limits*. Washington, 1964.

Ott, L. *Fundamentals of Catholic Dogma*, tr. P. Lynch, 4 ed. St. Louis, 1960.

Pieper, J. *Guide to Thomas Aquinas*, tr. R. and C. Winston. New York, 1962.

Pius XII. *Humani Generis*. New York, 1950.

Rahner, K., S.J. *Theological Investigations I*, tr. C. Ernst, O.P. Baltimore, 1961.

————. *Theological Investigations II*, tr. K. Kruger. Baltimore, 1963.

————. *The Christian Commitment*, tr. C. Hastings. New York, 1963.

Ryan, Sister M. Rosalie, C.S.J. (ed.). *Contemporary New Testament Studies*. Collegeville, 1965.

Schillebeeckx, E., O.P. (ed.). *Who is Jesus of Nazareth?* "Concilium," vol. 11. New York, 1966.

Schnackenburg, R. *New Testament Theology Today*, tr. D. Askew. London, 1963.

Schoonenberg, P., S.J. *God's World in the Making*. Pittsburgh, 1964.

————. *Man and Sin*, tr. J. Donceel, S.J. Notre Dame, 1965.

Simpson, G. *This View of Life*. New York, 1964.

Thils, G. *Christian Attitudes*. Dublin, 1959.

Tomlin, E. *The Oriental Philosophers*. New York, 1963.

von Balthasar, H. Urs. *Word and Redemption*, tr. A. Littledale. New York, 1965.

Weil, S. *Gravity and Grace*, tr. A. Wills. New York, 1952.

ARTICLES

Auer, A. "The Christian Understanding of the World," tr. C. Gusmer, *The Christian and the World*, New York, 1965, 3–44.

Barrosse, T., C.S.C. "Death and Sin in Saint Paul's Epistle to the Romans," *The Catholic Biblical Quarterly* 15 (1953) 438–59.

Dumont, C., S.J. "La prédication du péché originel," *Nouvelle revue théologique* 83 (1961) 113–34.

Durig, W. "The Eucharist as Symbol of the Consecration of the

World," tr. L. Connolly, *The Christian and the World*, New York, 1965, 120–9.

Durrwell, F. X., C.SS.R. "Le Christ, premier et dernier," *Bible et vie chrétienne* 9 (1963) 16–28.

Lyonnet, S., S.J. "Le péché originel et l'exégèse de Rom. 5:12–14," *Recherches de science religieuse* 44 (1956) 63–84.

————. "The Redemption of the Universe," *Contemporary New Testament Studies*, ed. Sister M. Rosalie Ryan, C.S.J. Collegeville, 1965, 423–36.

McCallin, J. "Christological Unity of the 'De Civitate Dei,' " *Revue des études augustiniennes* 12 (1966) 85–109.

McIver, M. Emmanuel, O.S.U. "The Cosmic Dimensions of Salvation in the Thought of St. Paul," *Worship* 40 (1966) 156–64.

Metz, J. "A Believer's Look at the World," tr. H. Wansbrough, O.S.B., *The Christian and the World*. New York, 1965, 68–100.

van Caster, M., S.J. "Human and Christian Meaning of Work," *Lumen Vitae* 22 (1965) 283–306.

von Balthasar, H. Urs. "Spiritualität," *Geist und Leben* 31 (1958) 340–52, translated and condensed as "The One True Spirituality of the Church," *Theology Digest* 10 (1962) 189–94; translated in full in H. Urs von Balthasar, *Word and Redemption*, tr. A. Littledale, New York, 1965, 87–108.

INDEX

228

participates in Christogenesis, 99;
value of, 125-126; and obligation
to build the world, 172-179; and
Christian detachment, 196-202.
See *effort, action, activity*

enthusiasm for life, 74. See *motivation*

entropy, 49 fn. 26; moral entropy, 148 fn. 20

ethics, see *morality*

Eucharist, 105, 120-138; and the world, 133-138

evil, 140-147, 167, 202-208; moral evil, 147-153. See *sin*

evolution, idea of, 8, 35-37; Teilhard's theory of, 28, 33-82, 185-190; considered as a movement of spiritualization, 49 fn. 26; man is evolution become conscious, 52; socialization the most important mechanism of human evolution, 54; converging, 64-72, 118, 143, 157; personalizing, 171

excentration, 204-206, 213

expiation, 140, 155-156, 170-173, 197. See *reparation*

failure, 143-147, 203-206

faith, 25-28, 82-88, 208; in Christ, 6, 215; in man, 6, 215; in progress, 11, 12, 19, 215; in the world, 16, 25-28, 216; Christian, 25-28, 82-88, 92, 179; in God, 25, 100, 216; human faith, 28, 77; supernatural, 76-77, 83, 94; theological, 83

Fall, 154-155, 160

family, 180

fascism, 12, 58

Fathers of the Church, Greek, 30

fidelity, 151, 174, 178

finality, metaphysical, 37, 44

First Mover, 78, 137

focal point of evolution, 66-72, 97

Forward, the, 26, 103-104, 170-171, 215-216

Francoeur, R., 39 fn. 9

freedom, man's is gradually increasing, 54, 61, 161; God is First Mover in the order of human freedom, 78; God's freedom, 117-118; 164-165; union of the Christian's freedom to God's creative action, 123; statistical necessity of sin does not minimize human freedom, 150; degree of freedom of the first human generation, 161; Christian's obligation to develop his own freedom, 180

God, existence of, 28

God-Omega, 78, 81

Gospel, 18, 185, 191, 197, 207

grace, 83, 92, 199

gratuity, of creation, 21, 106, 117, 164; of Incarnation, 117, 164; of the Parousia, 211

Grenet, P., 39 fn. 9

groping, evolutionary, 45, 54, 149

guarantee of a successful outcome for evolution, 68-69, 74-75, 94

hell, 149-153

heredity, 45, 53; social heredity, 54

holiness, 20, 181, 207-208

hominization, 90

hope, 178

Hopkins, G. M., 115 fn. 28

Host, Eucharistic, 130-133

human point of view, 6, 8-16, 18, 25

human sense, 187-188

Humani Generis, 159

Husserl, Edmund, 38 fn. 8

hyperphysics, 41, 47 fn. 24, 86

hypothesis, 76, 82-83, 107, 110, 153, 156, 158, 189-192; evolution as a scientific hypothesis, 37, 40